D0919583

Selected Writings
in
BRITISH INTELLECTUAL HISTORY

Recently, if one heard Leslie Stephen mentioned, it would be only in relation to his actual, not his literary, offspring. But the father of Virginia Woolf himself made quite a mark in literature; Stephen (1832–1904) ranks with Matthew Arnold as one of Victorian England's most important men of letters. He followed William Thackeray as editor of the distinguished *Cornhill Magazine,* encouraging and publishing such writers as Hardy, Stevenson, and James. Undoubtedly Stephen's finest editorial achievement was the remarkable (British) *Dictionary of National Biography,* which he helped conceive and plan and of which he edited the first twenty-six volumes.

Stephen's own witty and penetrating works, however, surpass even his accomplishments as an editor. His clarity of mind, strengthened by his early mathematical studies at Cambridge, enabled Stephen to tease out strands of reasoning in individual writings and in the philosophical character of an age. His masterpiece, *English Thought in the Eighteenth Century,* started a reevaluation of rationalist philosophy and eighteenth-century culture that established Stephen's reputation as a scholar and thinker. From the first, critics recognized his stylistic grace—his ability as a sensitive and clever writer.

Classics of British Historical Literature

JOHN CLIVE, EDITOR

In this volume, Noël Annan has selected essays
and complete chapters from larger works that show
Stephen at his best in depicting and dissecting
varieties of philosophical thought, and illustrate
his approach to the history of ideas. He includes
four chapters from the famous *English Thought in
the Eighteenth Century;* a related essay, "English
Literature and Society in the Eighteenth Century";
a chapter on Johnson and another on Wordsworth
from *Hours in a Library;* and two other slightly
different works: "Thoughts on Criticism, by a
Critic," which reveals what Stephen thought the
duty of a literary critic should be and how criticism
in general should function, and "Poisonous
Opinions," from *An Agnostic's Apology,* which
Annan describes as "one of the finest statements
written in the Victorian age of the case for freedom
of expression."

LESLIE STEPHEN

Selected Writings
in
BRITISH INTELLECTUAL HISTORY

Edited and with an Introduction by
NOËL ANNAN

The University of Chicago Press
CHICAGO AND LONDON

NOËL ANNAN, Vice-Chancellor of the University
of London, is the author of *Leslie Stephen: His
Thought and Character in Relation to His Times.*

The University of Chicago Press, Chicago 60637
The University of Chicago Press, Ltd., London
© 1979 by the University of Chicago
All rights reserved. Published 1979
Printed in the United States of America

84 83 82 81 80 79   5 4 3 2 1

Library of Congress Cataloging in Publication Data

Stephen, Leslie, Sir, 1832–1904.
Selected writings in British intellectual history.

(Classics of British historical literature)
Bibliography: p.
Includes index.
1. England—Intellectual life—18th century—
Collected works.   I. Annan, Noel Gilroy Annan,
Baron, 1916–   II. Title.
DA485.S74 1979   941   78-13218
ISBN 0-226-77255-1

Contents

2084713

Series Editor's Preface   vii
Editor's Introduction   xi
Bibliographical Note   xxix

1. English Thought in the Eighteenth Century
   The Philosophical Basis: Introductory   1
   Butler's 'Analogy'   20
   David Hume   50
   William Warburton   83
2. English Literature and Society in the
   Eighteenth Century   110
3. Thoughts on Criticism, by a Critic   153
4. Hours in a Library
   Doctor Johnson's Writings   172
   Wordsworth's Ethics   197
5. An Agnostic's Apology: Poisonous Opinions   228

   Notes   291

Series Editor's Preface

This series of reprints has one major purpose: to put into the hands of students and other interested readers outstanding—and sometimes neglected—works dealing with British history which have either gone out of print or are obtainable only at a forbiddingly high price.

The phrase Classics of British Historical Literature requires some explanation, in view of the fact that the two companion series published by the University of Chicago Press are entitled Classic European Historians and Classic American Historians. Why, then, introduce the word *literature* into the title of this series?

One reason is obvious. History, if it is to live beyond its own generation, must be memorably written. The greatest British historians—Clarendon, Gibbon, Hume, Carlyle, Macaulay—survive today, not merely because they contributed to the cumulative historical knowledge about their subjects, but because they were masters of style and literary artists as well. And even historians of the second rank, if they deserve to survive, are able to do so only because they can still be read with pleasure. To emphasize this truth at the present time, when much eminently solid and worthy academic history suffers from being almost totally unreadable, seems worth doing.

The other reason for including the word *literature* in the title of the series has to do with its scope. To read history is to learn about the past. But if, in trying to learn about the British past, one were to restrict oneself to the reading of formal works of history, one would miss a great deal. Often a historical novel, a sociological inquiry, or an account of events and institutions couched in semifictional form teaches us just as much about the past as does the "history" that calls itself by that name. And, frequently, these "informal" historical works turn out to be less well known than their merit deserves. By calling this series Classics of British Historical Literature it will be possible to include such books without doing violence to the usual nomenclature.

Intellectual history has come upon bad days in our time. Philosophers are mainly interested in language and logic; historians devote themselves chiefly to social history; and excellence in the realm of the history of ideas has become a rare thing. It is particularly useful and instructive, then, to observe in Leslie Stephen a master of the art both of depicting and dissecting the thought of the past. Stephen was by no means unaware, as the selections here reprinted from his pioneering *English Literature and Society in the Eighteenth Century* show, of the way in which thought and ideas are ineluctably related to their social setting. Yet, as Noël Annan (whose masterly biography of Stephen remains the starting point for any consideration of him) points out in his Introduction, the great strength of Stephen's approach was his conviction, faithfully carried out in practice, that the intellectual historian's first duty was to examine and, if necessary, to question the method of argument, the consistency, and the coherence of those thinkers of the past who were his subjects. Many of today's intellectual historians find themselves either incapable of doing this or, if capable, reluctant to undertake it. The example of Stephen shows what can and ought to be done.

One point might be added to Annan's excellent introduction, and that concerns Stephen's capacities as a stylist. He invariably writes with elegance, and often with humor. One need only read him on Butler ("'hell is probable enough to be worth avoiding"), on Johnson's *Rambler* ("'is there not some danger ... that the mind will be benumbed with perpetual torpidity by the influence of this soporific sapience?''), and on the regret for youth's lost pleasures, which "resembles too often the maudlin meditation of a fast young man over his morning's soda-water," to be persuaded of his grace and wit as a writer. In this sphere, too, today's intellectual historians might well choose Stephen as a model. Others can just enjoy reading him.

JOHN CLIVE

Editor's Introduction

Leslie Stephen was the second most important man of letters in the late Victorian age. Not the first. That place of honor belongs to Matthew Arnold.

Early Victorian England presented men and women interested in people and general ideas with the spectacle of Newman's crisis of conscience and the conflict between the way in which Carlyle and Mill interpreted the world. Late Victorian England presented many more alternatives to intellectuals. There were sages such as Ruskin and Pater, eloquent scientists such as Huxley and Tyndall, and philosophers of the stature of T. H. Green, F. H. Bradley, and Henry Sidgwick. There was a great social scientist in the shape of Alfred Marshall and pioneers of new subjects, such as J. A. Symonds and Henry Maine. The new age demanded interpreters; and there appeared, as editors of the serious periodicals, Morley of the *Fortnightly,* Hutton of the *Spectator,* and—most original of all—Bagehot of the *Economist.* They were all more successful as editors than was Stephen with the *Cornhill.* Yet none of them covered such a wide range of topics with such authority as Stephen did. He was a historian of thought, the first critic to tackle the English novel, a commentator on his time, and a biographer of immense distinction. He was not a sage among the sages. He adjudicated between them with authority.

In the twentieth century, we expect historians and critics to be found in the universities. They were often found there in nineteenth-century Germany, but in England and America the universities were not yet the places where one was most likely to find the most original and seminal minds. In England amateurs undertood mammoth tasks of scholarship such as now would engage teams of research assistants guided by a succession of scholars. It is often said that Stephen's greatest monument is the *Dictionary of National Biography,* a gigantic editorial undertaking of which Stephen edited the first twenty-six volumes; yet Stephen would have been astonished if anyone had suggested that this was a full-time task. During most of the years of research on the biographies he wrote and drudgery on those he edited, he was also running the *Cornhill* and writing dozens of books and articles on thought, literature, and biography, as well as an original (if unsuccessful) work on ethics. Toward the end of his life he wrote a three-volume study of the English Utilitarians. But his masterpiece in the history of ideas was the two-volume *English Thought in the Eighteenth Century,* which established his reputation as scholar and thinker.

Leslie Stephen was the great-grandson of a Scotsman who had come south to England and had failed. His grandfather, James, thus thrown on the world, scraped into the legal profession, got to the West Indies, made some money, and returned to become a legal luminary and a dedicated opponent of slavery. In so doing he became an intimate of William Wilberforce, Zachary Macaulay, and that group of earnest Evangelicals called the Clapham Sect, who carried through Parliament the legislation which first abolished the slave trade and then freed the slaves in the British dominions. In 1832 he died, the same year his grandson Leslie was born; but he lived to see his third son, Sir James Stephen, Leslie's father, take up the cause of the slaves. As permanent secretary in the civil service at the Colonial Office, Leslie's father drafted the emancipation bill; and the power he wielded over ministers led his enemies to nickname him "Mr. Over-Secretary Stephen."

This senior civil servant had married the daughter of another family well known within the Clapham Sect, the

Venns; and thus by intermarriage the Stephens moved inexorably into an even larger connection than the Clapham Sect, into a circle of like-minded intellectual families intermarrying among themselves—families such as the Trevelyans, Macaulays, Arnolds, Darwins, Wedgwoods, Sidgwicks, Hodgkins, Huxleys, Haldanes, and Butlers, who became dons, headmasters, and editors of periodicals or who held senior posts in the new civil service, which could be entered only through competitive examination. Leslie Stephen was born into the professional middle class and into a talented family, into a clan which was establishing itself as an aristocracy of the intellect by dominating so many of the eminent positions within the cultural establishment. As such, these families were quietly but emphatically self-confident. They had no connection with the nobility nor yearning to join it, and therefore saw no reason to fawn upon it. But they lived on terms of ease with the landed classes and met them without affectation, because in England there was never a social chasm, recognized by both sides and established by custom and sometimes by law, as there was on the continent of Europe, between the aristocracy and landed gentry and the professional middle classes.

Yet it would be a mistake to picture the Stephens as moving in a circle of brilliant talkers or aspiring to become the leaders of an intelligentsia; still further from the truth to see a resemblance between them and the "superfluous men" of the Russian intelligentsia of the forties. To keep one's distance from the ruling class is a very different thing from being subversive toward the social order of one's country. Nor did Sir James Stephen care much for the society of clever men, and he was not to be found at Macaulay's breakfast table. Although John Stuart Mill, the jurist John Austen, and others among the Utilitarian philanthropists often visited him, he preferred on the whole the company of his kinsmen, the Venns and the Diceys. His home was a Christian home. His children were brought up in an atmosphere suffused with gentle Christian piety, never fanatical or partisan, as some homes were in the years of conflict between Tractarians and Evangelists or between High and Dry Anglicans and the

Nonconformist communions. The family was, nevertheless, somewhat austere. Sir James Stephen was not a man to do anything for pleasure; indeed, if he found himself enjoying anything overmuch, he would at once abandon it. "He once smoked a cigar," wrote his son, "and found it so delicious that he never smoked again." Though childhood did not mean visits to the theater or dances, the Stephens were otherwise liberal in outlook and mild Evangelicals. The children were not required to become prigs. To be sincere, rather than to exhibit patent virtues or membership in do-good organizations, was the text the family held most dear. The first duty of man was to search the heart and then to speak one's mind.

Leslie Stephen eventually broke with his Christian upbringing and became the most outspoken agnostic of his day. But his was not the rebellion of youth. When he graduated from Cambridge with first-class honors in mathematics, he realized that if he wanted to stay there as a fellow of his college, he would have to be ordained a clergyman of the Church of England. There is no evidence that he hesitated for a moment. In those days, when most fellowships could be held only by those in holy orders, it was the natural thing to do if one wanted to follow an academic career.

In 1854, when he became a fellow of his college, Stephen would not have considered himself as belonging to the Evangelical party in the Anglican church: that party would have been associated in his mind too much with bigotry and persecution, and he already considered himself more a follower of F. D. Maurice and Broad Church principles. But the truth was that he was not particularly concerned with religious controversy or parties. Taking holy orders in those days so as to be appointed to a fellowship pretty well corresponded to the obligation today to take a Ph.D. in order to obtain a post at a university; it was a professional qualification. No one thought you needed an academic accolade: that had been given when you graduated as a wrangler, as the first-class men in mathematics were called. To take holy orders was to obtain a qualification in morality, enabling one to become a professional teacher of the elite; for the prime purpose of Oxford and Cambridge in Stephen's time was not to advance knowledge through research, nor even to provide good academic teachers; it was to educate men who would be of service to Church and State. Men did not think an undergraduate was educated solely by training his intellect. Education was regarded as being a moral exercise. You trained a boy not through giving him courses on ethics or theology but by compulsory chapel, at which the tenets of the Christian faith, illustrated in sermons, and the precepts embodied in the marvelous prose of the Book of Common Prayer were supposed through constant repetition to make a lasting impression on the mind. People also believed that the mere experience of living within a college community persuaded young men to lead regular and diligent lives. The pervading influence in achieving these ends was supposed to be the young dons, all of them bachelors, who lived in college, tutored the undergraduates in classics or mathematics until a college living fell vacant to which they could move—and there marry. Educational theories—our own no less than those of the past—bear a somewhat tenuous relationship to reality, and Leslie Stephen was to write some trenchant and amusing passages which threw doubt on the notion that the fubsy dons, quite a number of whom, being far from young, preferred to stay on into a restful middle age solaced by port, were inspiring guides to youth, or even conversed with them. But it was this theory which explains why Leslie Stephen became a clergyman.

Stephen did more perhaps than any other single don during the century to change the notion of this moral training. During the ten years that he was a fellow of Trinity Hall, he made games and athletic pursuits into a cult. Famous as a walker, the fifty miles to London for a dinner and fifty miles back being as nothing to him, he was even more famous as a rowing coach. Athletics and mountaineering in the Alps were other diversions which he popularized. He was an entirely new type of don, someone who invited undergraduates to his room, entertained them, sympathized with their pursuits, and influenced their lives by example, not by preaching at them.

Yet there was more to his days than coaching pupils in mathematics in the morning and coaching them on the river in the afternoon. Indeed mathematics no longer occupied his leisure hours. A few years after he became a fellow, Stephen was reading modern philosophy ardently, and he must have won a reputation for knowing something about it, since in 1861 he was appointed an examiner for the newly instituted first degree in philosophy—or as it was called significantly in Cambridge, the "moral sciences."

Then came the change of heart which changed his life. Between 1859 and 1864 he lost his faith in Christianity. Most likely the continuous effort of scrutinizing the logic of the argument in the books he was reading began the process of making him consider what he himself actually believed. Certainly the reception of Darwin's *Origin of Species* in 1859 confirmed any doubts he may have had before that date. By 1862 he told the Master of his college that he could no longer conduct the chapel service. To him there was only one course open for an honest man to take. He resigned his fellowship and two years later left Cambridge for London.

I record these biographical facts because they give us a glimpse of Stephen's mind and of the character which shaped that mind. It was no accident that Stephen chose to call his first collection of articles *Essays in Freethinking and Plainspeaking*. Nor should we be surprised that the title means what it says. When Stephen evaluated a thinker, he did not genuflect or equivocate or display any hesitant respect or hedge and counterbalance his own judgments. Nor did he refer much to the judgments of other scholars, still less enter into dispute with them. He did not even justify his own approach to the work at hand. But this self-confidence is deceptive. He had as hearty a skepticism of the value of his own work as he had for those about whom he wrote. Vanity of vanities, saith the Preacher; and no one was quicker than Stephen to declare there was no new thing under the sun. He expressed his own judgment forcibly, but he was the last to suggest that he had said the last word. He spoke his mind because he knew his audience to be those families with whom he had grown up and whose children went to Oxford and

Cambridge. They and those serious book-reading subscribers to the Victorian periodicals in Scotland and the north of England expected to have clear and trenchant opinions put before them.

Stephen had a sharp eye for cant. The hypocritical, whining language which has lost all its meaning through repetition and affects to express emotions which in fact have long since evaporated, if they indeed ever burned bright, was anathema to him. But there was another kind of cant which Stephen was adept in uncovering. That was the unconscious kind which emanates because the speaker has ceased to use his mind and assumes a certain comfortable state of affairs to exist when in reality it does not. For instance, the way in which dons defended the curriculum at the public schools or the university and declared that the routine of college life, with its chapel services and hall dinner, elevated the character, when the majority of undergraduates were devoured by boredom and wasted their time and substance with never a goal in sight, seemed to Stephen astonishing and worthy of some tart comment. There was a resemblance between the don who coached the college boat with such fury, as if to say, "You may despise this as childish if you like, but it's more honest and valuable as a means of training character than the more usual affectations of the young or for that matter of their seniors," and the man of letters who, analyzing the writings of some eighteenth-century theologian or philosopher, audibly groaned when he detected a non sequitur in his argument or came across some proposition which flew in the face of common sense.

The most important biographical fact is naturally his confident agnosticism. Confident because Stephen said quite simply: "You cannot believe in any meaningful sense of the word belief these so-called dogmas of the church." This was the citadel from which he went to war as an intellectual historian. He advanced from the premise that the truth of any religion, but in particular Christianity, could not be demonstrated. Although he was as scrupulous in dissecting the flaws in the utilitarianism of John Stuart Mill or the positivism of Auguste Comte or the political economy of

Adam Smith and Ricardo as he was in exposing the errors of some miserable Deist, he stands foursquare in the tradition of Victorian rationalism. Stephen was very far from measuring thinkers against some rationalist yardstick. That is why he is superior to the Comtean positivist Frederic Harrison, or to those two historians of the rationalist movement, J. M. Robertson and A. W. Benn, who aspired to write for the nineteenth century the kind of history of ideas which Stephen wrote for the eighteenth century. But his greater critical ability and his determination to expose error in whatever quarter it appeared, could not disguise his own commitment to empiricism. At the time Stephen began to publish, so it may have appeared to some,[1] the reaction against rationalism which had swept in on the successive waves of Coleridgean intuitive thought, German idealist philosophy, the Oxford movement, Roman Catholic ultramontanism, and, above all, of Carlyle and the romantic movement, had submerged Locke, Hartley, and Hume and all their appendages. But in fact there were always two broad highways of thought along which men trudged throughout nineteenth-century England. There was the religious and romantic highway, relying on intuitionist psychology, and there was the scarcely less powerful philosophic radicalism of Bentham and James Mill, always being reinforced, first by the political economists, then by the natural scientists, and then again by the second generation of utilitarians, John Stuart Mill and Henry Sidgwick. Neither highway ever disappeared into the sands. But Stephen signposted his chosen road and, reminding his contemporaries whence it came, forecast whither it would go.

There is, however, a puzzle within *English Thought in the Eighteenth Century* which was first detected by John Bicknell, who has written the best article on Stephen as a historian of ideas.[2] Bicknell noted that Stephen's introduction to that work maintains that "the immediate causes of change are to be sought rather in social development than in the activity of a few speculative minds. A complete history of thought would therefore have to take into account the social influences, as well as the logical bearing, of the varying phases of opinion."[3] Yet, having led the reader to the top of Pisgah and spread the Promised Land before him, Stephen then makes it clear that he at any rate will not lead him into it. He confines himself to the logic of the thinkers whom he analyzes, considering "the successive controversies as of a continuous debate in which each writer starts from positions determined by the previous course of the discussion."[4] Bicknell solves the puzzle by remarking sagaciously that the introduction to a book, far from being the first words on the virgin sheets of paper which lie on a writer's desk, is usually the very last part of the book ever to be written. He then shows that Stephen's great work was very much a tract for the times. Stephen wanted to convince his readers that many of the eighteenth-century thinkers had anticipated the freethinkers of their own time. In the essays he wrote in the sixties Stephen was even more explicit than he was in his history; here he takes pleasure in suggesting that Shaftesbury was the Matthew Arnold of his day, Clarke a Dean Mansel, and Mandeville a Darwin.[5] His contemporaries could hardly have failed to feel the thrust of Stephen's argument. Few could have been left in much doubt that Stephen regarded the attempts by the orthodox to sustain the truth of Christianity as unsuccessful, and the attempts of the Deists to substitute for it a rational religion founded on nature as no less ruinous. Almost in an aside Stephen conceded that the conditions in the eighteenth century hardly favored the discovery of arguments which would convince men that revealed religion was false. That was why the work had to be done all over again in his own generation.

Another reason why it had to be done all over again is that rationalism is such a bloodless, abstract creed. Bicknell concludes his article by remarking that Stephen poses a question: How could those who believe in reason make contact with the mass of men and capture their hearts as Wesley had done? To Stephen, Methodism and the Evangelical movement had put the clock back. Could one discover, therefore, some hitherto unperceived emotional strength in rationalism which would satisfy the longing that men feel and that was at present assuaged by religion? Not, surely, through some phoney cooked-up rite such as Comte's Religion of Humanity.

Stephen's fears were justified. The last years of his life coincided with the rise of new religious movements—Christian Science, Theosophy, Spiritualism, and dozens of fundamentalist sects. But it was not these which were going to dash the hopes of Stephen's kind of rationalist. It was the rise of nationalism, the consciousness of belonging to a special ethnic and linguistic community among mankind, which has made diplomacy in our time a nightmare and "rational" solutions to political problems unattainable. The enormous power that nationalism was to have over men's minds was not foreseen by the thinkers of Stephen's time; those who noted the phenomenon considered it to be an agreeable and worthy kind of loyalty. Nor could they conceive that it could take the form of an irrational and fanatical political movement, fascism, which would plunge Europe into a second world war and rejoice in trampling upon the kind of society Stephen believed in.

But there did appear a rationalist creed which captivated the imagination of thousands of intellectuals in the century after Stephen's death and which satisfied all too successfully his hope of a logical coherent body of thought which at the same time imbued its adherents with something of the same passion inspiring evangelists of the Church Militant. This was Marxism. Marxism arguably also satisfied that hope, which he expressed in the Introduction to *English Thought in the Eighteenth Century* and never really fulfilled, of relating ideas to the society in which they flourished. What would he have thought of this creed? It is unprofitable to speculate what a man long dead would have made of the intellectual and political movements of another age, but if we are to judge from the way Stephen denounced Taine—whose methodology of criticizing English literature should on the face of it have appealed to him—he would have found in Marxism the same unacceptable willingness to torture facts and use double-speak as he disliked in Taine.

Several other movements have liked to think of Stephen as their ancestor. He was claimed body and soul, bag and baggage by the Leavises as a precursor of their own interpretation of English cultural history.[6] According to them the true line of responsible, serious Cambridge thought descended from Stephen to themselves. The culture of Russell, Keynes, and Bloomsbury was to them a deplorable corruption of a great tradition, and it was a virtue to refer habitually to Virginia Woolf as "the clever daughter of Sir Leslie Stephen" in order to place and dismiss her. To anyone with a historical mind this pretension is fraudulent. The strands in Stephen's thought are too varied and intertwined to sustain such a narrow interpretation of his ideas.

If, then, we ask what Stephen himself considered the true substitute for religion—what would inspire men to follow reason and what the eighteenth-century rationalists had lacked—the answer he gave was clear. It was the sense men have that this is right and that is wrong which should, ideally, be a sufficient inspiration and comfort. The living duty to discriminate between good and evil was for Stephen as moving as the quest for the Holy Grail. The rationalist should not be guided solely by the light of reason and the operation of logic. Accusing Shaftesbury of facile optimism or Mandeville of cynicism, Stephen rends those eighteenth-century rationalists whom at first sight he might have been expected to welcome as allies, and praises such Christians as Butler for facing candidly the question of evil in the world, or Johnson for humility, masked though it often was by his famous manner. Johnson— high Tory, terrified of hell, superstitious, the man who dealt with Berkeley's theory of the nonexistence of matter by kicking a stone and saying "I refute it thus"—was dearly loved by Stephen because, upholder of law and order as he was, he hated cruelty and injustice as much as he hated anarchy; because he despised optimism but, finding the world miserable and tormenting, never abused it or gave way to self-pity; because he loathed cant, hypocrisy, and pretence and, underneath the bullying veneer, considered himself the humblest of God's creatures. These were some of the virtues which Stephen wanted rationalists to insist must be revealed in any vision of life which they wanted to substitute for the religious vision. Whether he was writing biography, criticizing a thinker, or judging a novelist, Stephen was always doing so as a moralist to whom virtue and vice were so unambiguous that there was scarcely any need to ask his reader to identify them.

Aware though he was of the power of metaphysical systems over men's minds, Stephen believed too fundamentally in the March of Mind, the gradual elimination of error and folly in the light of new knowledge, for him to grasp how deeply, in fact, traditional morality was sustained by metaphysics. He knew well that faith leads all too often to hideous perversions in political practice, to war, torture, and intolerance. He even sensed that when men yearn for a faith, they do so in order to relieve themselves from the responsibility of moral decision; they want to unload their problems onto a historical process or a psychoanalytical explanation of their own discontents. Stephen denounced his eighteenth-century thinkers for thinking that morality consists in avoiding extremes. The doctrine of the golden mean does not open the gate to a moral and harmonious life. But he was orthodox enough to believe that all good ends can be reconciled and that all moral conflicts ultimately are resolvable. Holding this belief, he was therefore no precursor of pluralism; nor did he detach himself from the dilemmas in which a moralist of his persuasion must logically find himself.

Stephen, then, considers that a historian of thought should concern himself first with the logical consistency of the writer he is examining. He should pursue his argument, or lack of it, relentlessly in order to see whether it stands up to close and exact scrutiny. Stephen is uninterested in what interested Lovejoy, the genealogy of ideas. His first question is always the same; do the concepts the writer holds make sense? Next he asks whether the writer's morality—his implicit recognition of what is right and wrong, and his ability to judge the state of the world in the light of that morality—stands up to a different kind of scrutiny. The scrutiny here is not that of a philosopher, crucial though it is to understand the foundations of ethics. The scrutiny Stephen imposed resembles what many people today expect literary critics to give us. Only by peering into the intricacies of character to show how men live in practice can one demonstrate that they can experience joy. Only by acquiring the highest number of good attributes can one show that the sorrows that life brings can be endured.

To resurrect the ideas of the past in order to bring them to the seat of judgment is unfashionable today. Is it not applying to the past the criteria of the present? Is not historical hindsight a self-flattering type of judgment? What have we here but another Whig interpretation of past thinkers? Possibly. One cannot forever use the same approach, and inevitably new questions begin to be asked. And questions which either take for granted the pluralist interpretation of ideas or alternatively operate within a neo-Marxist interpretation of society are not likely to be concerned with the objective truth of propositions. But Stephen's method has one immense advantage. He asks his reader to judge not whether the work in question is interesting or illuminates the society in which the writer lived or reflects the social movements and aspirations of the times. He asks him whether it is true. He asks him what are the consequences of holding the doctrine or embracing the vision of life which the work displays. Stephen's method was after all followed by most historians of ideas in Britain until after World War II, and in America G. H. Sabine's great textbook on political thought is a triumphant vindication of his approach. There is indeed a great deal to be said for compelling people to declare how they stand in relation to a system of ideas. Stephen agreed readily enough that the impersonal forces of history in some respects dictate the prevailing moral code and erect what he called a "municipal law" for each age. But he also declared that there exists a "law of nature" in which all municipal laws can be subsumed. How this law of nature is to be discovered or justified, Stephen does not say; but throughout his writing he shows that for him Mill had said the last word. The intellectual conflicts of each age leave behind a nugget of pure gold which succeeding ages can convert into their own currency.

All his mature life Stephen wrestled with the relationship between the municipal laws and the law of nature. Here he is pondering the problem in 1900, four years before he died, in his three volume history of the English Utilitarians:

To give an account of [how the creeds current among mankind were determined by the social conditions as well as helped to determine them] it is necessary to specify the various circumstances which may lead to the survival of error, and to the partial views of truth taken by men of different idiosyncrasies working upon different data and moved by different passions and prepossessions. A history written upon these terms would show primarily what, as a fact, were the dominant beliefs during a given period and state, which survived, which disappeared, and which were transformed or engrafted upon other systems of thought. This would of course raise the question of the truth or falsehood of the doctrines as well as of their vitality; for the truth is at least one essential condition of permanent vitality.[7]

Stephen, as so often when he reaches this point in expounding his methodology, becomes diffuse. Let us therefore return to the puzzle which tickled John Bicknell's fancy when he noticed that the method advocated in the Introduction to Stephen's *English Thought in the Eighteenth Century* bore little relation to the method employed throughout the two volumes. Bicknell, it will be remembered, ascribed this to the fact that introductions get written after the author finishes his book, not when he begins it. But perhaps we can find in Stephen's own writing the reason why he failed ever to do what he believed he ought to be doing. In the last book he ever wrote, his Ford lectures, *English Literature and Society in the Eighteenth Century,* once again he stated the problem and walked round it; but solve it he could not. Why did he fail?

"Truths have been discovered and lost because the world was not ripe for them." Stephen's words can be applied to his own failure. Men wanted to relate ideas to society, but they did not yet know how to do so. To begin with, Darwin's triumph mesmerized them. If Darwin had revealed the laws of natural selection and the evolution of the species, then surely the next step was to discover the laws of social evolution. The social Darwinists claimed to do just that: to explain why society had developed the way that it had and to predict the way it was going to develop in the future. Marx himself believed that he was doing for society what Darwin had done for nature.

But it is not Marx's laws of political evolution—the inevitable displacement of the middle class by the proletariat as rulers—which has won him enduring fame as a social analyst. It is his perception of the *relationship* of economic forms and forces to the class structure, and both to the political, intellectual, religious, and artistic culture of society which we so admire today as an insight of astonishing originality. Even so it took another generation of social scientists to deepen our sense of these relationships and remove them from political polemic and praxis. The first modern sociologists, Weber and Durkheim, the economist Alfred Marshall and the functional, and later the structuralist, anthropologists of the twentieth century had to publish and be interpreted before people discovered how to make the kind of analysis which was so dear to Stephen's heart. It took men nearly a century to abandon the positivist interpretation of society which Comte and Mill employed and which Stephen implicitly accepted. It took hundreds of books and thousands of articles to dissipate the notion that society must be interpreted primarily through the individual. A new conceptual scheme of reference had to be woven like a spider's web to catch, despatch, and devour lazy ideas of a past age so that a new and wily attack could be made on Stephen's problem of relating literature to thought and both to society. It could not have been done earlier. Indeed, when it began to be done, principally by Marxist scholars, the crudity of their interpretations in treating ideas and art as a mere superstructure repelled dispassionate scholars. It even ultimately repelled Marxists such as Lukacs. Nor have some of the attempts by sociologists of literature in the post-Weber era been all that happy: literature has been imprisoned and then pressed to death by the fearful weight the sociological concepts imposed upon it. But Stephen would have found much satisfaction in the way today's scholars relate ideas and art to the times. What Ian Watt did for Defoe, for example, seems to me to be the kind of analysis which Stephen wanted done.[8]

The extracts from Leslie Stephen's works which I have collected illustrate the way he approached the history of ideas. The book begins with his Introduction to his most famous work, *English Thought in the Eighteenth Century,* and it should be read with John Bicknell's comments in mind. Then follow three studies of writers, selected from the same work. The essay on Bishop Butler illustrates Stephen's candor and fairness of mind; that on Hume, his admiration for clarity and empiricism; and that on Warburton, his method of dissecting an argument. The next extract is taken from the beginning of *English Literature and Society in the Eighteenth Century*, the book Stephen wrote at the end of his life and his final attempt to put into practice the method which he advocated in the Introduction with which these extracts start. Here he tries to show how the literature of those days could have been written only then, so impregnated is it with the ethos and assumptions of that society.

The next article illustrates what Stephen thought was the duty of a literary critic. It is his sole attempt to analyze the function of criticism; and since so many of his writings were in effect essays in literary criticism, he cannot be judged as a historian of ideas without considering what he thought criticism is about.

Although Stephen would have hoped that his most important contribution to moral philosophy was contained in the *Science of Ethics*, in fact his studies of the morality of certain writers was far more valuable. His essays on Johnson and Wordsworth show him at his best in moral analysis. In these essays one can see how scrupulous Stephen was in weighing what he must have found unsatisfactory as philosophy yet enchanting as morality. He does not expect a poet to exhibit the same internal coherence of thought as a philosopher or theologian. His first concern is to tell the reader what the writer was about, how to get inside his ideas, and through sympathy understand him. Only then does he make judgments; and he was never afraid to indulge his sense of humor.

The last essay is one of the finest statements written in the Victorian age of the case for freedom of expression. This essay illustrates Stephen's power to explore the liberal tradition and produce what to my mind is an even more cogent argument for freedom of expression than Mill made in his essay *On Liberty*. Inevitably, since Stephen wrote, other arguments have to be met and countered; and anyone wanting a more up to date defence should read Isaiah Berlin's *Four Essays on Freedom*.

"Poisonous Opinions" is as essential a prop to Stephen's ideas as *An Agnostic's Apology*, the title of the book in which it appears. Stephen, as a historian of thought, was a positivist. Like Comte and Mill he assumed that truth is a unity. Every change in society is preceded by a change in men's beliefs and in their store of knowledge. The operative word is *preceded*. Changes in knowledge come first; changes in society second. Human falsehood is the enemy of human progress. That is why there must be free thinking and plain speaking.

Stephen has his limitations. Detesting affectation, he used his trenchant humorous irony to deprecate not only sloppy thinking in others but his own calling. He was a little too circumspect, too ready to deal with authors so long as they were stone dead and too unwilling to venture a judgment on the living, too eager to pride himself on being a bit of a philistine and think he was doing Arnold a service by declaring that although old Mat had said some hard things about philistines, he really cannot have meant it since he could hardly have despaired of that genial Caliban, the Middle Class, to which they both belonged. Nor can it be denied that the great German historiographical movement which made so little impact upon British historians until the end of the nineteenth century, displayed a sophistication unknown to Stephen. But then in England neither was anyone else a professional historian in the German sense. Hallam, Macaulay, Froude, and Lecky were all amateurs. Until history took root in the universities, it could not be otherwise; and when this occurred, Stubbs at Oxford and at Cambridge the great Maitland, Stephen's biographer, set new standards in their treatment of sources.

But Stephen was a great man of letters. Maitland would never out of friendship have written of his accomplishments as a historian of ideas, as he did, and complimented him on his "audacity" in covering such a vast field in the eighteenth century. Stephen had marvelous gifts which often put the professional historian to shame. His clarity of mind, strengthened by his mathematical training, enabled him to tease out the strands of reasoning in a writer; and his own dialectical powers, exercised with charm as well as skill, make his reader feel that he is being taken by the elbow through difficulties, rather than frog-marched into comprehension. The term *man of letters* has fallen into disrepute in our time. Yet how much we owe to amateurs, to men such as H. L. Mencken or Edmund Wilson, whose natural talents and readiness to express views springing from wide reading and reflection shame scholarly caution and obsession with problems of method which so often end by paralyzing the writer and smothering the reader. Despite the fact that in old age Stephen liked to maintain that philosophical thought and imaginative literature could have no history, since they are no more than "the noise the wheels make as they go round,"[9] his achievement is a standing rebuke to those who would reduce history to an analysis of social movements in which men and women and what they believe their destiny to be are insignificant. Stephen knew that human beings are at the mercy of the impersonal forces of history but are not totally their playthings. As a historian, he praised those who through their writing left some mark upon their age so that their times would not be forgotten or despised by the generations to come. As a man, he praised those with the courage and endurance to confront whatever life dealt them and to go on working until the end. It is not an ignoble creed, and he lived up to it.

NOËL ANNAN

Bibliographical Note

Works by Leslie Stephen

A checklist of Stephen's writings will be found in S. A. O. Ullmann's edition of Stephen's *Men, Books and Mountains* (1956). The most important works to read, considering Stephen as an intellectual historian, are the following:

> *History of English Thought in the Eighteenth Century.* 2 vols. 1876. 3d ed., 1902.
> *The English Utilitarians.* 3 vols. 1900.
> *English Literature and Society in the Eighteenth Century.* 1904.
> *Hobbes.* 1904.
> *Essays on Freethinking and Plainspeaking.* 1905 ed.
> *An Agnostic's Apology.* 1893.
> *Studies of a Biographer.* 4 vols. 1907.
> *Hours in a Library.* 4 vols. 1907.

Works about Leslie Stephen

The commemorative biography of Stephen was written by the great medieval and legal historian F. W. Maitland, *The Life and Letters of Leslie Stephen* (1906). A fragment of autobiography which he wrote for his children has now been edited by Alan Bell and published as *Sir Leslie Stephen's Mausoleum*

Book (1977). There is also a short account of his life by Quentin Bell in *Virginia Woolf*, 1:1–86.

The following are recommended for further reading on Leslie Stephen as a historian of ideas:

Nöel Annan. *Leslie Stephen: His Thought and Character in Relation to His Times.* 1951.

John W. Bicknell. "Leslie Stephen's 'English Thought in the Eighteenth Century': A Tract for the Times." *Victorian Studies,* vol. 6, no. 2 (December 1962). Also unpublished doctoral thesis, Cornell University, 1950.

Alan Brown. *The Metaphysical Society.* 1947.

Sidney A. Burrell. *Some Modern Historians of Britain,* ed. Herman Ansubel. 1951.

Phyllis Grosskurth. "Leslie Stephen." In *Writers and Their Work.* 1968.

H. Sidgwick. Review of Stephen's "Science of Ethics" in *Mind,* 1882.

David D. Zink. *Leslie Stephen,* chap. 3. 1972.

1

English Thought in the Eighteenth Century

The Philosophical Basis: Introductory

1. Between the years 1739 and 1752 David Hume published philosophical speculations destined, by the admission of friends and foes, to form a turning-point in the history of thought. His first book 'fell dead-born from the press;' few of its successors had a much better fate. The uneducated masses were, of course, beyond his reach; amongst the educated minority he had but few readers; and amongst the few readers still fewer who could appreciate his thoughts. The attempted answers are a sufficient proof that even the leaders of opinion were impenetrable to his logic. Men of the highest reputation completely failed to understand his importance. Warburton and Johnson were successively dictators in the literary world. Warburton attacked Hume with a superb unconsciousness of their true proportions which has now become amusing. Johnson thought that Hume's speculations were a case of 'milking the bull'[1]—that is to say, of a morbid love of change involving a preference of new error to old truth —and imagined that he had been confuted by Beattie.[2]

If Hume impressed men of mark so slightly, we are tempted to doubt whether he can have affected the main

Reprinted from *History of English Thought in the Eighteenth Century* (1876), chaps. 1 (abridged), 5, 6, and 7.

current of thought. Yet, as we study the remarkable change in the whole tone and substance of our literature which synchronised with the appearance of Hume's writings, it is difficult to resist the impression that there is some causal relation. A cold blast of scepticism seems to have chilled the very marrow of speculative activity. Men have lost their interest in the deepest problems, or write as though paralysed by a half-suppressed consciousness of the presence of a great doubter.

2. The explanation of the apparent contradiction must doubtless be sought partly in the fact that Hume influenced a powerful though a small class. He appealed to a few thinkers, who might be considered as the brain of the social organism; and the effects were gradually propagated to the extremities of the system. The influence, indeed, of Hume's teaching is the more obscure because chiefly negative. It produced in many minds a languid scepticism which cared little for utterance, and might see, without proclaiming, the futility of Warburton's insolence or Johnson's dogmatic contempt. But the rapidity and extent of the transformation of the whole body of speculation points unmistakably to the working of influences too manifold and potent to be embodied in any single personality. The soul of the nation was stirred by impulses of which Hume was but one, though by far the ablest, interpreter; or, to speak in less mystical phrase, we must admit that thousands of inferior thinkers were dealing with the same problems which occupied Hume, and, though with far less acuteness or logical consistency, arriving at similar solutions. It is as if they felt what Hume saw, or perceived implicitly and obscurely what he brought out with the most explicit lucidity. What is the real nature of this process? How is it that a tacit intellectual co-operation is established between minds placed far apart in the scale of culture and natural acuteness? How is it that the thought of the intellectual leaders is obscurely reflected by so many darkened mirrors, even when we are unable to point to any direct and overt means of transmission? How far may we believe in the apparent unity of that shifting chaos of speculations of more or less independent thinkers, which forms what we vaguely describe as public opinion, or the spirit of the age?

2

3. Historians of philosophy naturally limit their attention to the ablest thinkers. They tell us how the torch was passed from hand to hand—from Descartes to Locke, from Locke to Hume, and from Hume to Kant. Men become leaders of thought in virtue of the fact that their opinions are in some degree influenced by reason. Thus the progress of speculation may be represented as determined by logical considerations. Each philosopher discovers some of the errors of his predecessor, and advances to some closer approximation to the truth. Though a superficial glance suggests that succeeding thinkers are related rather as antagonists than allies, more careful observation may show that each great man has contributed some permanent element of truth, and that there is thus a continuous, though a very tortuous, advance in speculation. Thought moves in a spiral curve, if not in a straight line. But, when we look beyond the narrow circle of illustrious philosophers, we are impressed with the conviction that other causes are at work besides those which are obvious to the logician. Doctrines vanish without a direct assault; they change in sympathy with a change in apparently remote departments of inquiry; superstitions, apparently suppressed, break out anew in slightly modified shapes; and we discover that a phase of thought, which we had imagined to involve a new departure, is but a superficial modification of an old order of ideas.

4. Before tracing the development of that particular movement of thought of which I am about to sketch the history, it may be well to consider this familiar phenomenon a little more closely. Our knowledge has, in some departments, passed into the scientific stage. It can be stated as a systematic body of established truths. It is consistent and certain. The primary axioms are fixed beyond the reach of scepticism; each subordinate proposition has its proper place; and the conclusions deduced are in perfect harmony. If the truths thus established do not conform to any observed phenomenon, we are entitled to infer confidently, not that the doctrine is wrong, but that some disturbing element has escaped our observation. Every new discovery fits into the old system, receiving and giving confirmation. We may arrange our first principles under some wider generalisation, but we are not

called upon to modify their essential truth. The typical case is, of course, that of the mathematical sciences. Euclid's propositions are as true as ever; and the doctrine about floating bodies, which Archimedes discovered in his bath, has not been refuted. The map of human knowledge has here become far wider and more detailed, but the outlines once laid down remain unaltered. If the intellect could thus have always passed from the known to the unknown—if, in every advance to new conquests, its base of operations had always been secure—the whole history of speculation would have been of a similar character.

5. History shows a very different state of facts. In many departments of thought the foundations are still insecure. Men are wrangling as fiercely as ever over metaphysical problems substantially identical with those which perplexed the most ancient Greek sages. The controversial battle has raged backwards and forwards over the old ground, till general weariness, rather than victory, seems likely to conclude the strife. One reason is plain. Some theory about phenomena not yet accurately investigated is necessary in the earliest periods. Before the regularity of the order of nature had ever been asserted, men assumed at every step some principle in which it was more or less implied. When astronomy was scarcely in the embryonic stage, savage races must have had some views as to the recurrence of times and seasons. Even the brutes, we must suppose, have some implicit recognition of the simplest sequences of events; and in the lowest human intellect there are the rudiments of scientific knowledge. But these rudiments are strangely distorted by innumerable errors. In other words, before we know, we are naturally prompted to guess. We must lay down postulates before we arrive at axioms. Most of these, we must suppose, will possess an element of truth. A belief which brought a man into too direct collision with facts would soon disappear along with the believer. An erroneous postulate, however, may survive, if not so mischievous as to be fatal to the agent. Others may stand the test of verification by experience, and may finally take their place as accepted and ultimate truths. The greater number, perhaps, will be materially modified, or will gradu-

ally disappear, leaving behind them a residuum of truth. Thus the progress of the intellect necessarily involves a conflict. It implies destruction as correlative to growth. The history of thought is in great part a history of the gradual emancipation of the mind from the errors spontaneously generated by its first childlike attempts at speculation. Doctrines which once appeared to be simply expressions of immediate observation have contained a hypothetical element, gradually dissolved by contact with facts.

6. To hasten this slow progress of disintegration, to dissolve the old associations of ideas, and bring about their crystallisation round a new framework of theory, is a task to be performed slowly and tentatively even by the acutest intellects. Even when the reason has performed its part, the imagination lags behind. We may be convinced of the truth of every separate step in a scientific demonstration, and even be able to grasp it as a whole, and yet the concrete picture which habitually rises before our mind's eye may express the crude old theories which we have ostensibly abandoned. In ordinary moods, we are still in the days of the old astronomy, and unable to believe in the antipodes; and in movements of poetical feeling, we easily return to the mental condition of the believers in the solar myths. Old conceptions are preserved to us in the very structure of language; the mass of mankind still preserves its childish imaginations; and every one of us has repeated on a small scale the history of the race. We start as infants with fetish worship; we consider our nursery to be the centre of the universe; and learn but slowly and with difficulty to conform our imaginative constructions to scientific truths. It is no wonder, then, if the belief, even of cultivated minds, is often a heterogeneous mixture of elements representing various stages of thought; whilst in different social strata we may find specimens of opinions derived from every age of mankind.

7. When opinion has passed into this heterogeneous state, the first step has been taken towards a complete transformation. The two characteristic instincts of the philosopher are the desire for certainty and the desire for harmony. The few in whom a love of speculative truth amounts to a passion seek

on the one hand for a solid foundation of unassailable truths, and on the other endeavour to bring all departments of knowledge into agreement with established principles. In some minds the desire for unity of system is the more strongly developed; in others the desire for conformity to facts; and during the earlier stages of inquiry the two instincts must be frequently in conflict. So long as our knowledge is imperfect, we shall often have to choose between a want of symmetry and a want of accuracy. In time, we may hope that a definitive philosophy will give full satisfaction to both instincts. That time is doubtless distant; and the more distant because, with the mass of mankind, the love of speculative truth is amongst the weakest of impulses. It is only by slow degrees that the philosopher can hope to disperse the existing prejudices, and extend the borders of his intellectual cosmos over the ancient realms of chaos. We may hope that in the end he will be triumphant; for he has the advantage that his conquests, if slow, are permanent; and the gradual adaptation of the race to its medium, which is the underlying law of development, implies that there is a tendency towards a growing conformity between the world of thought and the world of facts. It is not that every change implies the substitution of truth for error, but that, in the ceaseless struggle, truth has at least the one point in its favour—that when once reached it is more likely to be permanently held. Each established truth may serve as a nucleus round which all further discoveries may gradually group themselves.

8. The purely intellectual impulse is thus of the highest importance, though it corresponds to a feeble desire. When once the process has begun, when a foothold has been obtained by the pioneers of intellectual progress, the process will continue, though often slowly and obscurely, unless the spirit of inquiry be extinguished by tyranny or atrophied by some process of social decay. That the process should be generally slow and obscure follows from the general law of persistence. Old customs and institutions, even of the most trivial kind, linger long after their origin has been forgotten and some new justification has been invented for them. Forms of language and of thought have a similar vitality, and

persist long after they are recognised as cumbrous and mis-leading. Every change must originate with some individual who, by virtue of his originality, must be in imperfect sympathy with the mass of his contemporaries. Nor can any man, however versatile his intellect, accommodate his mind easily or speedily to a new method and a new order of ideas.

9. A new opinion emerges, as a rule, in regard to some particular fragment of a creed. An acute thinker detects an error of logic, or a want of correspondence between theory and fact. Whilst correcting the error, he does not appreciate the importance of the principles involved. He fancies that he is removing a morbid excrescence when he is cutting into a growth vitally connected with the whole organism. Controversies, which are afterwards seen to involve radically antagonistic conceptions of philosophy, begin by some special and minor corollary. The superficial fissure extends deeper and deeper, until the whole mass is rent in twain. The controversy which began at the Reformation appeared at first to turn upon the interpretation of a few texts: it has spread, until we see that it implicitly involved discussions as to the ultimate groundwork of all human knowledge. Two different modes of conceiving the universe and regulating life were struggling for the mastery. The most heterogeneous forms of opinion are involved, as such controversies develop themselves and affect minds in the most various stages of culture. The less acute intellects accept incongruous solutions, and admit a principle in one case, which they arbitrarily reject in cases logically identical. Illustrations might be given from every department of thought. One man believes that prayers can retard eclipses; a second laughs at his superstition, but holds that they can hasten fine weather; a third rejects these views, but clings to the belief that the course of a plague, or the issue of a battle, or the development of a character, may be influenced by the same method. People believe in miracles which happened a thousand years ago who would ridicule a miraculous story of to-day. Politicians hold that the suffrage is the inherent right of every human being; and add arbitrary limitations which exclude half or nine-tenths of the species. Free-trade is admitted to be beneficial to each of two prov-

inces or two federal states, and denied to be beneficial if the
states become nations. The normal attitude of thought is to
be heterogeneous, and therefore unstable. When the key of
the position is won, a battle has still to be fought over every
subordinate position. Philosophers, however, may congratu-
late themselves upon the inconsistency of mankind; for if it
were generally admitted that a principle which is true in one
case must be true in all similar cases, philosophy would be
crushed in the shell by the antipathies aroused. Philosophers
may win their way step by step, because the ordinary mind
deals only with special cases, and cares little for the ultimate
logical consequences.

10. But philosophers themselves are subject to the same
illusions in a scarcely inferior degree. The vulgar accept incoherent conglomerates of inconsistent theories. The philosopher has a more refined procedure for softening the process of
transition. The ordinary process is familiar in the history of
law. Old rules which are too narrow or clumsy for complex
states of society are modified by judicial interpretation without avowed alteration. Legal fictions grow up without a recognition of their fictitious character, as the natural result of
the attempt to bring a new class of facts under the old
formula. The original nucleus is lost to sight under a mass of
accretions and adaptations. Rationalising is the same process
in theology or philosophy. At each particular step it seems
that the old rubric is being expanded or confirmed, and that
its deeper meaning is being brought out by disregarding
trifling changes in the letter; and though the initial stage of a
theory may differ widely from the final, and even, in some
most important cases, be almost its logical contradictory, the
change at any given moment may be imperceptible. This may
perhaps be regarded as the normal process. It is conceivable
that the whole series of our conceptions of the universe, from
the most savage to the most philosophical, might have been
traversed by a continuous and imperceptible process. There
are, indeed, critical points at which the change forces itself
upon our consciousness, and at which the system, gradually
overloaded by the accumulation of new observations and
interpretations, requires a complete reorganisation. But the

great cause of abrupt changes is the fact that the process proceeds at varying rates in different social strata. The vulgar are still plunged in gross superstitions, from which the educated have definitively emerged. A conflict arises between inconsistent modes of thought, as a conflict arises between different systems of law, when two races at different points of the scale of development are brought into contact. The philosophic doctrine, misunderstood by the ruder intellect, gives rise to a crude scepticism, which is but another form of superstition, and the attempt to accommodate the hostile systems, no longer unconsciously carried out, but consciously adopted as a device for evading responsibility, may at times lead to downright dishonesty and disregard of the great virtue of intellectual candour.

11. Another process, however, is illustrated by the exceptional class of minds which really delights in novelty. Since truths and errors have become indissolubly associated, the thinker who perceives the error is tempted to abandon the truth. If moral teaching has been for ages connected with a belief in hell, the thinker who sees that hell is a figment sometimes infers that the moral law is not obligatory. The ordinary comment upon such cases is that an excess of credulity engenders an excess of scepticism. Though such oscillations occur, it is more important to observe that we easily exaggerate their amplitude. The most unflinching sceptic really carries with him far more than he knows of the old methods and conceptions. He inherits the ancient framework of theory and, unable to find a place in it for his new doctrine, cuts away a large fragment to make room for the favourite dogma. To his contemporaries this sacrilegious act appears to be the most important; it is the mark by which they recognise his peculiar character; to observers at a distance it may appear that his conservatism is really more remarkable than his destructiveness. They wonder more that he should have retained so much than that he should have rejected so much. He follows the old method or retains the old conception, though he sees its futility for attaining the old ends. The discord is the result of an incomplete transformation of thought. He gives up hell, but he admits that hell is the only

sanction for morality. He retains the old conception of the limited duration of history, though he rejects the old cosmogony which served to justify the conception. He is, therefore, forced to admit a catastrophe, though disbelieving in the mythology which reconciled the imagination to the catastrophe. We are doubtful whether to be more surprised at the boldness which rejected the old explanation, or at the timidity which retained the old assumptions of fact. The common taunt as to the credulity of sceptics is suggested by such cases. The heretic propounds a heterogeneous system of thought; he admits the validity of part of the orthodox case, whilst explicitly denying the validity of another part. He is, therefore, led into contradictions as glaring as those which he has discovered in the established scheme, whilst their novelty renders them more offensive. The old misconceptions are sanctioned by long association; the contrasts in the novel system of thought are still marked by the glaring crudity of raw conjecture. Thus it constantly happens that the innovator falls into an apparent excess of scepticism simply because he has retained too much of the traditional method. He sees that the old paths are crossed by impassable chasms; and has not yet discovered the existence of other roads to the ancient truths. The general tendency to persistence of ideas is, therefore, illustrated even when we come upon apparent exceptions, though here the shock of transition is intensified, instead of softened, by the tendency to adhere to ancient forms.

12. So far, we have been considering the purely intellectual influences which govern the gradual transformation of accepted theories. The love of abstract truth, the love of consistency, and even the intellectual curiosity which seeks to extend the boundaries of knowledge, are motives which can only be operative in minds of exceptional activity. Any intellectual impulse, however, necessarily sets up a whole series of other changes more appreciable by the ordinary understanding, and is in turn modified by their influence. The logician may work out his problems without regard to ulterior consequences; but these consequences are the exclusive or predominating considerations in determining the acceptance of

his theories by the great mass of mankind. Nor does any creed really flourish in which the faith of the few is not stimulated by the adhesion of the many. What, then, are the main influences, outside of the more logical instincts, which most obviously affect the progress of a new system of thought?

The most obvious of all is the application of any given theory to the material wants of mankind. No creed, as I have said, can be permanent which does not imply an approximate recognition of many facts. A tribe which had an unlimited faith in the efficacy of charms against poisonous plants or savage beasts would be speedily extinguished. Nature would effectually persecute such heretics. But it is also true that a race may be capable of maintaining itself in spite of the grossest superstitions, or mankind would not be in existence. The savage believes in his charms, but he believes more profoundly in his bow and arrows; and thus, many races survive to the present day which still preserve the intellectual habits of the remotest prehistoric past. Still, an increase of knowledge is, so far, an increase of power. The race which possesses some simple acquaintance with rudimentary truths as to the properties of iron has a point in its favour in the great game of life. It will, probably, end by extirpating its neighbours. And, passing to the other extreme of civilisation, the direct utilitarian value of scientific knowledge has become a great source of power. Not less than in the earlier stages, the race which knows most of the physical laws, and can apply them most effectually, has an advantage in that struggle for existence which is not less keen because its character is concealed amongst civilised races. The more direct influence upon the progress of opinion is equally clear. Not only does the most scientific race flourish, but it comes to believe in science. We may denounce, and very rightly, those coarse forms of utilitarianism which imply an excessive love of mere material advantages; but it is not to be forgotten that the prestige acquired by modern science depends in great measure upon its application to purposes of direct utility. Railways and telegraphs are not everything. Most true! but the prospect of bringing the ordinary creeds of mankind into harmony with scientific conclusions depends, in no small

11

degree, upon the general respect for men of science; and that respect, again, depends materially upon the fact that men of science can point to such tangible results as railroads and telegraphs. We need not fear to admit that, if there is a greater chance now than formerly of the ablest intellects acquiring a definite supremacy, and resisting the constant tendency of mankind to lapse into superstition, it is in great degree because such conquests over the material world can be appreciated even by the ignorant, and reflect credit upon that system of thought with which they are associated. This utilitarian tendency of modern science is, at the present day, the first and most direct influence in the transformation of opinion.

13. But the influence of a change in the pervading modes of thought acts in other, and perhaps more potent, though less obvious, methods. There is a correlation between the creeds of a society and its political and social organisation. The belief in the supernatural sanctity of a king or a caste, the prevalence of some ethical views as to the nature of marriage, or the true ends of national existence, are essentially necessary for the preservation of a certain order. If the belief is modified, the order becomes unstable or disappears. The forces of cohesion by which men are held together take a different form. Society may thus be radically altered by the influence of opinions which have apparently little bearing upon social questions. It would not be extravagant to say that Mr. Darwin's observations upon the breeds of pigeons have had a reaction upon the structure of European society. It is, however, as clear as it is more important, to remark that the social development reacts upon the creeds. If, for any reason, as from the stimulus caused by a geographical or a scientific discovery, or by the simple accumulation of wealth, a large class becomes dissatisfied with its position, the attempt to remodel its relations to the whole may involve an attack upon the theories implied in the social order. When a natural organ becomes unfitted for its task—when, for example, the rule of a king or a priesthood becomes intolerable, the religion which sanctions their authority will itself be questioned. No great social change, it is probable, can be carried out

without stimulating some such process. Or, again, when two races at different stages of progress are brought into contact, not only do the ideas current in each directly affect the ideas of the other, but the whole constitution may be changed, and a redistribution of power modify the theories upon which power reposes. A struggle between two different types of government forces upon each nation a consciousness of its own peculiarities, and may intensify or weaken its characteristic beliefs. The mere realisation of the truth that other forms of faith beside the Christian were actually flourishing in a great part of the world profoundly altered the established creeds during the period which followed the reawakening of modern Europe. The extension of commercial activity thus influenced the spiritual life. Any great shock, in short, to the social order, or any new relation to the external world, may react upon the creed. If such changes do not suggest new thoughts, they provide a favourable opportunity for the application of new thoughts. The stirring of the soil gives a chance for the growth of the new seeds of thought. Beliefs which have been dormant, or popular only amongst philosophers, suddenly start into reality, and pass from the sphere of remote speculation to that of immediate practice. The more closely we examine recent developments of opinion, the more, I believe, we shall be convinced that the immediate causes of change are to be sought rather in social development than in the activity of a few speculative minds. A complete history of thought would therefore have to take into account the social influences, as well as the logical bearing, of the varying phases of opinion.

14. The fact becomes more striking when we remember that the creed of a race shapes other manifestations besides its industrial activities and its discharge of social functions. It regulates the play of the imagination, and provides expression for the emotions. Life is not entirely occupied in satisfying our material wants, and co-operating or struggling with our fellows. We dream as well as act. We must provide some channel for the emotions generated by contemplation of the world and of ourselves. A creed is partly an attempt at a systematic statement of our knowledge, real or supposed, and

partly a more or less poetical embodiment of the feelings which have no direct relation to our actions. In the earlier stages of development the distinction scarcely appears. A child does not distinguish between its dreams and realities. Its fancies and its observations are inextricably blended; and it cannot lie because it cannot speak the truth. In the infancy of the race, its history is its poetry; it cannot distinguish between the mythology which represents a vague conjecture and the traditions which more or less record facts. The attempt to separate the two elements is the more difficult because, as I have said, the imagination lags behind the reason, and persists in reproducing the old dreams in indissoluble union with speculations as to facts. When the emotions are roused, the old mode of conceiving the universe revives; and any attempt to dispute its accuracy is resented as needlessly cruel. The new order, constructed by the reason, remains colourless and uninteresting, because the old associations have not yet gathered round it.

15. Wordsworth expresses the familiar sentiment when he wishes that he could be 'a pagan suckled in some creed outworn.' The sight of Proteus and Triton might restore to the world the long-vanished charm. Now, as far as science is concerned, we are tempted to say that Wordsworth is simply wrong. The Greek mythology gave an inaccurate representation of the facts. The more accurately we know them the better for us. A slight acquaintance with the law of storms is far more useful to the sailor than any guess about a mysterious being, capriciously raising the waves, and capable, perhaps, of being propitiated by charms. From the purely utilitarian point of view, we are the better off the closer the correspondence between our beliefs and the external realities. But, further, we are tempted to say the same even in a poetical sense. Why should Wordsworth regret Proteus and Triton? Because the Greek inferred from the sea the existence of beings the contemplation of whose power and beauty was a source of delight to him? But, in the first place, the facts are to Wordsworth what they were to the Greek. If the Greek thought the sea lovely in colour or form, the colour and the form remain. The imaginary being in whom the phenomena

were embodied could only be known through the phenomena. The beauty is beautiful still, though we no longer infer
an imaginary cause. Nothing is lost but a dream, and a
dream, which, by its nature, could only reflect the reality.
Why not love the sea instead of loving Proteus, who is but the
sea personified? And, secondly, we must add that the dream
reflects the painful as well as the pleasurable emotions. When
the superstition was a living reality, instead of a poetical
plaything, we may be sure that it expressed horror as well as
delight. The sailor, imagining a treacherous deity lurking
beneath the waves, saw new cause for dread, and would often
have been glad enough to learn that Proteus was a figment.

16. So far as the myth is simply a rough statement of
observed facts, we may admit that its disappearance is a clear
gain. We may admit, too, that ultimately its disappearance
will not be even a loss to the imagination. When the imaginative synthesis has overtaken the logical, when the bare
framework of formulae has gathered round it the necessary
associations, we may be able to express our emotions directly
as well as by the intervention of a crude hypothesis. And,
further, we may agree that accurate knowledge does not
ultimately alter the apparent balance of pain and pleasure in
the world. The new view will gain as much by dispersing the
old gloomy forebodings as it will lose by dispersing chimerical
hopes. But it must be also admitted that there is an interval,
and a very long interval, of comparatively depressing sentiment. The evil is not that a charm has departed, but that we
have lost a mode of expressing our emotions. The old symbols
have ceased to be interesting, and we have not gained a new
set of symbols. The fact, therefore, that we have dispersed the
gloomy along with the cheerful superstitions is not, in this
sense, relevant. The mind is quite as much in need of an
expression for its fears as of an expression for its hopes. We
invert the relation of cause and effect when we consider that
our emotions are determined by our imaginative creeds. We
are not melancholy because we believe in hell, but we believe
in hell because we are melancholy. The hard facts of the
world, the misery which is blended with every form of human
life and every spring of human action, force us to blend

lamentation with rejoicing. A race, struggling for life, pressed by cold, hunger, disease, and the attacks of enemies, may try to console itself by a dreamland of future happiness, but it must also find expression for its forebodings. No creed, therefore, has a widely spread or continuous vitality which has not embodied all moods of the human mind. Sheer optimism is the least vigorous of beliefs. Believe in a beneficent Creator, and you must also believe in human depravity, and the continued activity of the Devil. Manichæism may be disavowed in words. It cannot be exiled from the actual belief of mankind. And thus the loss which Wordsworth might fairly lament was not the loss of a mistaken theory about facts, nor the loss of a consoling prospect for the future, but the loss of a system of symbols which could enable him to express readily and vigorously every mood produced by the vicissitudes of human life. In time the loss may be replaced, the new language may be learnt; we may be content with direct vision, instead of mixing facts with dreams; but the process is slow, and, till it is completed, the new belief will not have the old power over the mind. The symbols which have been associated with the hopes and fears, with the loftiest aspirations and warmest affections of so many generations, may be proved to be only symbols; but they long retain their power over the imagination. Not only respect for the feelings of our neighbours, but our spontaneous impulses, will tempt us to worship at the shrines in whose gods we no longer believe. The idol may be but a log of wood; yet, if it has been for ages the tutelary deity of a race, they will be slow in discovering that it is possible to express their natural sentiment in any form but that of homage to the old god. The importance of some outward and visible symbol of an emotion is evident in all religious and political history—so evident, that many people hold the symbol to be everything, and the symbolised nothing. Some day patriotism may justify itself, but it cannot yet be expressed except in the form of devotion to some traditional fetish, or to a particular flag. The flag you say is but a bit of coloured cloth. Why not manufacture one as it is wanted? Unluckily, or luckily, it is as hard to create a new symbol as to obtain currency for a new word.

17. Thus the gradual ebbing of an ancient faith leaves a painful discord between the imagination and the reason. The idols gradually lose their sanctity; but they are cherished by poets long after they are disowned by philosophers, and the poet has the greatest immediate influence with the many. In the normal case, therefore, we may assume that the imagination exercises, on the whole, a retarding influence. Science has to appeal to its utilitarian triumphs in order to gain allies against the ancient idolatry. There are, however, times when the emotions take side with the intellect; when the old symbols have become for large classes associated with an oppressive power, and have been turned to account for obviously degrading purposes by their official representatives. These are the periods of the moral earthquakes, which destroy an existing order. It must, however, be repeated that, even in such cases, the most vehement reformers generally retain more than they know of the old spirit. They are attacking rather some corollaries than the vital part of the ancient creed; and an alliance produced by temporary community of purpose between the leaders of the intellectual and the popular revolt may not be so intimate as it appears.

The ultimate victory of truth is a consoling, we may hope that it is a sound, doctrine. If the race gradually accommodates itself to its environment, it should follow that the beliefs of the race gravitate towards that form in which the mind becomes an accurate reflection of the external universe. The closer the correspondence between facts and our mental representation of facts, the more vigorous and permanent should be the creed which emerges. But great forces may work slowly; and it is only after many disturbances and long-continued oscillations that the world is moved from one position of equilibrium to another. Progress is the rare exception: races may remain in the lowest barbarism, or their development be arrested at some more advanced stage during periods far surpassing that of recorded history; actual decay may alternate with progress, and even true progress implies some admixture of decay. The intellectual activity of the acuter intellects, however feeble may be its immediate influence, is the great force which stimulates and guarantees every advance of the race. It is of course opposed by a vast force of inertia. The ordinary mind is indifferent to the thoughts which occupy the philosopher, unless they promise an immediate material result. Mankind resent nothing so much as the intrusion upon them of a new and disturbing truth. The huge dead weight of stupidity and indolence is always ready to smother audacious inquiries. Men of more imagination and finer emotional sensibility are equally inclined to hate the inventor of intellectual novelties. To them the reason presents itself as an 'all-corroding' force, wantonly sapping the foundations of belief, and desecrating all holy symbols. The daring speculator, sufficiently tasked by the effort to escape from his own prejudices, has a hard struggle against this spontaneous alliance of the grosser and finer natures. His motives are often obscure or hateful, and his theories unintelligible. And yet, if not forcibly silenced, he can find a sufficient fulcrum from which to move the world. He can point, and with increasing confidence, to the immediate practical utility of many of his discoveries. Though a respect for abstract logic is rare, there is such a thing as the logic of facts. Theories once worked into the popular mind, in regard to certain particular cases, spread slowly to the most closely analogous cases, though their wider application is still regarded with horror. His alliance, moreover, though distrusted, is necessary. If the higher intellect of a race is alienated, the popular creed is doomed to decay. The light may be quenched, but only at the cost of ensuring the corruption of creeds, which from that moment lose the principle of vitality. And, finally, the social changes which result from the growth of knowledge and the conquest of the material world necessarily react upon the moral and intellectual order. When the ancient creed no longer satisfies the aspirations of mankind, the philosopher has his chance, and too often fails to turn it to account. For the value of his creed will be tested, not by pure logic, but by trying its efficacy upon men's minds and hearts. The question will be, not only whether the philosophic doctrine can convince the reason, but whether it can satisfy the imagination; whether it can afford rules for controlling disorderly passions, and provide a sufficiently vivid imagery for the expression of emotions. Undoubtedly there is a kind of implicit logic in this process. The truer and more complete the creed, the greater, *ceteris paribus*, the chance that it can effectively influence mankind at large. But it may be that men are not yet educated up to the necessary degree of culture, and the higher creed may be ousted by a doctrine less complete and satisfactory, but better fitted for assimilation by the ordinary intellect. The power of the doctrine is tested, we may say, by feeling and acting rather than by reasoning. Will it work? That is the essential question, which is not always answered completely by proving that it is true. In a progressive society a creed which is not advancing is retiring. Unless it is making new conquests, it is falling into disorganisation. And though one condition of its power is that it should satisfy the keenest intellects, it is also a condition of its full vigour that the enthusiasm of the leaders should be reflected and intensified by their less intelligent followers.

In studying the development of a system of thought, it is essential to remember these conditions, though they may not be the most prominent or the most easily assigned. The logical strength and weakness of the various creeds which were struggling for the mastery during the eighteenth century, goes some way to explain the course of the intellectual history; but no explanation can be complete which does not take into account the social conditions which determined their reception. Truths have been discovered and lost because the world was not ripe for them. If Hume's scepticism was a potent influence at the time, it was not because similar doubts had never occurred to other thinkers, or never been expressed by them, but because the social conditions happened to be favourable to their development. Though I propose to deal chiefly with the logical conditions in the following pages, I shall endeavour to indicate briefly what

was that peculiar phase of thought amongst the less accomplished thinkers which decided the fate of the various germs
of thought cast upon a more or less fruitful soil.

Butler's 'Analogy'

1. Joseph Butler belonged to the exceedingly small class of
men who find in abstract speculation not merely the main
employment, but almost the sole enjoyment, of their lives. He
stands out in strange contrast to the pushing patronage-
hunters of his generation. Amongst the clergy, Berkeley
alone was his equal, as, in some respects, Berkeley was greatly
his superior in speculative power. But Berkeley was impelled
by his ardent benevolence into active occupations, whilst
Butler passed his days, like a certain philosopher mentioned
by Voltaire, in profound meditation. In David Hume the
purely intellectual temperament was still more strikingly
manifested. Hume's philosophical curiosity or love of truth—
whatever we please to call it—was freer from any alloy of
ulterior motive. But if Hume gained as a philosopher, he lost
as a practical teacher of mankind, by his want of that deep
moral earnestness which is Butler's great claim upon our
respect. Butler stood apart from the world. Good prefer-
ments, indeed, were showered upon the solitary thinker,
without solicitation of his own. He had the fortune to be
introduced to Queen Caroline, the only member of the Han-
overian family in that age who loved and appreciated intellectual excellence. Her favour presented him, when already in
possession—thanks to an earlier patron—of 'one of the richest parsonages in England,' to the rather incongruous dignity
of a bishopric. The poverty of the see of Bristol was eked out
by the revenues of the deanery of St. Paul's; and, shortly
before his death, he was translated to Durham. He used his
wealth liberally, as one to whom earthly possessions were of
little importance, and seems to have discharged his episcopal
duties conscientiously, and even admirably, if judged by the
lax standard of the time. In those days bishops had leisure.
The most characteristic anecdote related of him comes from

Dean Tucker, whom he distinguished by his friendship at Bristol. The bishop was accustomed to walk in his garden through many hours of the night; and, on one occasion, he suddenly turned to his companion Tucker, and put the well-known question, whether nations might not go mad as well as individuals? Butler did not escape the ordinary penalties of singularity. His contemporaries, puzzled by his ascetic and meditative life, thought there must be something wrong about an episcopal recluse who, to say the truth, would have been more in his element in a monastic cell, or in the chair of a German university, than in the seat of an eighteenth-century bishop. When he put up a cross in his chapel, and was convicted of reading the Lives of the Saints, the problem seemed to be solved, and he was set down as a papist.

2. Butler was born May 18, 1692, and died June 16, 1752. The two books upon which his fame rests, the 'Sermons' and the 'Analogy,' were published in 1726 and 1736 respectively. They are remarkable amongst other things for the fact that they produced no contemporary controversy. The industry of a biographer has only hunted up a single pamphlet,[3] by one Bott, in which the 'Analogy' was attacked. And yet the books indicate an absorbing preoccupation in the controversies of the day. Butler has deeply pondered the ordinary arguments; he has brooded over them, worked them out, and set down his conclusions, as tersely—often, it must be added, as clumsily—as possible. The 'Analogy' has been built up like a coral reef by slow accretions of carefully digested matter. The style corresponds to the method. We may say, if we choose to be paradoxical, that the 'Analogy' is an almost unique example of a book which has survived, not merely in spite of, but almost by reason of, its faults of style. The paradox, indeed, holds only in so far as the faulty language is indicative of the effort to pack thought more closely than it will easily go. The defect results from a good motive. But it is also characteristic of the lonely thinker who forgets the necessity of expounding with sufficient clearness the arguments which have long been familiar to himself. And, in this sense, it is indicative of a more serious weakness. Butler's mind, like the mind of every recluse, was apt to run in grooves. He endeavoured, as he tells

us, to answer by anticipation every difficulty that could be suggested. But, unfortunately, he has always considered them from the same point of view. He has not verified his arguments by varying the centre of thought or contemplating his system from the outside. And thus his reasoning often reminds us of those knots which bind the faster the more they are pulled in a given direction, but fall asunder at the first strain from another quarter. The pursuit of truth, as he told Clarke, was the object of his life. Every page confirms his veracity. And yet the same letter shows the strong prepossessions with which he started. He is anxious, he says, to discover a demonstrative proof of the existence of God—doubtless, a most natural and innocent desire. Yet it is a desire which suggests the question, what would be his course if such a proof should not be forthcoming? Would he have the rare intellectual courage which enables a man to face the most appalling consequences? Might he not share the weakness of Don Quixote, and unconsciously resolve not to put his newly framed armour to too severe a test? That some hidden weakness was lurking in his argument is suggested from a remarkable peculiarity of the 'Analogy.' It is a rare instance of a theological argument which may, with some plausibility, be called original; it has ever since its publication retained a high place in our literature; and many men of great ability, and in widely different schools of thought, have ascribed to it a profound influence upon their minds. James Mill and Dr. Newman, at the opposite poles of speculation, are typical examples of the lines of thought which may diverge from this common centre. And yet the book, like its author, remains, in some sense, isolated. It does not seem, so far as I can judge, to have materially affected the contemporary currents of thought. It has found more admirers than imitators, and the mine which it opened has not been extensively worked. One explanation is suggested by the names just mentioned. Though Butler is habitually described as amongst the ablest champions of Christianity, he has probably made few converts, and has clearly helped some thinkers towards scepticism. The fact is, as we shall see, that his reasoning is open to applications which he never suspected. The absence of that

22

power of looking through other men's eyes which can rarely be acquired by a lonely thinker, blinded him to one side of the question. The 'Analogy' impresses us in literature like some mass of rock-piercing strata of a different formation, unmovable and undecayed, but yet solitary, exceptional, and barren.

3. Butler's aim is, in brief, to countermine the ordinary deist position. Fragmentary anticipations of his argument are to be found scattered here and there through many contemporary writers. But, as I have said, they are wanting in philosophical breadth and consistency. The orthodox reasoner of the time is beset by a difficulty which expresses his equivocal position. He half admits and half denies the deist assumptions. He professes to believe in such a God of nature as the deist postulates—a God whose attributes are discoverable by reason, and whose law is the embodiment of reason. But when this conception is confronted with the historical Deity of Jewish and Christian mythology, he begins to retract, and he asserts that, as a matter of fact, God has not been discovered by reason, and cannot be shown to have governed men according to the laws of reason. This is substantially to admit an irremovable discrepancy between theory and observation, and to cover it by the decent name of mystery. The difficulty could only be removed by looking more closely into the assumptions which both sides accepted with a suspicious facility. Before we can argue safely from our conceptions of the Deity, we must ask what they are, and how are they determined. Two assumptions, in fact, are made on all sides; first, that there is a God; and, secondly, that he is the God of the rationalists—the God, that is, whose attributes were demonstrated by Clarke, and accepted by Tindal. To take those doctrines for granted is to beg the ultimate questions of philosophy, and therefore to be inevitably superficial. The whole aim of Butler's book is summed up in his treatment of the secondary assumption as to the divine character. He takes for granted the assumption of the divine existence. We believe, he says substantially, in a God of nature, but the God of nature is such a God as nature reveals, and not the God who is described by your *a priori* specula-

tions. God, as known to us by the analogy of nature—that is to say, by that kind of imperfect induction which alone is available in these deep problems—is no longer different from the God revealed to us in the Bible; on the contrary, he appears, so far as our faculties can be trusted, to be the very same Being. The difficulty, therefore, of the orthodox argument disappears; and, instead of half granting and half admitting the appeal to reason, we can admit it frankly and unreservedly.

4. Meanwhile, Butler passes lightly over the ultimate problem. He takes it 'for proved, that there is an intelligent Author of nature, and natural Governor of the world.'[4] He accepts the validity of all the ordinary reasonings upon which this doctrine has been based; the arguments, that is, from analogy, from final causes, from abstract reasoning, from tradition, and from general consent.[4] He elsewhere accepts, in particular, the argument of Descartes or Anselm, derived from the necessary existence of an archetype corresponding to our idea of 'an infinite and immense eternal Being.'[5] Butler, therefore, does not address himself to atheists, if such there be, who dogmatically deny the existence of God; nor to the undoubtedly numerous class who, neither denying nor affirming, hold that our vision is limited to this world by a veil of impenetrable mystery. He excludes as chimerical the dark doubts which, to many readers, are the most conspicuous results of his arguments, and he assumes that all arguments for a God must make for such a God as his theory implies. A pressing difficulty is thus unconsciously evaded. Butler does not renounce the *a priori* line of reasoning, though it was probably a sense of its difficulties which led him to seek for a more tangible ground of controversy. He is content to leave it to others to discover the essential nature and attributes of the Deity; but, far from rebuking their presumption, or from suspecting any possible discrepancy between himself and them, he fully accepts their conclusions. His task is the collateral one of discovering in what character the Deity actually manifests himself to men. The difficulty, therefore, of the ordinary theologian is not so much solved as transferred to another application. For the difficulty of proving

that the God of nature is also the God of revelation, we have with Butler the difficulty of believing that the God known equally through nature and revelation can be the God of abstract speculation. In neglecting to face this question, or even to understand that any such question can arise, Butler, though going deeper than his less thoughtful colleagues, fails to probe the real depths of the question; and he lays himself open to a retort from a scepticism which is not afraid to pass beyond the limits of accepted theology. A writer who would raise a firm system of belief must follow Descartes' principle of doubting whatever can be doubted. He must look carefully to every foundation of belief.

5. The belief in God and the belief in a soul are with Butler the primary articles of natural religion. The first is assumed; the validity of the second is examined in the first chapter of the 'Analogy.' Though hesitatingly and in cautious language, he is here forced to interweave a proof of different character with the ordinary tissue of his argument. This rather heterogeneous element was due immediately to Clarke. A curious controversy between Clarke and Collins had for its pretext a singular crotchet of the learned nonjuror Dodwell. Dodwell's brain, bewildered with excessive reading, and crammed with obsolete theological curiosities, had excogitated a strange doctrine as to the natural mortality of the soul. Baptism by the successors of the Apostles could alone confer immortality. The souls of dissenters, it would seem, were to be revived by an express exertion of divine power, with a view to receiving their dues, whilst the souls of those who had never heard of Christ might be mercifully dismissed to insensibility. Clarke, instead of treating this absurdity with pity or contempt, wrote a solemn remonstrance to its author (1706); and Collins, as in the similar case of Whiston, caught at an opportunity of assailing established dogmas under cover of supporting an indisputably Christian writer. Four pamphlets by Collins received four elaborate replies from Clarke. As usual, the controversy gathered heat, and lost in relevancy towards the conclusion. Clarke's main argument is simple enough. Though drawn from the common armoury of his school, it is still used by controversialists

with little modification. The soul cannot be material, for the properties of any aggregate of particles can be but the sum of the properties of the separate particles. As separate particles cannot think, no aggregate of particles can think. There must be an immaterial subject in which thought inheres, and as thought is an 'individual power'—incapable, that is, of analysis into simpler elements—this subject must be 'indiscerptible,' and therefore naturally immortal.

The argument, in short, is the familiar doctrine of Descartes, elaborated into quasi-mathematical shape,[6] and rendered more precise by help of the distinction between primary and secondary qualities. The mathematical qualities are inherent in matter. Others, like sound or smell, are not really qualities of matter, but modes of the thinking substance; others again, like 'magnetism and electricity,' are general names which express 'the effects of some determinations of certain streams of matter.'[6] Consciousness obviously cannot belong to either class of derivative qualities, nor can it be put in the same category with motion and figure, which, indeed, are but the formula for the opposite pole of existence. As consciousness must be a quality of something, and cannot be a quality of matter, the something must be immaterial.

6. Collins's reply is ineffective, in so far as he seems to admit the assumptions on which the conclusion is virtually given. He does not anticipate Berkeley's denial of matter, or rest, as a modern upholder of his position would do, upon our necessary inability to penetrate to the ultimate essences of things. At times he seems to change weapons with his antagonist. 'As far as I can judge,' he says, 'all this talk of the essences of things being unknown is a perfect mistake;'[7] and he accordingly pronounces the essence of matter to be solidity. Relying upon such hand-to-mouth modes of argument, he generally (in my judgment at least) leaves the logical victory with Clarke; though here and there he hits the true difficulties of his antagonist's position. He attempts, for example, to show that the production of 'roundness' from particles not themselves round is analogous to the production of thought from unthinking matter. Clarke fairly replies,

26

though after some needless argumentation, that the difference between the whole and its parts is merely in the abstract name and not in the thing.[8] Clarke, too, has an equal advantage in maintaining against Collins that it is impossible to regard thought as a 'mode of motion.' Any mode of combining things regarded as external to ourselves must result in an external product. To call motion thought is, in fact, to confuse the radical opposition of subjective and objective; and so long as Collins falls in with Clarke's fundamental method of representing that opposition as embodied in the distinction between primary and secondary qualities, he in vain attempts to give an air of plausibility to his escape from Clarke's conclusion. Elsewhere, as in the illustration of the egg, which runs through two or three letters, he presses his antagonist harder.[9] That consciousness does in fact arise from certain collocations of matter is a fact which Clarke struggles to evade rather awkwardly by the hypothesis of an 'immaterial principle' somehow added to the embryo.[10] But Collins does not seem to have a sufficiently firm grasp of principles to turn his opponent's weakness to account. The question recurs at intervals, though it is one of those which seem to be generally passed over in silence by a kind of tacit agreement. Andrew Baxter published a long 'Enquiry into the Soul' some years afterwards, which may be read by persons curious to study the effect of exploded metaphysics on a feeble, though ingenious, intellect; and Hume's posthumous essay, or notes for an essay, on the Immortality of the Soul, contains some rather obvious criticisms on the accepted doctrine. It is enough to notice Butler's reasoning.

7. Butler's correspondence with Clarke, a few years later, seems to imply that he was more or less sensible to the hollowness of the ground. In reference to one of Clarke's ontological arguments, Butler, then (1713) a student at Tewkesbury, asks the significant question—What is space? His doubts were not pressed very far, nor does he conceal his anxiety to be relieved from them. They would have taken him to the root of the questions suggested by Clarke's whole philosophical method. Butler, however, seems to have thought that a sound thread of argument might be extricated

from the web of questionable metaphysics. 'It has been argued,' he says, referring in a note to Clarke's letters, 'and, for anything appearing to the contrary, justly,'[11] that the unity of consciousness implies the unity of the conscious being; or, at least, as he presently says, with characteristic caution, there is 'no more difficulty in conceiving' the being to be a unit 'than in conceiving it to be a compound.'[12] In this case, our organised bodies would be no more parts of ourselves than any surrounding matter. Though 'experimental observations' cannot prove the doctrine, they 'fall in with it,'[13] and we are therefore somehow enabled to 'conclude certainly that our gross organized bodies ... are no parts of ourselves.'[13] Thus he persuades himself that our eyes and feet are in reality no more than glasses and crutches;[14] and, consequently, though the destruction of our bodies destroys the proof of our vitality, there is no ground to think that it destroys the living agents themselves. The familiar argument from the case of animals is met by the familiar appeal *ad ignorantiam,* and by the more specific argument that the higher intellectual faculties appear to be, in some way, independent of our senses.[15]

8. The discussion is characteristic of Butler's whole method. Whatever plausibility it possesses, is due to the preliminary assumption of the unity and separate existence of the soul. Butler's admission that this assumption is not proved by observation, but falls in with it, is equivalent to saying that observation does not contradict it. But neither, it is plain, can observation really confirm it. Nobody would argue in the sphere of observation that, because a man can in some sense do without his legs, he can therefore survive in some sense without his brain; or that because parts of the organism are not essential to life, therefore the whole organism is superfluous. The whole hypothesis of an independent entity called the soul is simply irrelevant from the scientific point of view; and to infer from its being not upset that it is confirmed is a palpable fallacy. Butler, however, by dwelling exclusively upon the absence of direct contradiction, and sinking the absence of confirmation, converts absolute ignorance into the likeness of some degree of positive knowledge. He obtains,

that is, a delusive appearance of independent scientific grounds for what is really a purely *a priori* deduction. He finds it desirable, however, to add that the credibility of a future state answers 'all the purposes of religion' as a demonstrative proof would do.[16] The chances are so awful that we cannot afford to neglect them. If there is no presumption against the existence of heaven and hell, there is a presumption for it; or, at least, a plain reason for acting as though it were a fact. The doctrine of probability which we thus meet at the beginning of Butler's whole argument colours the whole book. It is his unique distinction amongst theologians that, whilst writhing in the jaws of a dilemma, he refrains from positively denying that any dilemma exists. Yet even Butler will not admit that the doubts which he allows to be possible should influence our conduct. And thus he is encouraged to attempt the impossible feat of transmuting blank ignorance into some semblance of positive knowledge. The difficulty in one shape or another underlies his whole argument.

9. The essential data for a creed being thus provided, Butler has to turn them to account. His thesis is, as we have seen, that the God of nature resembles the God of revelation. He disperses with true insight one class of fallacies which had gathered round the question. The ordinary language implied an untenable distinction between divine and natural. Divines, for example, thought that some heresy lurked in the assertion that the rewards and penalties of another state would be the 'natural' consequences of our actions.[17] Butler sees the distinction to be unphilosophical. All God's commands are at once divine and natural. 'Natural' can only mean 'stated, fixed, or settled.'[18] Civil government is itself natural, if natural be taken in this wider sense; and civil punishments are, therefore, part of the 'natural' punishment of sin.[19] Butler, of course, guards himself from too unreserved an acceptance of his own principles. 'For aught we know,' he says, future punishment may be the 'natural consequence of vice,'[20] in the same sense as the present punishments. 'For aught I see,' we are afterwards told, it comes to the same thing whether this be the case or not.[21] He disposes

in the same way of the equally futile distinction between positive and moral precepts, which reflected the ordinary assumption of an arbitrary element in the divine nature. 'Moral precepts,' he says, 'are precepts the reason of which we see; positive precepts are precepts the reason of which we do not see.'[22] He is of course, careful to add that 'there is not altogether so much reason for the determination of this question' (as to the relative claims of the two classes of commands) 'as some people seem to think.'[23] To make an unnecessary assumption, however undeniable, would apparently have been torture to his strangely cautious understanding.

10. So far the case seems to be clear. The laws of nature are the laws of God, and the distinctions drawn by divines who feared lest God should be lost in nature were plainly irrelevant. Yet Butler is, of course, equally alive to that danger. His God must be a real governor, separate from the universe. God's conduct, as he says (though he does not hold the dogma to be strictly relevant to his argument) must be determined by a certain 'moral fitness and unfitness of actions prior to all will whatever.'[24] Something must exist outside of God. Some material must be provided upon which the divine will may operate. And yet, if nature be related to God as the effect to the cause, how are we to infer anything from nature but a counterpart of nature? From the ontological point of view, we have a difficulty in distinguishing between God and pure being. From Butler's experiential point of view, it seems to be equally difficult to distinguish between God and the sum of all the forces of the universe. It is necessary for his purpose to show that the Author of nature has 'some character or other;'[25] something, as he explains, analogous to that which in men we call 'temper, taste, disposition, practical principles; that whole frame of mind from which we act in one way rather than another.'[25] We are able to assign character to individuals and classes, because we can stand outside them, compare them with some external standard, or measure them by each other. But how is this method to be applied to the Whole? Where is our fixed element in this shifting phenomena of experience which will enable us to determine their

relation not to each other, but to the absolute and eternal? If all exists by God's will, how can the observation of particular existences reveal a special purpose distinct from the general will implied in creation? Divines had boldly argued from the immunity of vice in this world to its punishment in the next. Given some independent source of knowledge as to the attributes of God, the argument might be valid; but from the bare fact by itself we can only reach such a conclusion by inverting all the canons of induction. The whole pith of the 'Analogy' is given by the answer to this difficulty. The mere fact of injustice in this world cannot, as Butler sees, prove justice in the next. Why, as one of his objectors asks—and Butler's objectors are never men of straw—should we not suppose that 'things may be now going on throughout the universe, and may go on hereafter, in the same mixed way as here at present upon earth?'[26] Butler's reply admits in substance that we cannot infer from the world as we see it anything but a similar world; but we may, he thinks, show that the facts fall in with a doctrine which implies a very different world. The 'usual known arguments' in behalf of a future state of retribution are, in his opinion, 'plainly unanswerable.'[27] Though he renounces direct proof, he thinks that he can discover a confirmation of them in experience. What, for example, if some system could be detected amidst the apparent uncertainty of distribution? He has remarked that the good and bad tendencies of virtue and vice are 'essential, and founded in the nature of things, whereas the hindrances to their becoming effect are, in numberless cases, not necessary but artificial only.'[28] Does not this observation make it probable that, in another world, the tendencies will work themselves out more clearly? The argument seems to involve a distinction between natural and artificial as arbitrary as those which Butler has exposed. We must, however, look more minutely into the argument, to see how he conceives the question.

11. A striking chapter is devoted to prove that we can dimly discern a vast providential scheme.[29] Since we see only a part, we may infer that all objections to its justice and

wisdom are founded in our ignorance; and yet we can see enough to be certain that it exists. The vast mass of observable phenomena is not a chaos, but an organised system. Besides simply enumerating facts, we can detect principles of arrangement which will justify a partial induction. Man is intelligible, so far as he is intelligible, as a fraction, not as an integer; the world is one province of an ordered universe. The hypothesis of a divine government supplies the necessary clue to the bewildering labyrinth. This world and the next tally in such a manner that our observations, though imperfect, give dim indications of the complementary sphere. The relation between this and a very different set of theories is significant. It is evident, says Butler, that the 'course of things which comes within our view, is connected with somewhat, past, present, and future, beyond it. So that we are placed, as one may speak, in the middle of a scheme, not a fixed, but a progressive one, every way incomprehensible; incomprehensible, in a manner equally, with respect to what has been, what now is, and what shall be hereafter.'[30] Men accustomed to regard the world as the scene of a gradual evolution may adapt the phrase to their own purposes. We may perceive, they might say, in the midst of mysteries, a tendency to the development of certain social and intellectual types, which it is our duty to forward or to retard. But Butler has in view a different series. The successive terms are not the savage, the civilised being, and the ideal man of the golden age to come; but corrupt man—man perfected here by grace, or ruined by rejecting it, and man in a state of final reward or punishment. His induction, one may say, cuts the line of scientific induction at right angles. It must then be justified by some extra-scientific assumption. The scientific series remains within the limits of experience. The first terms, already known by observation, contain the law which will be revealed to future observers. Butler's series contains a transcendental element. To verify it we must be able to discover a standing-point outside the world of the senses; and find an absolute scale upon which to measure the relation of God to man.

12. The second and third chapters of the first part show us how this external standing-point is to be attained. Butler

starts from the undeniable fact that happiness depends in great measure upon conduct. We are enabled 'to foresee,' he says, 'with more or less clearness, that, if we act so and so, we shall have such enjoyments; if so and so, such sufferings.'[31] 'This,' an objector replies, 'is to be ascribed to the general course of nature.' 'True,' says Butler, 'that is the very thing I am contending for.'[31] The course of nature is the order of things appointed by the Author of nature. God or nature—the two words are so far interchangeable—has affixed pain and pleasure to different courses of action. This, in theological language, is to admit that God governs us. It matters not whether we suppose God to be always acting directly or that his laws operate without further intervention. If the laws of civil magistrates operated automatically and unerringly, we should still be under their government, though in a much higher degree. Here, then, is a solid statement of undeniable fact. God governs. Further, God is a moral governor. The penalties which he inflicts are affixed to vicious courses, and the rewards to virtuous courses. Of the general fact, Butler admits no doubt. Neither is it doubtful that, perplexing as may be the distribution of happiness and misery, virtue *as such* is rewarded, and vice *as such* punished. The nature with which we are endowed, and the power which we can exercise over others, provide certain sanctions; amongst which we must reckon the penalties of civil governors, and the hopes and fears of futurity, which—whatever their origin—undoubtedly exist. Our intuitive moral judgment entitles us to set aside apparently conflicting cases, in which impulses, implanted in us for good purposes, have been perverted to the punishment of the good and reward of the bad. And, finally, the intrinsic excellence of virtue is illustrated by the hypothetical case of a perfectly virtuous kingdom, which must bring the whole world under its empire, either 'by what must be allowed to be just conquest,'[32] or by the voluntary submission of less happily constituted races. The argument would fall in with an exposition of the doctrine of 'the survival of the fittest;' and indeed the statement is substantially that races will flourish as they adapt themselves to the laws of nature.

13. This is the main substance of Butler's constructive argument, and its suggests an obvious criticism. The bare statement that happiness and misery follow certain courses is almost trivial. It receives a peculiar colouring in Butler's hands, from his introduction of the words reward and punishment. How then do we know that the suffering which follows sin is a divinely inflicted punishment, whilst the suffering implied in self-sacrifice or submission to tyranny is merely a proof of the perversion of natural instincts? To answer that question, we must know what is meant by virtue. The utilitarian answer—soon to be explicitly given by Hume —is obvious. Virtue is that which promotes the happiness of mankind. To show, then, that virtue is conducive to happiness is to show that virtue is virtue. Temperance, for example, is virtuous because, and in so far as, it is conducive to health. To represent health as a divine reward annexed to temperance is to fall into the error of the person who wondered at the goodness of providence in bringing navigable rivers by large towns. The statement, indeed, becomes more complex in regard to the social virtues, where the motive of the individual may conflict with the interests of the race. A modern disciple of the derivative school of morality would say that the moral law is substantially a code of rules, worked out by more or less conscious experience, which express the most obvious conditions of general well-being. So far as they are accurately known, the effect of observing them must be to increase the general sum of happiness. That part of morality which coincides with personal prudence must generally increase the happiness of the individual. The 'altruist' instincts will not have that effect so uniformly, because the present social order is far from allowing a perfect harmony between the individual and the whole organism. Still, as Butler very rightly argues, the mass will approve, and to that extent reward, qualities which they recognise as plainly beneficial to themselves; and the fact of our mutual dependence implies, as a condition of social existence, that the interests of the mass and of its units must coincide through a great part of our relations. Justice will make the just man happier, because it secures one essential condition of happiness, namely, the

goodwill of his fellows. A similar inversion naturally follows whenever a scientific view is substituted for a view based upon the doctrine of final causes. What to Butler seems to be a mysterious harmony, appears in a derivative system of morality as the necessary result of the conditions of existence. Any special inference as to a supposed intention of the Divine legislator disappears or melts into the general consideration of a fixed order in the universe. Butler's blindness to this very obvious inversion of his argument is explained by the fact that he contemplated utilitarianism only in its crudest form, as sanctioning individual selfishness.³³ The social virtues of veracity, justice, and public spirit, which Hume described as 'artificial,' appeared to him as necessarily implying the existence of an independent moral faculty, inasmuch as their immediate motive was unselfish. Their rewards, therefore, seemed to be annexed by a divine regulation, even when he goes far towards explaining their natural origin.

14. Here, then, is that absolute standing-point which Butler needed. His essential doctrine is the independent system of morality. Without it, his arguments crumble; with it, we can understand their plausibility. Denying that the consequences of an action are directly or indirectly the determining causes of its morality, the consequences, so far as they affect the agent, appear to him to be plainly rewards or punishments, annexed by the Divine Governor. The God whom Butler worships is, in fact, the human conscience deified. The evidence of his existence and interest in the world rests not on certain miracles wrought some centuries ago in Palestine, but on that great standing miracle—the oracle implanted in every man's breast. For what can be more miraculous than an infallible faculty, not derived from others or developed by the pressure of society and the external world, but absolute, authoritative, and inexplicable? Each of us is provided by nature with a compass pointing undeviatingly to celestial regions. By that gift we can recognise the giver and understand his character. The character of the God of nature is summed up by saying that he loves virtue and hates vice. Having proved this, our course is clear. We can trace the great outlines of the providential scheme. The world is no longer a

scene where forces are steadily working for inscrutable ends, wielded by a Being of whose character, if he has a character, we have not the dimmest conception; where we can only say that the races succeed best which are most in harmony with the conditions; and where, if we can vaguely forecast the future of the race, we can see no traces of care for individuals. To Butler the individual is the centre of interest. God is the Almighty chemist, testing all men in his crucibles; the pro-cess—in what Butler calls the state of probation—either strengthens or weakens the qualities in which he delights; he places the thrice-tried jewels in the cabinet of heaven; and throws aside the rest upon the heap of refuse called hell.

15. Will this theory fit the facts? Can we regard this world as a forcing-house, in which qualities primarily suited for another world are stimulated to activity? The discipline of life clearly trains the race in habits which are useful here, what-ever they may be hereafter. Butler seizes upon this fact as affording an instructive analogy. After describing the process by which prudence is fostered in our temporal capacity,[34] he adds: 'Substitute now the word future for temporal, and virtue for prudence, and it' (the description of our state of trial in our temporal capacity) 'will be just as proper a de-scription of our state of trial in our religious capacity, so analogous are they to each other.'[35] Are they not rather identical? Virtue, on Butler's showing, would seem to be distinguished from prudence—if any distinction be necessary —by the circumstance that prudence guards us against tem-poral, as virtue against spiritual, dangers. The likeness, in-deed, is so marked that Butler anticipates, though he properly repels, the charge, that with him virtue is but a discipline and strengthening of self-love.[36] The likeness or identity of the two leads, however, to a serious difficulty. In the case of prudence, we evidently mean by 'discipline' that the conditions of our existence are such as to make prudence useful. Must it not mean the same in the case of virtue? The process described as the moral government of God, means that, on the whole, virtue is useful in this world. Butler, it is true, regards virtue as a plant intended to flourish more vigorously in another world. The Almighty gardener is culti-

vating plants of an odour too ethereal for our earthly perceptions. If, in fact, this could be made out with any show of
plausibility; if, that is, we could prove that the discipline of
this life tended to develop qualities fitted for another life,
Butler's argument would be forcible. But, unfortunately, this
is just what the 'Analogy' cannot possibly prove, or even tend
to prove. The very meaning of the supposed discipline is that
virtue is advantageous under existing conditions. The whole
evidence open to him by the very nature of his argument is
the tendency of the present state to encourage virtue. So far
as virtue is not profitable here, his argument collapses. And
yet his conclusion is only plausible so far as it is profitable in a
different state from this. If, in short, he could point to some
quality, encouraged by the existing conditions, and yet not
useful under present conditions, his case would have a certain
support. But as qualities are encouraged just so far as they are
useful—as the utility is the sole evidence of the supposed
encouragement—he is in a dilemma, from which there is no
escape.

16. Indeed, he states the theory himself. 'Our nature,' he
says, 'corresponds to our external condition. Without this
correspondence, there would be no possibility of any such
thing as human life and happiness; which life and happiness
are, therefore, a *result* from our nature and condition jointly;
meaning by human life, not living in the literal sense, but
the whole complex notion commonly understood by those
words.'[37] A modern evolutionist could not say more plainly
that happiness results from the harmony between the organism and its environment, and the natural inference is that
the science of morality is simply a statement of the rules by
which that harmony is promoted. It remains true, of course,
that, as Butler labours to show with much ingenuity, qualities strengthened by our discipline in this life may be useful
in another life. Meanwhile, it cannot be argued, from the
mere absence of harmony here, that there must be harmony
elsewhere; or that, because, under existing conditions, many
virtues run to waste, and conduct regulated by a regard to
general rules produces misery instead of happiness in particular cases, the wasted qualities will be turned to account in a

different order. Butler is too logical to draw this as an inference, though he seems to countenance the opinion inculcated. He is content to argue, in his usual method, that the assumed utility of virtue in the next world is consistent with the facts of observation, without saying explicitly that observation suggests or necessitates the assumption.

17. Meanwhile, he tries to turn the facts to account in a rather startling way. 'The present state,' he says, 'is so far from proving in effect a discipline of virtue to the generality of men, that, on the contrary, they seem to make it a discipline of vice.' The garden of the Lord produces more weeds than flowers. And what is the explanation? Of the numerous seeds prepared for growth, 'we do not see that one in a million actually' comes to perfection. 'Yet,' he adds, 'no one who does not deny all final causes, will deny' that these seeds answer the end for which they were designed by nature. 'And,' he concludes, 'I cannot forbear adding, though it is not to the present purpose, that the *appearance* of such an amazing *waste* in nature, with respect to these seeds and bodies, by foreign causes, is to us as unaccountable as, what is much more terrible, the present and future ruin of so many moral agents by themselves, *i.e.* by vice.'[38] The fact, thus candidly acknowledged by Butler, throws a strange light upon his theory. It is one of the facts which science takes into account as explaining the gradual adaptation of the race to its new conditions of life. From Butler's point of view, it seems to imply either that the plan of the Almighty is a failure, or that he is not a benevolent agent. The world is a state of probation, and it is a probation which ruins the vast majority of those who undergo it. The dying out of drunkards may explain how the race gradually increases in sobriety; but the death of ten drunkards, to say nothing of the punishment of their posterity, seems to be a strangely awkward way of teaching one man to be sober in a world where, so far as we know, there is to be no more drinking. Butler suggests what no one can deny, that such qualities as 'veracity, justice, and charity' may be useful elsewhere.[39] So, for anything we can tell, may temperance, soberness, and chastity. Yet, admitting the possibility, and admitting that the state of probation

38

here may be the prologue to a state in which there is no probation, we see that Butler has once more succeeded in proving only that the facts do not necessarily contradict the theory. The whole appearance of plausibility is obtained by stating undeniable facts in his own language, and then assuming that, because they can be so stated, the theory embodied in the language is confirmed. Call the evil consequences of vice its punishment; the development of character under the action of circumstances, probation; take for granted the existence of a moral governor, and a separate and indestructible entity called the soul; and, undoubtedly, theology will give an interpretation of the facts which, though it may conflict with our preconceived notions of divine benevolence, does not conflict with the facts observed.

18. The great difficulty remains. Butler's God is revealed through conscience. Does his conscience reveal a just God? This is the old and familiar difficulty, which has tasked the ingenuity of innumerable thinkers. Why does the potter complain of his pots? Is it divine or childish to set puppets in motion, and be angry because they do not work out the supposed design? Who is to blame if we, feeble creatures of circumstance, are such as circumstances, or, if you will, the divine system of government, has made us? Because we have strayed where we had no light, and been fused by a probationary fire too hot for our constitutions, are we to be everlastingly tortured? Butler's treatment of this ever-recurring problem is probably the weakest part of his argument. He argues that the opinion of fatalism or necessity is not necessarily opposed to religion, or rather that the 'absurd supposition,' as he calls it, of 'universal necessity,' must be reconcilable to religion, that is, to his theological system, if it be reconcilable to facts given by experience.[40] The statement indicates at once a confusion between two really contradictory theories. 'Universal necessity' makes 'fatalism' impossible; for fatalism assumes what necessity excludes, the existence of an arbitrary element in the universe. Butler, for example, argues at length, and for a moment a humorous smile seems to flit across his grave countenance, that a boy brought up without fear or shame would 'be the plague of all about him

39

and of himself too, even to his own destruction.'[41] There cannot be a doubt of it. If the boy thought that he was not blamable for lying because a dark power, called fate, moved his tongue; or that he might as well jump out of the window as walk through the door, because fate had decided whether he should die or live, that boy would soon cease to plague anybody in this world. The hypothesis, however, of a fate which determines certain points in the chain of events, and does not determine the intermediate points, is not only absurd in itself, but radically opposed to the doctrine of necessity. 'Necessity' would make the boy jump out of the window if he was to be killed, or walk out of the door if he was to live. As a fatalist, the boy might be right in holding that he was not to be blamed for lying, because acting under outward compulsion. As a necessitarian he would be illogical. Praise and blame are as much matters of necessity as anything else, and indeed are only intelligible on the assumption that acts are caused; and that lying, therefore, implies a certain disposition. The two doctrines clash irreconcilably, and Butler's confusion between them is one more proof of his feebleness in dealing with purely metaphysical questions. In this respect he is but a child compared with such men as Hume, Hobbes, or Jonathan Edwards.

19. Butler's position, however, is instructive. He remarks very truly that the doctrine of necessity does not explain 'how things came to be and to continue as they are,' but only adds the circumstance that they could not have been otherwise.[42] The necessitarians and the advocates of free-will would alike infer an architect from a house, whether the architect were conceived as a free or a necessary agent. It would appear, then, that the doctrine of necessity, consistently carried out, has no practical bearing; like an atmosphere pressing equally in all directions, it leaves the previous equilibrium unaltered; affecting no truth, or all truth equally, it will not affect our view of facts. The doctrine of necessity, it would be more accurate to say, so far as it is equivalent to the assertion of universal causation, gives an essential postulate for all reasonings about fact, but does not affect one reason more than another. Necessity, regarded as an external entity, compel-

ling events to conform to their laws, is a metaphysical figment, which causes nothing but confusion. It is in this sense,
however, that Butler takes the doctrine. His 'necessity' is a
dark power, coercing God and man alike. It belongs to the
super-divine sphere—if the phrase may be used—where
exists the eternal and immutable nature of things by which
even God's will is determined. Butler argues that such a
necessity would destroy all morality. Destroying the injustice
of the murder, it would destroy also the injustice of punishing murder.[43] And thus the Divine judge must be excused on
the very plea which we advance to excuse the criminal.

20. The responsibility, it would be more accurate to say, is
transferred to the new God called Necessity. If, however,
Necessity, as in the more profound theology, means God's
will, the answer becomes irrelevant. God, being subject to no
external coercions, cannot be excused because he forces himself to punish. The argument really involves a confusion
which lies at the root of Butler's method. His contention is in
substance that the doctrine of necessity, and, therefore, its
scientific successor, the doctrine of universal causation, must
destroy the conception of desert—which from his point of
view is an essential part of the conception of morality—as
between man and man, along with the conception of desert
as between man and God. The fallacy is clear. In speaking of
desert between two agents, we imply that they are subject to a
law which defines their relations, and that the action in
respect of which desert accrues is independent of the will of
the agent obliged. But the conception fails us when one
agent is supposed to be both the sole source of law and the
determining cause of the character and surroundings of the
other. The category which is applicable to the conduct of
finite beings breaks down when one being is supposed infinite. Man can have no rights as against God. A sovereign
power can do no legal wrong, because law means that which
the sovereign wills. God can do no moral wrong, because,
however we settle the question of precedence, his will and the
moral law necessarily coincide. Regard God as the sole cause,
and the words just and unjust can have no reference to him,
whilst they retain their full meaning in regard to human

beings. We may still ask whether he is, or is not, benevolent, but not, in any proper sense of the words, whether he is or is not just. Butler does not contemplate this mode of conceiving the case. He assumes that a doctrine which deprives desert of an absolute meaning must also destroy its relative meaning. His God, I have said, is revealed by conscience. He is the God of whom our hearts tell us that he will punish our sins; and, therefore, the God who leaves to us a certain sphere of independent action. When the conceptions applicable to the case of a finite moral governor are transferred to the case of an infinite cause, contradictions necessarily emerge. The doctrine of the penal character of suffering, which is intelligible in one case, becomes monstrous in the other; and thus Butler's assumption of the first article of his creed allows him to overlook the fact that the God proved by ontological reasoning is really a different being from the God assumed by the conscience.

21. From this want of philosophical clearness his final reply to objectors becomes strangely unsatisfactory. Government by reward and punishment, the necessitarian is supposed to say, 'must go upon supposition that we are free and not necessary agents. And it is incredible that the Author of nature should govern us upon a supposition as true which he knows to be false; and, therefore, absurd to think that he will reward and punish us for our actions hereafter; especially that he will do it under the notion that they are of good or ill desert.' Butler replies: 'The whole constitution and course of things' shows 'beyond doubt that the conclusion from this argument is false, wherever the fallacy lies.' The fallacy lies, as he thinks, in the belief that we are necessary agents. If that belief be right, the fallacy must lie in the assumption 'that it is incredible necessary agents should be rewarded or punished.'[44] And why? Because, as a matter of fact, God does reward and punish 'even brute creatures,' and punishes and rewards men in respect of actions to which the sense of desert has been annexed. Butler's identification of suffering with punishment has become so indelible, that he thus treats it as simple matter of fact; and is appalled by no conclusion to which it leads when for the conception of a Governor we

substitute the conception of a Creator and Sustainer of the universe.

22. To Butler, of course, the difficulty is masked by the theory of free-will—the device by which most theologians justify God's wrath with the work of his own hands. Thinkers who proceeded by a different method saw that the device was in any case insufficient. When God is presented as equivalent in nature, it matters little whether we do or do not concede to man that trifling capacity for modifying his destiny which we call free-will. The utmost amplitude that we can conceive implies but a kind of futile wriggling upon the hook implanted in our vitals and drawn by irresistible power. Let the will be 'free,' yet we must admit, and Butler's theory of 'probation' emphasises the fact, that nature turns out murderers as regularly as rattlesnakes. The omniscient and omnipotent Being who made and exposed us to temptation must surely have known, or at least have formed a shrewd suspicion about, our probable fate. No evasion can blind us to the true bearing of Butler's statement. God made men liable to sin; he placed them where they were certain to sin; he damns them everlastingly for sinning. This is the road by which the 'Analogy' leads to Atheism. If this be the logical result of accepting theories, better believe in no God at all. If nature reveals to us a being who acts upon such principles, and will probably carry them out more systematically in another world, let us dispel the hideous nightmare by holding that God and a future life are priestly fictions. Butler appeals to conscience, and conscience, as interpreted by him, reveals Almighty injustice seated on the throne of the universe. If suffering is punishment, and punishment distributed as recklessly as suffering, belief in theology becomes an insult to humanity.

23. These consequences, however, are comparatively in the background in the first part of the 'Analogy;' for there our attention is fixed chiefly on the appearances of distributive justice. They recur in a darker shape in the second part, which deals with revealed religion. Butler, though he takes a deeper view than his contemporaries of the significance of Christianity, has no special qualifications for dealing with historical evidence. His most original remarks apply to the theory of

the Atonement, and it is probably this part of the 'Analogy' upon which the wisdom of succeeding divines has most delighted to dwell. The argument is simple. That we should suffer for the sin of our parents is only in accordance with the general course of providence.[45] The scheme of redemption is equally conformable to observation; for 'vicarious punishment is a providential appointment of every day's experience.'[46] Human punishments are sufferings inflicted upon the criminal on account of his crimes. The chief argument of the first part of the 'Analogy' relies upon the statement that this is approximately true of divine punishments. We are now invited to attend to a different, and it would seem contradictory, series of facts. Divine punishments sometimes strike the virtuous person on account of his virtue; they often miss the vicious person on account of his vice; they constantly and systematically strike the innocent person instead of the guilty; and the penalty is not even roughly proportioned to the offence. Why, because they resemble punishment in one respect, should we call them punishments at all? Simply because Butler's conscience has told him that a certain Being is the avenger of sin; because he has identified this Being with nature, and has therefore inferred that wherever nature produces pleasure or pain, they are produced as sanctioning the criminal law of the universe. Happiness and misery are but the reflections of divine gratitude or vengeance, and therefore divine rewards and penalties appear to be inflicted pretty nearly at random.

24. The difficulty is exaggerated in the second part of the book because it is not diminished. 'What men require,' says Butler, with unusual unfairness, 'is to have all difficulties cleared.'[47] What they really expect is that a divine revelation should make some difficulties clearer. Revelation, if it did not solve the enigma, might at least show it to be soluble. In answer to a similar difficulty, Butler complains that the absence of proof is turned into a positive argument; or, as he elsewhere says, 'over and above the force of each particular difficulty or objection, these difficulties and objections are turned into positive arguments against the truth of revelation.'[48] Butler may be exposed to a similar retort; for when he

argues that 'speculative difficulties' are probationary in the same sense as 'external temptations,' he comes near converting the deficiency of proof into a positive ground of belief.[49] Such reasoning provokes the criticism most commonly directed against the 'Analogy.' It is an attempt to meet difficulties, by suggesting equal or greater difficulties. It should, therefore, lead to scepticism rather than to conviction. Butler, as usual, anticipates and tries to meet the objection. It is a 'poor thing,' says the objector, 'to solve difficulties in revelation by saying that there are the same in natural religion.'[50] Butler's reply is more obscure than usual, and has an air of depression very unlike the triumphant summing up of the ordinary controversialist. It is a poor thing, perhaps; but the epithet poor may be applied to most things in human life. 'It is most readily acknowledged,' he says again, 'that the foregoing treatise is not satisfactory, very far from it; but so would any natural institution of life appear if reduced into a system, together with its evidence.' The last words, obscure even for Butler, reflect the general perplexity produced by his contemplation of this troublous world. He retires upon the one main principle of his book. We are under the moral government of God. That is plain, whatever is doubtful. The argument, he admits, proves the credibility, not the reasonableness, of religion; except in so far as the existence of the laws is a sufficient proof of their wisdom and justice. At any rate, there is proof enough to make obedience judicious. In matters of health or money, we have to act upon insufficient evidence. Why not in matters of salvation? Hell is probable enough to be worth avoiding.[51]

25. Of revelation, as of natural religion, Butler has shown that it does not contradict the testimony of facts. That conclusion is, with him, equivalent to a strong presumption in its favour. The plausibility of such a theory is obvious in this, as in the other case. Religious theories have been suggested to men by the observation of facts, and are an attempt to state them as coloured by the imagination. There is nothing, therefore, surprising to us in the circumstance that a religious doctrine which has embodied the conclusions of many generations of the most civilised races and the greatest of intel-

lects, should give a statement not obviously in conflict with universal experience. That it should be so far tenable was a condition of its existence, and is therefore no proof of its supernatural origin. Butler, who only contemplated as possible the alternatives of a divine inspiration or direct imposture, just as he held that morality must be revealed through an independent faculty or regarded as a human fiction, naturally estimated the value of this coherence between fact and theory by a different scale. And yet there is a wide gulf, even from his own point of view, between his arguments and the acceptance of an implicit belief in Christian revelation. He seems to have shown at most that it may be true. His version of the facts will stand till a better has been suggested; and whilst it stands, it is wise to act upon it. The gulf, however, was filled in Butler's mind by a series of tacit assumptions. He has taken for granted, as I have pointed out, the answers to the most vital questions of philosophy. He tells us[52] that he has omitted to rely upon the two great doctrines of the freedom of the will and the independent origin of morality, because, though he held them, they were disputed by his antagonists. Yet, as we have seen, they are implicitly assumed throughout; and, in addition to them, he assumes the doctrines of the existence of God and of the soul; and assumes, moreover, that those doctrines can be established in the sense required for his argument. Grant that there is a God who is a moral governor, and a soul which is an immortal entity; that the soul is in some sense independent of God and circumstances, and that morality is not determined by the conditions of human life; and Butler has shown that the facts of observation may be fitted into his framework of theory. Regarding those assumptions as having a strong *a priori* probability, and further holding that the Christian doctrine is practically the only alternative to Atheism, he thinks that this argument is not only negatively strong, but may in some sense stand by itself. It may force even those who start by denying the truth of Christianity to admit 'the absurdity of all attempts to prove Christianity false, the plain undoubted credibility of it;' and he adds, rather vaguely, a hope that it will prove 'a good deal more.'[53] The *Conclusion* reiterates his

46

position. God's existence being proved by the indications of design, infidelity is the result of attending to the difficulties involved in Christianity and neglecting those involved in natural religion. The case fairly stated, it is plain that 'there is not any peculiar presumption against Christianity.' Even doubt implies that there is some evidence in its favour, and enough to compel our serious attention. The lowest degree of opinion possible to the candid mind is a 'serious apprehension' that Christianity may be true, 'joined with doubt whether it be so;' and even such a state of mind about Christianity 'lays persons under the strongest obligations in regard to it throughout the whole of their life; a regard, not the same exactly, but in many respects the same with what a full conviction of its truth would lay men under.' That is the last effort to represent doubt as a ground for action.

26. Butler, in spite of all the eulogies of his admirers, was no philosopher in the strict sense of that word. The essence of his method, as of that of the common-sense school, to whom he is most nearly related, is to pass by those ultimate problems which are strictly called philosophical. The attempt to frame a religious theory without thoroughly sounding its foundations led to the inevitable result. Butler fails to understand that his assertions read by the light of a different set of assumptions would lead to a totally different result. His conclusions appear to some minds to be a *reductio ad absurdum* of his principles. Even theologians should be slow to praise the philosophical acuteness of a writer whose defence of Christianity is so easily convertible into an attack upon theology. It is not upon this side that we must look for the secret of Butler's greatness. His attitude is impressive from the moral side alone; but from that side its grandeur is undeniable. In the 'Analogy,' as distinctly as in the Sermons, the deification of the conscience is the beginning, middle, and end of Butler's preaching. Duty is his last word. Whatever doubts and troubles beset him, he adheres to the firm conviction that the secret of the universe is revealed, so far as it is revealed, through morality. Removing the colouring of theological dogma, his doctrine thus becomes a lofty stoicism. Whatever happens, and whatever prospects are re-

vealed, he will hold to this creed. Read by the light of this belief, all suffering becomes punishment. The difficulty of reconciling this with the actual distribution of happiness presses upon him; but all difficulties must be faced. The doctrine seems to imply that God is unjust. The conclusion is horrible, and, of course, 'there must be a mistake somewhere;' but it cannot be in his original principle. The doctrines learnt from revelation increase the difficulty, but never overwhelm his faith. Men suffer here, as Butler urges, and suffer 'irremediably' for a certain amount of folly and vice. Here, however, we have the remedy of death—a remedy not available to save us from the Almighty avenger. If, then, suffering be punishment, analogy suggests that everlasting torture will punish the misdeeds of the most frail and sorely tempted. We must believe it rather than give up our moral conception. God Almighty, maker of all things and ruler of all men, came down from heaven in bodily form, and conveyed a message of unspeakable moment. He gave it only to a few, but he is always partial. The message said that God would punish the good for the crimes of the wicked. That is not surprising, for it is a matter of everyday experience; if I get drunk, my son has the gout. The message confirms our darkest forebodings of the future; otherwise, could it be in analogy with our observations? God, then, has said, Let there be light, and there is no light—no light, or rather darkness visible, such as 'serves only to discover sounds of woe.' Well, if nature is a riddle, how should the message of the God of nature be clear?

27. This is hardly a caricature of Butler's arguments, though it is an interpretation of them into different dialect. And if they have—as is undeniable—a revolting side, they are also imposing by the sheer tenacity with which, in spite of perplexity and confusion, Butler clings to the one great dogma, that God hates sin. However differently stated in systems of more philosophical width, the conviction must always survive, and Butler's firm grasp of it gives a kind of sublimity to his troubled utterance. Moreover, it enables him to give due weight to the facts overlooked by his opponents. As against Deism, the force of Butler's argument is undeniable. Nature

has its dark side. It is not that amiable power which fluent metaphysicians constructed out of *a priori* guesses. Their creed in the long run turned out to be mere moonshine. His is, at least, an impressive statement of certain truths, though they are seen in a distorted form through the traditional haze. No religion can be powerful which does not give forcible expression to men's conviction of the prevalence of natural and moral evil, and of their intimate connection. The shallow optimism of the deists blinked the obvious facts. Butler recognised them manfully, in spite of the additional horrors of the nightmares which haunted his imagination. There is such a thing as evil in the world, he seems to say, and the worst of evils is vice. The philosophy might be improved; but the very want of a philosophy makes his vigorous grasp of such truths the more impressive. Butler's influence is thus an indirect testimony to the fact that no vigorous creed can be reconciled with a tacit denial of the evils which disturb the world and perplex the intellect.

28. Butler has been compared to Pascal. Infinitely inferior in beauty of style, and greatly inferior in logical clearness and width of view, as Butler is to Pascal, there is a certain resemblance. Butler and Pascal are both sensible, as the noblest minds are alone sensible, to the sad discords of the universe. To both of them it seemed to be a scene of blind misery and confusion. Pascal, in despair, pronounces man's intellect to be helpless, and does his best to prostrate himself before an earthly idol. Butler, trained in a manlier school, refused to commit intellectual suicide. Reason, he says, is feeble; he disdains to conceal how feeble; and yet he resolves painfully and hesitatingly to grope out a path by this feeble guidance. He is as far from joyful confidence as from blank despair. He staggers out of Doubting Castle with trembling knees and wearied limbs. He puzzles out his track by such guidance as he can find, and that guidance is in substance that, whatever fails, a man must try to do his duty. That belief, if nothing else, is of heavenly origin. So doubting a pilgrim could hardly guide others authoritatively; he is no Greatheart, nor has his voice the true spirit-stirring ring of a born leader of men. Christian advocates praise him, declare his arguments to be

irrefragable, and find an easier path for themselves. We can but honour him as an honest and brave man—honest enough to admit the existence of doubts, and brave enough not to be paralyzed by their existence.

David Hume

1. 'I flatter myself,' says Hume, in the Essay upon Miracles, 'that I have discovered an argument, of a like nature' (the reference is to Tillotson's argument on transubstantiation), 'which, if just, will, with the wise and learned, be an everlasting check to all kind of superstitious delusion, and, consequently, will be useful as long as the world endures.'[54] This preliminary trumpet-flourish, intended probably to startle the drowsy champions of the faith into some consciousness of the philosopher's claims, has been as nearly fulfilled as could have been expected. Hume's argument, neglected for the moment, soon attracted the assaults of theologians.[55] Since his day eager apologists have denounced it, reasoned against it, passed it under the most rigid examination, and loudly and frequently proclaimed the discovery of some fatal flaw. The fact that the argument is being answered to this day proves that its efficacy is not exhausted. Every new assault is a tacit admission that previous assaults have not demolished the hostile works. It is needless to enquire how far this particular logical *crux* has contributed to the decay amongst rational thinkers of a belief in the miraculous. That belief forms part of a system of thought, and grows faint as the general system loses its hold upon the intellect. The prominence given to the essay, except as an admirable specimen of the dialectical art, may, therefore, be easily exaggerated. No single essay has sapped the bases of belief. On the other hand, the essay is but a small part of Hume's attack upon the fundamental dogmas of theology. His popular reputation, indeed, is almost exclusively based upon it; he is known as the author of this particular dilemma; all else that he wrote is ignored; and so exclusively has attention been fixed upon these particular pages, that few of his assailants take any

notice even of the immediately succeeding essay,[56] which forms with it a complete and connected argument.

2. Various causes may be given for this neglect. Hume does not himself give any intimation that the Essay on Miracles requires (if, indeed, it does strictly require) any supplement. The essay gives a direct and tangible issue for the popular disputant. A tricky or illogical, though not consciously unfair, antagonist might feel that the argument was more manageable when detached from its setting, or might be unable to appreciate the wider philosophical considerations; or, possibly, might not have taken the trouble to read any farther in so scandalous a performance. But it is also true that there exists a kind of tacit consent to pass by the questions raised by Hume's other writings upon theology. We dare not face them. Our cowardice and our better feelings shrink from the possibilities of a negative reply. Our belief may be too faint to allow of a keen interest in the discussion, or we have too much at stake, and are appalled by what appears to be a complete disintegration of the universe. The doubts which may chill our hearts are forbidden to pass our lips. Argue this or that theological dogma, if you please; even dispute the value of Christianity as compared with pure theism, but do not ask the tremendous questions which lie beyond—Is there a God? or, rather, have we any means of knowing whether there be a God or not? What, again, do we mean by God in any case? Is the holiest of names but a periphrasis for our ignorance, or a name for some reality, apprehensible, however dimly, by human intelligence? Many men, we cannot doubt, have agreed with Hume's answer, though few have dared to confess their agreement publicly; but that kind of intellectual courage which faces such doubts in the ordinary spirit of scientific enquiry is only less rare than the courage which will proclaim to the world that they are insoluble. Our literature swarms with so-called demonstrations of the existence of God. The half-formed suspicion of their authors that the foundation of their reasonings may be unsound is rarely indicated by frank admissions, though betrayed in the dexterity with which they sidle past the ancient pitfalls, and the obstinacy with which they deny, not the validity, but even

the existence, of objections. Hume's reasonings were, until very recent times, the single example in our literature of a passionless and searching examination of the great problem.

3. The vigour of his mind is exhibited in these writings even more conspicuously than in his metaphysical arguments. His scepticism in metaphysics seems at times to be but half sincere, as scepticism must be which not only disputes certain dogmas, but throws doubt upon the validity of the reasoning process itself. The so-called scepticism of the theological essays is not in this sense sceptical; it admits the validity of reason in its own sphere, but seeks to demonstrate that theology lies outside of that sphere. In the metaphysical writings Hume throws doubt upon the validity of our belief in the invariable order of the universe. His theological writings are made more cogent by admitting that fundamental truth. The doubts which he expounds are not the mere playthings of philosophical fancy, which vanish when we leave the closet for the street. They are strong convictions seen from another side; and are as dogmatic, in one sense, as the theologian's in the opposite sense. From his various writings, the 'Treatise on Human Nature,' the 'Dialogues on Natural Religion,' the 'Philosophical Essays,' and the 'Natural History of Religion,' we may frame a complete and logically co-ordinated system of argument. J. S. Mill, the most distinguished of Hume's recent disciples, left behind him an essay upon theism, discussing the same vital problems with the advantage afforded by familiarity with subsequent speculation. Though more symmetrically arranged, it scarcely includes a single argument not explicitly stated or clearly indicated by Hume. It is marked, however, by one quality, curiously absent from Hume's colourless logic. A pathetic desire to find some remnant of truth in the ancient dogmas breathes throughout its pages, and is allowed to exercise a distorting influence upon its conclusions. In Hume there is no trace of such a sentiment. As a rule, he neither scoffs, nor sneers, nor regrets. The dogma under discussion seems neither to attract nor to repel him. Here and there we may trace too complacent a sense of his ingenuity, or a desire to administer a passing rebuff to the confidence of men like Warburton; but the stream of his

logic is generally as unruffled and limpid as though he were discussing a metaphysical puzzle unrelated to human passion, or undertaking an historical enquiry into the truth of some doubtful legend. This strange calmness is characteristic of the man and of his age; it is only possible to a consummate logician, arguing at a time when theology, though living amongst the masses, was being handed over by thinkers to the schools. We have in his pages the ultimate expression of the acutest scepticism of the eighteenth century; the one articulate English statement of a philosophical judgment upon the central questions at issue.

4. Let us endeavour to state Hume's reasonings as calmly as they were propounded. What are the appropriate methods of proving the first article of the theological creed? Kant, in the 'Critique of Pure Reason,' resolves all possible methods into the ontological, that of which Descartes' argument is the fullest expression; the cosmological, or the familiar argument from the necessity of a first cause; and the physico-theological, or the argument based upon the evidences of design. According to Kant, the last two arguments are ultimately resolvable into the first; and the first is, according to him, untenable. The pure reason cannot supply a basis for theology; a function which, however, is discharged by the practical reason. Kant's reasonings are stated with much greater scholastic precision than Hume's, and imply a more systematic conception of the relations of theology and philosophy; but they scarcely show greater acuteness, and they do not show an equally unbiassed attitude of mind. His scheme may enable us to condense Hume's arguments, dispersed through various essays, into a definite system of reasoning.

5. The belief in God may be regarded as an ultimate truth, above all need of demonstration. We know the existence of God, as we know our own existence, by direct intuition. This doctrine may take the mystical shape, or the common-sense shape, or it may appear as the ontological argument. The mystic is outside of argument. The vague yearning which sees no personal deity, and requires no logical apparatus of articulate demonstration, but recognises the divinity immanent in all nature through some supersensual

faculty, was beyond Hume's cognisance. The doctrine partakes more of the character of emotion than reason, and the mere logician is powerless either to assail or support it. As represented by the common-sense philosopher, who says dogmatically that a belief in God is a first principle, the doctrine is equally unassailable by argument. The believer must, in fact, say to the atheist, 'You lie,' or he must say, 'I have a faculty which you have not.' Locke put the dilemma in his controversy with Stillingfleet. The argument from universal consent, he says, which is the historical form of the same theory, must be useless; 'for, if anyone deny a God, such a perfect universality of consent is destroyed; and, if nobody does deny a God, what need of arguments to convince atheists?'[57] All serious argument implies the possibility of sincere dissent. Against an opponent of theism who is not really an atheist, we require not argument, but exhortations to truthfulness. If the believer claims a special faculty, the question arises, whose faculty is the more trustworthy? and the argument passes into some other form. Hume regarded all mystics as foolish 'enthusiasts,' represented at the time of writing only by such solitary recluses as Law, or by fanatical followers of Wesley. He would have thought it a mere waste of time to direct his batteries against them; and the common-sense philosophers did little more than give him the lie direct.

6. His whole philosophy, however, is the antithesis of the doctrine upon which reposed the ontological proof of Descartes, or the more familiar cosmological proof represented by Clarke. His scepticism is one continuous assault upon the validity of their methods; and the direct application is made, though with some veil of reticence, in the fourth part of the 'Treatise of Human Nature,' and more explicitly in the posthumous 'Dialogues on Natural Religion.' Abandoning the high *a priori* road, divines might betake themselves to the 'physico-theological' argument, generally described as the argument from final causes. A prolonged and most ingenious discussion of this theory forms the main substance of the Dialogues. Reasoners, again, who doubted the soundness of this mode of argument, or shrank from raising the fundamental questions involved, might retire to the moral argu-

ment, which, in one shape or other, has the strongest influence with many minds. The theory of the 'categorical imperative,' and the deduction of theology as a regulative principle of conduct, was not known to English thinkers, but it has a close affinity to the ethical doctrine of Clarke, and is represented to some extent in Butler's doctrine of the conscience. Hume's morality, if accepted, strikes at the root of this theory; and the application to Butler's argument is sufficiently indicated in the essay upon 'A Particular Providence and a Future State.' Finally, abandoning all strictly philosophical arguments, the divine might fall back upon the historical argument. He might appeal to experience at large, as showing that the idea of a supreme Deity must have been supernaturally implanted in men's minds, or to the particular experience embodied in the history of revelation. The answers to these arguments are given by Hume in the 'Natural History of Religion,' and in that Essay on Miracles, which alone excited any vehemence of controversy.

7. The whole cycle of reasoning is thus completed. Later developments of thought have presented some of the arguments assailed by Hume in a form intended to evade the destructive effects of his criticism. Whether that intention has or has not been successfully carried out is a question beyond my province. It is enough to say for the present that, whatever the value of Hume's reasonings, he has, at least, the high merit of having unflinchingly enquired into the profoundest of all questions, and of having dared to give the result of his enquiries without fear or favour. The want of intellectual courage displayed by his contemporaries is doubtless pardonable, in one sense. We cannot judge harshly of men who feared to injure a doctrine which, true or false, seemed to afford the only lasting consolation to suffering humanity, and the only sound basis for morality. But, in another sense, no cowardice is ever pardonable, for it is never pardoned by facts. Want of candour brings an inevitable penalty upon the race, if not upon the individual. The hollowness in theory and the impotence in practice of English speculation in the last half of the century, is but the natural consequence of the faint-heartedness which prevented En-

glish thinkers from looking facts in the face. The huge development of hypocrisy, of sham beliefs, and indolent scepticism, is the penalty which we have had to pay for our not daring to meet the doubts openly expressed by Hume, and by Hume alone.

8. Hume's scepticism cuts away the very base of ontological proof. The mind, according to him, is unable to rise one step beyond sensible experience. It can separate and combine the various 'impressions' and 'ideas;' it is utterly unable to create a single new idea, or penetrate to an ultimate world of realities. The 'substance' in which the qualities of the phenomenal world are thought to inhere is a concept emptied of all contents, and a word without a meaning. The external world, which supports the phenomena, is but a 'fiction' of the mind; the mind, which in the same way affords a substratum for the impressions, is itself a fiction; and the divine substance, which, according to the Cartesians, causes the correlation between these two fictions, must—that is the natural inference—be equally a fiction. Impressions and ideas, combining and separating in infinite variety, being the sole realities; the bond which unites, and the substratum which supports them, must be essentially unknowable, for knowledge itself is but an association of ideas. Dismiss these doubts, attempt to frame ontological propositions, and the fallacy manifests itself afresh in the futility of the dogma which emerges. Under the form of examining Bayle's criticism upon the 'hideous hypothesis' of Spinoza,[58] Hume exhibits the inevitable antinomies, which beset the reason in its endeavour to soar beyond experience, and, therefore, on his assumption, to transcend itself.[59] Metaphysicians had insisted upon the utterly disparate character of mind and matter. The two could not be brought into relation, except by the verbal explanation of the divine power. It was only necessary, then, to exhibit this antithesis, to show that the doctrine was inconceivable. Mind cannot be resolved into matter, therefore materialism is absurd. But neither can mind be brought into contact with matter, unless mind be itself extended. Therefore spiritualism is equally absurd.[60] The external universe, said Bayle, in answer to Spinoza, in all

its complex variety, cannot be a simple indivisible substance. Neither, then, can the soul, whose ideas, by the hypothesis, reflect every conceivable modification of the external universe, be a simple indivisible substance.[61] Whatever may be said of the assumed object, may be said of the impression by which it is represented. Matter and motion, it was argued again, however varied, could still be nothing but motion and matter. Hume's theory of causation destroys the argument. Causes and effects are but names for conjoined phenomena, and we cannot assert *a priori* that any two phenomena will or will not be conjoined. No position of bodies can produce motion, any more than it can produce thought; for, turn it which way you will, it is still but a position of bodies.[62] As thought and motion are, in fact, constantly united, motion may be, and on Hume's definition it actually is, the cause of thought. We must either assert that causal connection between two objects exists only where we can perceive the logical nexus between their ideas, or we must admit that uniform conjunction implies a causal relation. In the first case, there can be no 'cause or productive principle' in the universe, not even the Deity himself. For we have no 'idea' of the Deity, except from impressions, each of which appears to be an independent entity, and, therefore, includes no efficacy. If we still assert the Deity to be the one cause which supplies this defect, he must be the cause of every action, virtuous or vicious; and we fall into Pantheism. If we admit that uniform connection is sufficient to establish cause, we must then admit that anything may be the cause of anything;[62] and the argument against Materialism vanishes. Nominally retorting upon Bayle the objections to Spinozism, Hume is really extending Bayle's scepticism beyond its immediate purpose; and bringing out the contradictions which inevitably beset the attempt to treat of absolute substances supposed to exist in perfect simplicity and independence of all relations. His argument was shrouded by a thin veil of reticence, and the defects of style which mar the early treatise: and it dealt with considerations too abstract to impress the ordinary reasoner. In the posthumous Dialogues he comes to closer quarters with the popular theology.

9. The Dialogues are prefaced by an apology for adopting that form of argument. The true motives are obvious enough. Theologians might indulge in demonstrations. The sceptic finds it convenient to create personages to whose utterances he is not obviously pledged. Moreover, the form of the Dialogue itself implies an argument. The sceptic Philo mediates between the rigidly orthodox Demea and the more amenable Cleanthes. Demea and Cleanthes represent, in fact, two opposite schools of theology, and Philo finds in each of them an ally in his assault upon the other. We have already noticed the antithesis between Clarke and Waterland, or between Browne and Berkeley. When each divine accused his brother of sanctioning the first principles of Atheism, so keen an observer as Hume was not likely to overlook the advantage to himself. He could stand aside, like Faulconbridge in 'King John,' and watch France and Austria shoot in each other's faces. Demea, in fact, represents the *a priori* school, who at once assert the existence of God and exhaust themselves in assertions of the utter inconceivability of his attributes. Cleanthes, relying upon the argument from final causes, is forced to admit a certain analogy between the Divine workman whose purpose is revealed in his work, and the human observer who can understand his designs. The agreement of theologians is an agreement to use a common name, but the name covers radically inconsistent conceptions. The arguments of the anthropomorphist for a limited Deity tell against the ontological argument for an infinite Deity. The worship of nature can be no more made to square with the worship of Jehovah than with the worship of the supreme artisan. Hume is least antipathetic to the least exalted conception. He has a common ground with the reasoner from design, and resents the metaphysical arrogance which at once admits that its dogmas are unintelligible, and insists upon their acceptance. There is hope of a definite issue between ourselves and a reasoner who accepts our method. Between the *a priori* school and Hume's the opposition was vital, though in practice the ontologists might frame a theology of a more neutral tint than that of their rivals.

10. In the Dialogues, Hume deals briefly with the *a priori*

argument. Assuming the truth of his philosophy, it falls, as we have seen, to the ground. He states, however, distinctly the main ground of the difficulties to which it is exposed. Admitting ostensibly the necessity of a belief in God, he quotes Malebranche, and adds that he might have quoted any number of philosophical divines[63] in favour of the utter inconceivability of the divine nature. We call God a spirit to signify that he is not matter; but without venturing to imply that his nature has any resemblance to ours. We attribute to him thought, design, knowledge; but such words are used in a sense indefinitely distant from that which they bear when applied to mankind. Cleanthes, the advocate of final causes, asks Demea—the representative of the *a priori* theorists—how this doctrine differs from that of the sceptics or atheists, who declare the first cause to be unknown and unintelligible?[64] Men, he says, who assert that God can have no attributes corresponding to human ideas, that he is absolutely simple and immutable, are in fact atheists without knowing it. 'A mind whose acts and sentiments and ideas are not distinct and successive; one that is wholly simple and totally immutable, is a mind which has no thought, no reason, no will, no sentiment, no love, no hatred; or, in a word, is no mind at all.'[65] The ontologists may prove the existence of God; but God with them means pure Being—a blank, colourless, and useless conception.

11. But can it be proved? Hume lays down as a principle that it is evidently absurd to demonstrate a matter of fact, or to prove it by any arguments *a priori.*[66] 'Nothing is demonstrable, unless the contrary implies a contradiction. Nothing that is distinctly conceivable implies a contradiction. Whatever we conceive as existent, we can also conceive as nonexistent. There is no being, therefore, whose non-existence implies a contradiction. Consequently, there is no being whose existence is demonstrable. I propose this argument as entirely decisive, and am willing to rest the whole controversy upon it.'[67] This, in fact, is Hume's retort to the ontological argument of Descartes. It anticipates the more elaborate analysis of the same argument by Kant; and though it may need development, seems to be substantially unanswerable.

Reid characteristically admits its validity in regard to all truths concerning existence, excepting 'only the existence and attributes of the Supreme Being, which is the only necessary truth we know regarding existence.'[68] It is impossible, however, to assign a clear logical ground for this judicious exception. The Cartesian proof is really a subtle mode of begging the question. It is contradictory to speak of non-existing existence; and, therefore, if God be defined as the existing Being, his existence is, of course, necessary. But to transmute this logical necessity into an objective necessity is a mere juggle. It proves that God exists, *if* he exists; which is indeed a true, but not a fruitful, proposition. The argument, in fact, proves nothing, or simply asserts the apparently identical proposition that all existence exists. Every being which exists is known as related to and limited by other existences. From our experience of a particular existence, we may advance by help of such relations to other existences, beyond our immediate experience. But an existence, proved by *a priori* argument, and therefore independent of all relations to the facts of experience, can be nothing but the totality of all existence. The conclusion must be as wide as the premisses. From an argument, independent of all experience, we must infer an existence which does not affect experience, or which affects all experience equally. It has been attempted to revive the ontological argument thus assailed by Hume and Kant; but their criticism is at least decisive against its original form.

12. The 'cosmological' argument attempts to amend this plea by introducing a datum from experience. Something, it is admitted, exists; therefore, there is a necessary existence. Hume scarcely distinguishes this from the ontological argument with which, as Kant says, it is ultimately identical. In a short passage, however, he touches the vital point. Clarke had argued that matter could not be the self-existent Being, because any particle of matter might be conceived to be annihilated or altered. But it is equally possible, as Hume rejoins, to imagine the Deity to be non-existent, or his attributes to be altered. If that be impossible in fact, it is impossible in virtue of some unknown and inconceivable attributes, which may, therefore, be capable of union with matter. Or, if

we put the argument into the more familiar form of the 'first cause,' we are falling into another fallacy. To ask for the cause of an eternal succession is absurd, for cause implies priority of time. In the everlasting chain each link is caused by the preceding, and causes the succeeding. But the whole requires a cause? To call it a whole is an act of the mind which implies no difference in the nature of things. If I could show the cause of each individual in a collection of twenty particles, it would be absurd to ask for the cause of the whole twenty. That is given in giving the particular causes.[69] Hume sees, in fact, that the conception of causality which compels us to bind together all things as mutually conditioned by each other, cannot, without a logical trick, be transferred to the totality of being. If applicable at all, it would produce an infinite series; for, having determined the cause of the whole, we should have to ask for the cause of the cause. The application of the principle is in its very nature incapable of ever leading to an ultimate conclusion. It suggests only an infinite progression, reminding us once more of Locke's famous illustration of the Indian philosopher and his world-supporting elephant.[70]

13. Hume suggests this last difficulty in answer to the physico-theological disputant, whose argument, as we shall see, slides into the other. He concludes his brief argument against the *a priori* philosopher by the undeniable remark that such reasoning has never had much practical influence upon any minds except those of metaphysicians attempting to transplant the mathematical argument into an inappropriate sphere.[71] The argument from final causes, on the other hand, is the most popular pretext for belief, even where it has not been the efficient cause of belief. 'He that made the eye, shall he not see?' has been from of old the most effective retort upon the unbeliever. Kant says that it is hopeless to destroy the authority, even though he denies the demonstrative force, of this argument; and Hume himself admits that (in the character of Philo) he needs all his 'sceptical and metaphysical subtlety' to elude the grasp of the believer.[72] And yet it is plain that this celebrated argument involves another form of the same difficulty. The first steps of the

reasoning are enticingly plain and simple; but when we would reach the conclusion, we suddenly find a huge gulf yawning across our path. Remain in generalities: argue that the general order implies some vaster intelligence, underlying the whole universe, and the argument seems to be satisfactory, as, indeed, Hume seems to admit in some sense at the end of the treatise. He concludes, and apparently with sincerity, that we may admit as the final outcome of natural theology this 'simple, though somewhat ambiguous, at least undefined proposition; that the cause or causes of order in the universe probably have some remote analogy to human intelligence.'[73] But try to press the argument home, to grasp it in a tenable definite shape, and it crumbles in our hands. We can see it when we do not look at it directly. It affords a basis for a vague surmise, not for a distinct dogmatic belief.

14. Hume's argument is a little disordered by the exigencies of the Dialogue; and, perhaps, by his preference of literary effect to scholastic perfection of system. It may, however, be easily reduced to logical coherence. The real difficulty, as Hume very clearly sees, is that the argument, if valid, is in favour of some anthropomorphic conclusion; and that it loses its validity in proportion as it gains in dignity. This is the objection which Demea and Philo, the orthodox and the sceptic, concur in pressing upon Cleanthes, the upholder of its validity. You do not prove, they urge, the existence of God, but of a god or gods—a Demiurgus, not a Supreme Being. The objection may be evaded in two ways: we may either assert that the inference from the part to the whole is legitimate, in which case the argument melts into the *a priori* or ontological argument; or we may be content with proving the existence of a God, considered as a part of the universe and leave the subsequent transition to be tacitly effected. We have to choose between reaching a sufficiently wide conclusion and having a forcible argument. Thus, we may say a watch implies a maker, a house an architect, a book an author, and, therefore, the universe at large must have a contriver. Or, we may say, since the watch implies a maker, the eye equally implies a maker; and, from the numerous cases of a similar character, we gain a cumulative proof for the

existence of a being who has put together a number of natural contrivances, as men have put together their artificial contrivances. The distinction is not precisely made by Hume in this form, and some of his arguments may be applied to either hypothesis; but, by taking it into account, we shall be able to appreciate the argument more clearly without any real alteration of Hume's meaning.

15. The argument, as originally stated by Cleanthes, is that the world is 'nothing but one great machine, subdivided into an infinite number of lesser machines, which again admit of subdivisions, to a degree beyond what human senses can trace and explain.'[74] The adaptation of means to ends is throughout similar; and we are, therefore, justified in inferring the existence of a supreme contriver, with faculties in some sense resembling, though infinitely superior to, our own. The sceptic urges that analogy must grow weaker as the cases diverge, and that the supposed resemblance between a house and the universe is obviously too faint to justify more than a guess or conjecture.[75] Thought is but one of the forces which are operative throughout the universe; heat and cold, attraction and repulsion, are equally active causes. We are not justified in the wide jump from a minute part to the whole. Even assuming that we may argue from the *operations* of one part of nature upon another to the *origin* of the whole '(which never can be admitted), yet why select so minute, so weak, so bounded a principle, as the reason of animals is found to be upon this planet? What peculiar privilege has this little agitation of the brain, which we call thought, that we must thus make it the model of the universe?'[76] There are, he afterwards says, four principles—reason, instinct, generation, vegetation—each of which, or any one of a hundred others, might be selected for the analogy. 'The world resembles a machine, therefore it is a machine; therefore it rose from design'—that is the final-cause argument. Why not say, 'The world resembles an animal, therefore it is an animal; therefore it arose from generation'?[77] The steps in the last argument are not wider, and the analogy, says Hume, is more striking than in the first. And thus we have the old doctrine of the *anima mundi* or the ancient mythological fancies of

the origin of nature from animal birth. It is, indeed, easy to suggest an escape from such difficulties; but the escape is by changing the argument from design into the ontological argument, and a revival of all the old difficulties. The existence of reason, we must now say, implies the existence of a supreme creative faculty which includes, though it is not to be identified with, reason. We must, then, universalise our terms. The order observable in the universe implies, not the specific faculty of reason, but a divine mind, whose ideas correspond to the visible universe as the architect's plan corresponds to the house. Hume meets us again. Granting this, we have the old set of perplexities. The mental world requires a cause as much as the material world. Thought, as we know it, implies a machinery as curious as matter. Must we find a new cause for this ideal world, and so be led into an infinite progression; or shall we assert the existence of a self-ordering principle in ideas? But ideas may be disorganised as well as matter, and experience can tell us nothing of such an ultimate principle. It is, in fact, nothing better than those occult qualities assumed by the old physiologists, who would say that bread nourished by its nutritive faculty. It is but a 'more learned and elaborate way of expressing our ignorance.' At the end of all discussion we come to the inscrutable. An ideal system arranged without preceding design is no more explicable than a material one.[78]

16. Thus, if the argument be made apparently tenable by extending its terms, we find that we have but explained the universe by assuming a counterpart, itself equally in need of explanation. That, in spite of such reasoning, there remains an ineradicable impression that, in some undefinable sense, some mysterious power, to which reason bears an indefinable analogy, must underlie the visible world, is a doctrine not to be entirely dispelled; nor, as I have already said, does Hume appear to disavow it. His arguments might be met by the believers in later ontological systems; though no reasoning can express this shadowy belief in definite logical form, and still less frame from it an available system of theology. We shall presently see Hume's observations upon the gulf which yawns between such a philosophical theism, or, rather, pan-

theism, and the theism which alone can regulate men's lives, or alter their conceptions of fact.

17. Meanwhile, the popular argument escapes the difficulty by a different path. Man, it says, makes houses; God must have made the eye. Admit the force of the reasoning, and we are evidently proving the existence of a being, existing in time and space, and operating upon matter external to himself. The cause is proportional to the effect. From a finite effect we can only infer a finite cause; and from an imperfect effect an imperfect cause. The many difficulties in nature are explicable as an illusion produced by the limitation of our faculties if *a priori* reasoning has established the existence of a perfect creator; but when made the groundwork of an argument, they must imply that the creator has been at fault; or, at lowest, that we cannot tell whether he has or has not been at fault.[79] Not only does the argument go to prove a creator finite in power and imperfect in skill, but it does not even tend to prove his unity. If a city implies many men, why should not the universe imply many deities or demons?[80] The vaster we suppose the power, the less close the analogy. Polytheism, in short, with all its accompaniments of the grossest anthropomorphism, is the most natural, though not the necessary, inference from the argument, for the closer the resemblance discovered, the closer the likeness of the unknown cause to man.[81]

18. An objection is made by Cleanthes, which, indeed, forms a natural part of the argument from final causes. He argues from the brief course of modern history that the world must have had an origin in time; and, if an origin, then a maker. The sceptic replies that the argument suggests the probability of convulsions sufficient to have swept away the traces of former civilisations; and that, in fact, we have geological proofs throughout the world that every part of it has been covered with water. The most consistent explanation, then, is to suppose incessant and continuous change. An 'eternal inherent principle of order,' with 'great and continual revolutions and alterations,' will solve all difficulties as well as any other theory; and thus the argument is equally favourable to scepticism, polytheism, or theism.[82]

Another cosmogony is suggested which forms a kind of link between the 'old epicurean hypotheses' and modern systems of evolution. We may regard order as the condition of the continuous existence of a given state, not as its creative principle. 'Unguided matter' going through eternal revolutions will at times fall, so to speak, into positions of stable equilibrium. One of them when once reached will necessarily have a comparative permanence. Upon this hypothesis, it is vain to insist upon the uses of the parts in animals or vegetables, and their curious adjustment to each other. 'I would fain know how an animal could subsist unless its parts were so adjusted?'[83] The doctrine of final causes is here met by that doctrine of the survival of the fittest, or the correspondence between the organism and its medium, which in recent times has been its most fatal antagonist.

19. The argument thus appears to be unmanageable. It concludes, if it concludes for anything, for a finite and imperfect creator; and, if for a finite creator, then for any number of creators, or for the absence of any distinct creator. We are no longer seeking for the sole and supreme cause, but endeavoring to account for a set of adaptations, effected by some unknown agent acting under strict conditions and at some particular point. We have almost substituted an antiquarian investigation for a philosophical discussion. One mythology will serve for such a purpose as well as another. We admire a ship which has really been the gradual product of a system struck out by much botching and bungling; the world may have been made after the same fashion, or have been constructed by an infantile or superannuated or incapable deity.[84] In such arguments, says Hume, where we are guided by a finite analogy, it would be easy to suggest any number of systems, though the odds would be indefinitely great against right conjecture.[85]

20. The ambiguity of the argument is not its only defect. The theory, when pushed home, seems to contradict the very experience to which it appeals. In our experience, ideas are always copied from external objects, and mind is capable of affecting only that matter with which it is so conjoined that there is a reciprocal influence between them. The theory

reverses these and similar relations.[86] Hume, as we have seen, argues in various shapes, that, if we appeal to experience, generation, and not conscious construction, will be the mode in which complex organisms arise. By what right do we change our ground? What is the logic when articulately exhibited? The argument from experience in all ordinary cases is, upon Hume's theory, that the constant conjunction of two species generates the custom of inferring one from the other. This, and this alone, warrants me in attributing human works to intelligent action. But how can I be justified in making a similar inference in regard to objects 'single, individual, without parallel or specific resemblance'?[87] To afford grounds for the necessary induction, we ought to have had experience of the rise of several worlds. To ascertain that ours must have arisen from a thought and art resembling the human is simply ridiculous. The universe, as he puts it elsewhere,[88] is a unique effect. Our methods of investigation leave us helpless before such problems.

21. The more closely we scrutinize this imposing argument, the less we can trust it. It proves too much or too little. It lands us in downright anthropomorphism, or it leaves us with nothing but a vague doctrine. We may admit that the reasoning is compatible with the orthodox theory, we cannot hold that it proves it. And yet, if we admitted its value, we should be in face of a still more tremendous difficulty. Establish the existence of a first cause or a contriver, by appeals to reason or to experience, and we have still to ask whether we can discover a supreme moral ruler. Whether the world may have been made in this way or that is comparatively a question of curiosity. Whether it is governed by a ruler armed with the power and the will to secure our happiness is the real question. It is the consciousness of man's imbecility and weakness, says the orthodox Demea, that causes him to search for an all-powerful protector. That sentiment is the source, and strives to be the guarantee, of the religious instinct. The sceptic joins with Demea to enforce the old text of human misery; and Cleanthes struggles feebly to uphold the optimist view. Yet, granting all that he asserts, the sceptic urges unanswerably that a doubtful balance of happiness over mis-

ery is not what we should expect from infinite power, infinite wisdom, and infinite goodness. 'Why is there any misery at all in this world? Not by chance surely. From some cause then. Is it from the intention of the Deity? But he is perfectly benevolent. Is it contrary to his intention? But he is almighty.' Here, indeed, is the hopeless dilemma to which no answer can ever be suggested. 'Nothing,' as the sceptic Philo says, 'can shake the solidity of this reasoning, so short, so clear, so decisive; except we assert that these subjects exceed all human capacity, and that our common measures of truth and falsehood are not applicable to them'—a doctrine which the anthropomorphist Cleanthes has all along denied.[89] Here, says Philo, 'I find myself at ease in my argument.' In discussing the natural attributes, he felt that he was struggling against the obvious probabilities; but he adds: 'It is now your turn to tug the labouring oar, and to support your philosophical subtleties against the dictates of plain reason and experience.'[90]

22. Cleanthes replies by an anticipation of the theory which seems to have commended itself to Mill; he reverts to the doctrine of a limited deity already suggested as the logical result of the argument from design; and thinks that 'benevolence, regulated by wisdom and limited by necessity, may produce just such a world as the present.'[90] Philo replies by a more elaborate statement of his argument. Admitting, as before, that the facts are not incompatible with the orthodox theory, he denies that they have any tendency of themselves to suggest it. The misery of life may be attributed in great measure to four causes, all of which, so far as our limited powers entitle us to speak, might be removed.[91] The first is the employment of pain as well as pleasure to excite to action; the second, the fact that the world is conducted by general and inflexible laws, which could not, it is true, be abrogated without palpable inconvenience, but which might be suspended often enough to extirpate evil, or regulated by interferences compatible with our powers of prevision. A touch to Caligula's brain in his infancy might have made him into a Trajan, and human foresight would have been no more perplexed than by the apparent accidents of storm or sick-

ness.[92] Thirdly, it seems as though natural powers had been so frugally doled out as just to preserve existence. There is no such superfluous stock of endowments as might have been provided by an indulgent parent. But a little more industry, and the vast mass of evil which arises from idleness would be abolished. And, fourthly, the 'inaccurate workmanship' of all parts of the great machine is constantly producing evils. Storms arise in the moral and in the physical universe, and the secretions of the frame are constantly in excess or defect. There *may* be good reasons for these causes of evil, but what they may be, and whether they exist, is altogether beyond our knowledge; and thus, though we may save, we cannot establish, the orthodox conclusion as to the divine attributes.

23. The universe, in short, suggests to us a 'blind nature, impregnated by a great vivifying principle, and pouring forth from her lap, without discernment or parental care, her maimed and abortive children.'[93] Shall we adopt the Manichean principle as the best explanation of this strange mixture of good and ill? It is specious, and in some respects more probable than the common hypothesis, but scarcely compatible with the general uniformity. Cold and heat, moisture and drought, alternate in nature; but the alteration suggests rather indifference than conflict. Of four hypotheses in regard to the causes of the universe—that they are perfectly good, or perfectly bad, or good and bad in conflict, or indifferent—the two simple hypotheses are condemned by the mixture of phenomena; the hypothesis of conflict is condemned by their uniformity; the last hypothesis, therefore, that of indifference, 'seems by far the most probable.'[94]

24. Each man sees the universe coloured by his own temperament; and to Hume, in his speculative moments, it naturally appeared to be all but colourless. His final conclusion—so far as it can be taken as a serious expression of opinion—is equally characteristic. After all, he says, is it not a dispute about words? 'The theist allows that the original intelligence is very different from human reason; the atheist allows that the original principle of order bears some remote analogy to it.'[95] Where is the great difference? The misfortune is, however, that religion, as we know it, is something

very different from that calm assent to a hazy belief, which, on Hume's showing, should supplant our elaborate systems of dogma. The 'Dialogues' conclude with some pregnant remarks upon the important truth that the prevailing religions which are supposed to comfort man and restrain his passions, do, in fact, reflect his deepest melancholy and his worst feelings. The ordinary assumption, that beliefs are somehow imposed from without, instead of being generated from within, maintains a very erroneous estimate of their influence; and Hume's brief suggestions, if conceived in too hostile a spirit, go to the root of the matter.

25. Hume, as I have said, expressly takes notice that he does not assert facts to be incompatible with the theological solution, but only that they afford no presumption in its favour. It may be true, so far as we can say, that God is benevolent and omnipotent, or that his power or his benevolence is limited; any cosmogony, indeed, is compatible with our observations; to dogmatise in the negative sense is as incompatible with the sceptical view as to dogmatise in the positive sense. The denial of all certainty is, however, equivalent to a denial that theology can have any influence upon our lives. We could not, in any case, allow ourselves to be guided by the bare possibility that our actions may have influences which are, by their very nature, inscrutable. The possible truth of the Christian, or Pagan, or Epicurean solutions is, in the same way, too remote a contingency to be taken into account. Absolute ignorance can never be a ground for action. We cannot confute the Rosicrucian dreams of sylphs and invisible agents; we must act without reference to them. But the admitted possibility leaves room for an argument of a different kind from those hitherto considered. The argument from final causes is an argument from analogy; but analogy had been applied in a different sense by Butler. The Christian theory, he said, in substance, gives a view of the world similar to the view which is suggested by a fair interrogation of experience. If we assume for a moment the truth of the Christian dogma, it will fall in with our independent experience. The two views will coalesce and mutually strengthen each other. And if, as cannot be denied, there is

some independent evidence for Christianity, our provisional belief will be transmuted into something like certainty by this process. Introduce but an appreciable fragment of independent evidence, and our previously chaotic knowledge will crystallise round the nucleus. Though we do not profess to obtain a demonstration, our opinions may thus acquire a degree of probability sufficient to prompt us to action. Hume's reply to this theory is given in the essay on 'A Providence and a Future State.'

26. The essay,[96] written in Hume's most admirable style, is, in form, an imaginary defence of Epicurus against the ordinary accusations. Your tenets, say his accusers, are immoral; he replies that the tenets, however interesting to speculatists, have no bearing upon practice. It would be more accurate, of course, to say that their bearing upon society is confined to the destruction of opinions which are demonstrably false. The position taken by his opponents is that assumed by Cleanthes in the Dialogue. From the creation they infer an intelligent creator; and thence an intelligent government of the world. Hume starts by laying down the principle that the cause must be proportional to the effect. A definition of cause and effect, more accurate than Hume's, would strengthen his case, for we should then consider the effect and cause to be but the same phenomenon contemplated from different points of view. Hume, however, seizes the principle firmly enough, though his statement may be open to cavil. 'A body,' he says, 'of ten ounces raised in a scale may serve as a proof that the counterbalancing weight exceeds ten ounces, but can never afford a reason that it exceeds a hundred.'[97] Rather, we should say, the suspension of the weight proves the weight on the other side to be exactly ten ounces. It may be that the pressure is produced by the piston of a steam-hammer, which, in case of need, could exert a pressure of as many tons. That is merely to assert, that, under existing conditions, the pressure is ten ounces, though, under other conditions, the pressure might be indefinitely increased. 'The same rule,' as Hume continues, 'holds whether the cause assigned be brute unconscious matter, or a rational intelligent being.'[98] From one of Zeuxis' pictures, we

71

may safely infer that he possessed precisely the amount of artistic skill displayed; we cannot infer that he was also an architect or a sculptor. Applying the same principle to the case in point, we must allow that the gods, the supposed cause of the universe, possess the amount of skill and intelligence which appears in their workmanship. We can prove nothing further, unless we supply the defect of reason by flattery. We cannot 'mount up from the universe, the effect, to Jupiter, the cause, and then descend downwards to infer any new effect to that cause... The knowledge of the cause being derived solely from the effect, they must be adjusted exactly to each other; and the one can never refer to anything further, or be the foundation of any new inference and conclusion.'[99] Hence, though we may accept the religious hypothesis as accounting for the phenomena, 'no just reasoner will ever presume to infer from it any single fact, and alter or add to the phenomena in any single particular.'[100] The application to the case of Epicurus is obvious. He is accused of denying a supreme governor who rules the course of events, but he does not and cannot deny the course of events itself. As, then, the governor is only known through the events, every argument which is fairly deducible from the supposed cause is equally deducible from the effect.

27. The reply which would be made by any ordinary reasoner is obvious. From the painting, he would say, I infer that Zeuxis possesses *at least* the amount of skill displayed. He must have so much, he may have more in any degree. I infer, too, that Zeuxis has the qualities which would fit him to be an architect or a sculptor, if applied to that end. This is merely to say that, in different relations, Zeuxis would be a cause of different effects, which is to state a truism, if not to make an identical proposition. But, to avoid all appearance of quibbling, it is plain that my real inference is, that Zeuxis, under the given conditions, can produce precisely such a picture as that which I see: though I may infer that, under other conditions, he would produce better or worse, or entirely different works of art. The ground of this inference can be nothing but my experience of Zeuxis and other members of the species in varying relations. I learn from experience that a

man who can do this or that in one case, can do such and such things in another case. As Hume says, when we find 'that any work has proceeded from the skill and industry of man; as we are otherwise acquainted with the nature of the animal, we can draw a hundred inferences concerning what may be expected from him; and those inferences will all be founded in experience and observation.' But did we know man 'only from the single work or production which we examine, it were impossible for us to argue in this manner, because our knowledge of all the qualities which we ascribe to him, being in that case derived from the production, it is impossible they could point to anything further, or be the foundation of any new inference.'[101] Thus a footprint on the sand proves that there was probably another footmark, now obliterated, because we know independently that most men have two feet.[102] Here we mount from the effect to the cause, and, descending, infer alterations in the effect. But that is because other experiences enable us to strike into another chain of reasoning. We are not simply ascending and descending the same set of links.

28. The application is clear. The Deity is a single being in the universe; he is not comprehended under any species; he is known by one single effect, and from the very nature of the case, we are excluded from knowing what he would be in any other relation. The universe is the picture, and Zeuxis the deity; but in this case we cannot even in thought refer to other pictures; nor, if we could, would our inference be profitable. We must therefore always think of our Zeuxis as acting under the same relations as those in which he painted the picture. Zeuxis, as producer of that single effect, is, for us, the only Zeuxis.

29. Hume concludes the essay by asking the question, already noticed in the 'Dialogues,' whether the inference from a unique effect to a unique cause be legitimate? However that question be answered, the argument that such a cause can give us no more than is known in the effect is irrefragable, and in passing the argument overturns by a single stroke the laborious edifice raised by the patient ingenuity of Butler. What, he asks, are we to think of philosophers

who hold this life a mere passage to something further; and, what is more, to something contrasted with it; 'a porch which leads to a greater and more vastly different building; a prologue which serves only to introduce the piece, and give it more grace and propriety'?[103] Arguing from present phenomena, we can never, it is abundantly plain, infer anything dissimilar. The Deity may *possibly* be endowed with attributes which we have never seen exerted; but this is a mere possibility, and can never justify an inference. You argue, for example, from the marks of a moral government. 'Are there,' then, 'any marks of a distributive justice in this world? If you answer in the affirmative, I conclude that, since justice here exerts itself, it is satisfied. If you reply in the negative, I conclude that you have then no reason to ascribe justice, in our sense of it, to the gods. If you hold a medium between affirmation and negation, by saying that the justice of the gods, at present, exerts itself in part, but not in its full extent, I answer that you have no reason to give it any particular extent, but only so far as you can see it *at present* exert itself.'[104] The ordinary theologian calmly inferred that the next world would be the complement, instead of the continuation, of this, without troubling himself about the logic. Butler, looking at the world through certain preconceptions, painfully convinced himself, not indeed that the facts would justify the inference, but that they would bear being stated so as to harmonise with the theory, when once obtained. No colour can be given to any form of the argument, as I have already tried to show, unless we can find a standing-point outside of our experience, when judging of facts. Hume rightly asserts the feat to be impossible; and in his lucid statement, the facts fall into their proper order; and the plausibility of Butler's tortuous reasoning vanishes.[105] How are we to infer the whole from a part; to regard nature, the indifferent, and universal as taking sides in our petty conflicts?

30. That is the ever-recurring difficulty, which reappears in a thousand shapes throughout all theological controversy. If God is less than nature, he is not really God; if identified with nature, then he is not a God whom we can love, fear,

and worship. In the 'Dialogues' this difficulty, as we have seen, appears in the shape of a conflict between the anthropomorphic and the ontological conceptions. It may be approached from yet another side. If we fall into hopeless perplexities when discussing the logical basis of the belief, how are we to account for its historical origin? The belief was not originally suggested by metaphysicians, though they may sanction it as they sanction many others which have sprung up spontaneously. Was it, as the orthodox maintained, the result of a direct revelation, the memory of which was preserved by tradition, or can it be explained by any of the ordinary laws of our constitution? Hume's answer is given in the 'Natural History of Religion.'

31. This brief treatise, originally published in 1757, gives Hume's last views upon the philosophy of religion; for the 'Dialogues,' not published till after his death, had been already written. The fact illustrates his tendency to turn from abstract reasoning to historical methods. To Hume, of course, the various sources of information from which a history of primitive opinions could be now compiled, were not open. The whole method of modern enquiries into such matters was still unknown. He could see, as the most superficial view of history would suggest, that barbarism must have preceded civilisation, and that, 1,700 years ago, polytheism was, with scarcely an exception, the religion of the world. His speculations as to its nature and origin were suggested almost exclusively by the classical writers, or by his own observations of existing modes of thought amongst the ignorant and superstitious. The materials, however, though scanty enough for any minuteness of theory, were sufficient to suggest the main outlines of a scientific view. All ignorant nations are still polytheist; all history takes us back to an age of polytheism; in civilised countries, the vulgar are still polytheists. It is equally plain that the reasoning on which monotheism is ostensibly based implies a cultivated understanding. Polytheism, then, was the primitive religion. What may we conjecture of its origin? Reproduce in imagination the state of the primitive man, and the answer must be obvious. Our happiness depends upon a multitude of unknown causes,

whose laws were utterly obscure, and which could only be conceived in the vaguest way by a savage. Now we find in all men a tendency to transfer their own emotions to other objects. The tendency is illustrated in poetry, and has even forced its way into philosophy, and generated such fancies as the horror of a vacuum; and the whole series of sympathies and antipathies. What more natural, then, than that mankind should personify these unknown causes, upon which they so intimately depend, and attribute to them passions and feelings like their own?[106] In modern phrase, the origin of theology is to be sought in fetichism. We need look no further for an answer to our question. Gods so formed are, of course, anthropomorphic. They are not regarded as the creators of the world, but as invisible beings interfering in its affairs, like the fairies of our own popular mythology. Their worshippers treat them with strange disrespect, as befits beings composed of like materials to themselves.[107] Art takes advantage of these imaginary existences; poets embellish them with allegory; and heroes, remembered for their great deeds, are added to the pantheon, whilst their stories pass, with various distortions, into the great store of tradition.[108] Admitting the truth of hypotheses so obvious and so often verified, we come to a further conclusion. The reasons now given for theism are not the source of the belief. Nay, if you ask one of the vulgar at the present day for his reasons, he will not refer you to the order of nature, and the beautiful economy of final causes. He will tell you of sudden deaths, of famines or droughts, which he ascribes to the action of Providence. His reasons are the reverse of the official reasons. 'Such events,' says Hume, and it is one of his most pregnant remarks, 'such events as, with good reasoners, are the chief difficulties in admitting a supreme Providence, are with him the sole arguments for it.' The philosopher relies upon order; the vulgar rely upon the apparent exceptions to order. To deny special interposition is supposed to be a proof of infidelity; and yet a philosophical theist relies upon regularity and uniformity as the strongest proofs of design.[109]

32. If this be true, even of the less educated in theistical nations, it is clear that their theism does not arise from

argument. It is really due, says Hume, to the gradual promotion of some favoured deity, upon whom epithets of adoration are accumulated by his special worshippers, until infinity itself has been reached.[110] Are examples of the process required? Did not Jupiter rise to be the Optimus Maximus of the heathen? And the God of Abraham, Isaac and Jacob, the supreme Deity and Jehovah of the Jews? Has not the Virgin Mary usurped many of the divine attributes amongst the Catholics? Hume intimates, in a passage softened as it went through the press, that, in the same way, the Jewish God has been developed from the purely anthropomorphic conception indicated in the early chapters of Genesis.[111] He does not add, but his readers would be dull indeed not to infer, that a Jewish peasant has in the same way been elevated to union with the Supreme Being. The doctrine is confirmed by saying that the vulgar belief, however refined in words, is still essentially anthropomorphic; and that it is impossible to maintain a pure theism without stimulating a belief in inferior mediators to satisfy the popular imagination.[112] The remainder of the essay contains many interesting remarks upon the strange compromises which arise in the conflict between the philosophic and the vulgar conceptions. Superstition suggests dreadful attributes in the Deity; philosophy bids us lavish upon him the highest terms of praise. And thus a god may be verbally represented as the perfection of benevolence and wisdom, whilst, in fact, his conduct is represented as outraging all our notions of humanity and justice.[113] The divorce of religion from morality is a natural consequence of the desire to propitiate an imaginary being by services which will appear to be more religious as they have less utility to ourselves or our neighbours.[114] And thus, if the tendency to believe in invisible intelligences may be considered as a stamp set upon man by his Maker, we find that the beings actually created in virtue of this power are stained with caprice, absurdity, and immorality.[115] Religion is blended with hypocrisy; absurdities are blended with philosophy; without religion man is a brute, and yet ignorance is the mother of devotion; the morality inculcated by many religions is as pure as the practices which they sanction are corrupt; the hopes which they hold out are most comforting, but they are swallowed up by the more dreadful forebodings suggested. 'The whole is a riddle, an enigma, an inexplicable mystery. Doubt, uncertainty, suspense of judgment, appear the only result of our most accurate scrutiny concerning this subject. But such is the frailty of human reason, and such the irresistible contagion of opinion, that even this deliberate doubt could scarcely be upheld, did we not enlarge our view, and opposing one species of superstition to another, set them a-quarrelling; while we ourselves, during their fury and contention, happily make our escape into the calm, though obscure, regions of philosophy.'[116]

33. Hume has thus touched all the great lines of argument which have been made to converge upon the proofs of natural theology, and has pronounced them to be inconclusive and inconsistent. Neither the *a priori* nor the *a posteriori* reasoning can be made to hold water; the anthropomorphism implied in one set of theories is radically opposed to the ontological view implied in the other; if the proof could be made out, it would still lead to an essentially equivocal conclusion, which might be of speculative interest, but could have no bearing upon practice. And, finally, if we apply the historical method, we shall see that the fatal contradiction, which lies at the very root of natural theology, is but the inevitable consequence of its mode of development. Successive explanations of the order of the universe have led men through a complete circle of belief. The change which has made the sun instead of the earth the centre of our system, is not greater than the change which has made the deities the expression of the orderly, instead of an expression of the arbitrary, elements of the universe. But in theology men have retained a single name to express two antagonistic conceptions. The theory of final causes is, in fact, the natural expression of the transitional stage, in which the Supreme Being is conceived as interfering with an external universe, but yet as interfering upon a definite plan. What wonder that the conclusions which try to blend the primitive with the latest mode of thought should yield a fatal antinomy upon analysis! Through many of his arguments, Hume might claim the partial ap-

proval of orthodox divines. Before and since his time, distinguished theologians have exhausted language in proclaiming the utter inconceivability of the divine nature; others have insisted upon the incapacity of the unassisted reason to attain to a knowledge of God; and others, again, have denounced all the primitive religions as substantially equivalent to Atheism.[117] To combine their varying theories was to bring out the inherent difficulties of all theology. But another view remained. Theologians have accepted and gloried in the contradiction thus exposed. The familiar words 'very God of very man' remind us that the Christian Church has ordered us to accept this very contradiction as the groundwork of our faith on penalty of damnation. What Hume would have called nonsense, they have revered as mystery; and it must be admitted that the escape is, in one sense, complete. A man who really renounces reason cannot be reached by reasoning, though there is some difficulty in understanding why he believes, or what he means by believing. In one direction, however, he comes apparently to an issue with the sceptic. Mysteries, it is admitted, can be proved by revelation alone; and revelation, upon the ordinary theory, was to be proved by miracles. To consider the value of this method of proof is, therefore, the final task for Hume's ingenuity.

34. It would be superfluous to treat at length an argument which has been so frequently and elaborately discussed. I will content myself with briefly noticing its place in the general argument. The essay, I may say briefly, appears to me to be simply unanswerable if the premises implicitly admitted by Hume be accepted. Apparent success has been reached by tacitly shifting the issue, and discussing problems which may be interesting, but which are not the problem raised by Hume. Two modes of evasion have been commonly used, and to point out their nature will be to illustrate the position sufficiently. In the first place, the argument is often shifted from the question whether any evidence can prove a miracle, to the other question, whether there are *a priori* grounds for denying the possibility of miracles. It is tacitly taken for granted that, if a miracle is possible, the proof of a miracle is possible. Now the very purpose of Hume's argument is to set

aside as irrelevant the question as to the *a priori* possibility of miracles. And the endless discussions as to the meaning of natural laws, and the possibility of their being modified, imply a continuous *ignoratio elenchi*. Hume stated his argument in this form precisely to avoid such a hopeless controversy. In fact, Hume could not on his own principles deny that a being of indefinably superior powers to the human might effect the ordinary series of phenomena. If an extramundane being can, so to speak, impinge upon the world, we are bound by the theory of causation to anticipate novel effects. The reply, so far as a reply was required, to this hypothesis, is given in the essay on a 'Particular Providence.' It is simply that, if God be inferred solely from the order of the universe, we cannot logically attribute to him interferences with its order. When Paley calmly says, if we believe in God, there is no difficulty in believing miracles, Hume's answer is plain. If God is the cause of order, belief in him does not facilitate belief in miracles. On the contrary, pure theism, thus explained, really introduces a difficulty in the belief in miracles which is not apparent in Hume's theory of the arbitrary conjunction of cause and effect. The God required by Paley's hypothesis is really the anthropomorphic deity, whose existence is established by Paley's argument from design. If that argument survive Hume's objections, it undoubtedly removes the *a priori* difficulty of belief in miracles. But the difficulty still remains, whether their occurrence can be proved by testimony. Hume's dilemma remains in full force. We must always ask, for no other test can be suggested, whether it is more incredible that men should have made false statements, wilfully or otherwise, or that an event should have occurred which is opposed to a complete induction. To know that an event is miraculous is to know that it is opposed to such an induction; and, in that case, Hume's argument, as applied to any such evidence as can ever be contemplated, is conclusive. If the event be not known to be miraculous, then the evidence does not prove a miracle, but proves the existence of a previously unknown law of nature.

35. And here comes in the second mode of evasion. It is denied substantially that the events are miraculous. There is,

in a sense, much force in this argument. Undoubtedly, we are continually convinced by evidence, and rightly convinced, of the occurrence of phenomena which we had once supposed to be miraculous. Evidence might convince us that sickness may be cured by methods apparently inadequate to the effect. And it is precisely by such observations that we are led to suspect the soundness of Hume's reasoning. It must be admitted, too, that his favourite theory, that any cause might be joined to any effect, tends to obscure his argument and to perplex his statement. But the answer is obvious. Evidence may certainly prove strange events, but it cannot prove strictly miraculous effects. Now the supposed evidential force of the events in question depends upon their being really miraculous. If it is not contrary to the laws of nature that the dead should be raised or one loaf feed a thousand men, the occurrence of the fact does not prove that an Almighty Being has suspended the laws of nature. If such a phenomenon is contrary to the laws of nature, then a proof that the events had occurred would establish the interference; but, on the other hand, it must always be simpler to believe that the evidence is mistaken; for such a belief is obviously consistent with a belief in the uniformity of nature, which is the sole guarantee (whatever its origin) of our reasoning.

36. Really to evade Hume's reasoning is thus impossible. Its application to popular arguments of the day was, in any case, unanswerable. Theologians who rested not merely the proof of revealed theology, but the proof of all theology, upon miracles, could not even make a show of answering. In any other case, the statement that a man had been raised from the dead would admittedly prove that its author was a liar. The statement thus could not by any logical trick be made valid in the particular case of a religious theory. And this was, more or less avowedly, the position of many orthodox writers. Nor, in the next place, was any escape open to theologians who meant by God the supreme cause of the order of the universe. Their belief increased instead of diminishing the difficulty of the case. The only logical escape is for those who hold that the intervention of invisible beings of greater strength than human, but not strictly divine, is part

of the normal order of the universe. On such an hypothesis a belief in miracles might be tenable, because, strictly speaking, the miracles ceased to be miraculous. The conception, though disavowed by philosophers, was undoubtedly embodied in one form or other in the popular creeds of the day; and, therefore, the believers in the miraculous might evade Hume's dilemma. But since his time philosophical reasoners have been more and more driven either to pitiable evasions, or to take refuge in intellectual suicide.

37. It may still be asked, what was Hume's real belief? Did his theoretical scepticism follow him into actual life? That is a question for a biographer rather than for the historian of thought. There is a famous saying which has been attributed to the first Lord Shaftesbury, to Garth, to Humboldt, and probably to others. What is your religion? The religion of all sensible men. And what is the religion of all sensible men? Sensible men never tell. Hume quotes a similar saying of Bacon's. Atheists, says the philosopher, have now-a-days a double share of folly; for, not content with saying in their hearts that there is no God, they utter it with their lips, and are 'thereby guilty of multiplied indiscretion and imprudence.'[118] Hume so far adopted these precepts of worldly wisdom that he left his most outspoken writings for posthumous publication.[119] Yet Hume said enough to incur the vehement indignation both of the truly devout and of the believers in the supreme value of respectability. It is impossible to suppose that the acutest reasoner of his time would have considered his most finished work as a mere logical play, or that he should have encountered obloquy without the justification of sincerity. I have, therefore, no doubt that Hume was a sceptic in theology, that he fully recognised the impossibility of divining the great secret, and that he anticipated this part of what is now called the positive philosophy. Yet, as a true sceptic, he probably did not expect that the bulk of mankind would ever follow him in his conclusions. He felt that, although a rational system of theology capable of affecting men's lives be an impossibility, his own denial of its validity did not quite destroy the underlying sentiment. Though the old bonds were worthless, some mode of contem-

plating the universe as an organised whole was still requisite. A vague belief, too impalpable to be imprisoned in formulae or condensed into demonstrations, still survived in his mind, suggesting that there must be something behind the veil, and something, perhaps, bearing a remote analogy to human intelligence. How far such a belief can be justified, or, if justified, made the groundwork of an effective religion, is a question not precisely considered by Hume nor to be here discussed. We may be content to respect in Hume the most powerful assailant of the pretentious dogmatism and the timid avoidance of ultimate difficulties characteristic of his time.

William Warburton

1. In the course of the once celebrated controversy between Warburton and Lowth, Lowth made one hit which must have told forcibly upon his opponent. He quoted the following passage from Clarendon's History: 'Colonel Harrison was the son of a butcher near Nantwich, in Cheshire, and had been bred up in the place of a clerk, under a lawyer of good account in those parts; which kind of education introduces men into the language and practice of business, and, if it be not resisted by the great ingenuity of the person, inclines young men to more pride than any other kind of breeding, and disposes them to be pragmatical and insolent.' 'Now, my Lord,' says Lowth, 'as you have in your whole behaviour and in all your writings remarkably distinguished yourself by your humility, lenity, meekness, forbearance, candour, humanity, civility, decency, good manners, good temper, moderation with regard to the opinions of others, and a modest diffidence of your own, this unpromising circumstance of your early education' (Warburton had, like Harrison, been articled to an attorney) 'is so far from being a disgrace to you, that it highly redounds to your praise.'[120] Which piece of irony, pardonable, perhaps, as a retort to Warburton's sneers at Lowth's Oxford training, expresses the most conspicuous feature of Warburton's character—namely, that he was as

'proud, pragmatical, and insolent' as a man who brought to theological controversies the habits of mind acquired in an attorney's office might naturally be expected to show himself. Warburton, in fact, is the most perfect specimen of a type not unfrequent among clergymen. We may still, though less often than was once the case, observe a man in the pulpit who ought to be at the bar; and though the legal habits of mind may be an admirable corrective to certain theological tendencies, a frequent result of thus putting the round man in the square hole is to produce that incongruity which in another profession has given rise to the opprobrious term, sea-lawyer. Warburton, as we shall presently see, was a lawyer to the back-bone in more senses than one; but his most prominent and least amiable characteristic was the amazing litigiousness which suggested Lowth's sarcasm.

2. For many years together Warburton led the life of a terrier in a rat-pit, worrying all theological vermin. His life, as he himself observed in more dignified language, was 'a warfare upon earth; that is to say, with bigots and libertines, against whom I have denounced eternal war, like Hannibal against Rome, at the altar.'[121] Amongst bigots and libertines we must reckon everyone, Christian or infidel, whose faith differed by excess or defect from that of Warburton, and add that Warburton's form of faith was almost peculiar to himself. To entertain a different opinion, or to maintain the same opinion upon different grounds, gave an equal title to his hostility. He regrets, in one place, the necessity of assailing his friends. 'I have often asked myself,' he says, and nobody has ever answered the question, 'what I had to do to invent new arguments for religion, when the old ones had outlived so many generations of this mortal race of infidels and free-thinkers? Why did I not rather choose the high-road of literary honours, and pick out some poor critic or small philosopher of this school, to offer up at the shrine of violated sense and virtue?' In that case he thinks that he might 'have flourished in the favour of his superiors and the goodwill of all his brethren.'[122] According to himself, it was the love of TRUTH which carried him away. His creed had that unique merit which he ascribes to the Jewish religion—

namely, that it 'condemned every other religion for an imposture.'[123] To disagree with him was to be not merely a fool, but a rogue. So universal, indeed, was his intolerance of any difference of opinion, that bigot and libertine, wide as is the sweep of those damnatory epithets, can by no means include all the objects of his aversion. He makes frequent incursions into regions where abuse is not sanctified by theology. The argument set forth in the 'Divine Legation' wanders through all knowledge, sacred and profane, and every step brings him into collision with a fresh antagonist. Glancing at his table of contents, we find a series of such summaries as these:—'Sir Isaac Newton's chronology of the Egyptian empire confuted and shown to contradict all sacred and profane antiquity, and even the nature of things;' 'Herman Witsius' arguments examined and confuted;' a prophecy 'vindicated against the absurd interpretations of the Rabbins and Dr. Shuckford;' the Jews 'vindicated from the calumnious falsehoods of the poet Voltaire;' 'an objection of Mr. Collins examined and confuted;' 'the Bishop of London's discourse examined and confuted;'[124] and, in short, his course is marked, if we will take his word for it, by the corpses of his opponents. Deists, atheists, and pantheists are, of course, his natural prey. Hobbes, 'the infamous Spinoza,'[125] and Bayle, Shaftesbury, Collins, Toland, Tindal, Chubb, Morgan, and Mandeville, and, above all, his detested enemy Bolingbroke, are 'examined and confuted' till we are weary of the slaughter. But believers do not escape much better. If, as he elegantly expresses it, he 'trims Hume's jacket'[126] for not believing in the miracles, he belabours Wesley still more vigorously for believing that miracles are not extinct. From Conyers Middleton, who, indeed, escaped for some years as a personal friend, up to Sherlock and Lowth, he spared neither dignity nor orthodoxy. The rank and file of the controversial clergy, Sykes, and Stebbing, and Webster, fell before his 'desperate hook' like corn before the sickle. And when the boundless field of theological controversy was insufficient for his energies, he would fall foul of the poet Akenside for differing from him as to the proper use of ridicule, or of Crousaz for misinterpreting Pope's 'Essay on Man,' or of Bolingbroke for attacking the memory of Pope, or of a whole swarm of adversaries who gathered to defend Shakespeare from his audacious mangling. The innumerable hostilities which did not find a vent in any of these multitudinous conflicts struggled to light in notes on the 'Dunciad.' Probably no man who has lived in recent times has ever told so many of his fellow-creatures that they were unmitigated fools and liars. He stalks through the literary history of the eighteenth century, trailing behind him a whole series of ostentatious paradoxes, and bringing down his controversial shillelagh on the head of any luckless mortal who ventures to hint a modest dissent. There is, it cannot be denied, a certain charm about this everflowing and illimitable pugnacity. We have learnt to be so polite that it occasionally suggests itself that the creeds which excite our languid sympathy or antipathy are not very firmly held. It is at least amusing in this milder epoch to meet a gentleman who proposes to cudgel his opponents into Christianity and to thrust the Gospel down their throats at the point of the bludgeon.

3. Even Warburton, complex and many-sided as were his hostilities, was not above the necessity of finding allies. No man, though gifted with the most perverse ingenuity, can stand quite alone. Warburton formed two remarkable connections. As is not uncommon with men of boisterous temperament, both these friends were remarkable for qualities in which he was deficient. An alliance of two Warburtons would have formed a combination more explosive and unstable than any hitherto known to psychological chemistry. Pope and Hurd, his two friends, were suited to him by force of contrast. Warburton was well fitted to be Pope's bully, and Hurd to serve as the more decorous assistant of Warburton's vengeance. Pope seems to have been really touched by Warburton's blustering championship. It doubtless pleased him to discover that he had been in reality talking sound religious philosophy, when he had been too plausibly accused of versifying second-hand infidelity. The thin-skinned poet welcomed with infantile joy the alliance of his pachydermatous defender, and naturally inferred that the man who had discovered him to be an orthodox philosopher must be himself a

profound divine. Warburton took a natural pride in having cut out so rich a prize from under the guns of the infidel Bolingbroke; and raised himself in general esteem by acquiring a right of spiritual proprietorship in the literary ruler of the age.

4. The friendship with Hurd is more curious and characteristic. Hurd is a man for whom, though he has attracted a recent biographer,[127] animated by the ordinary biographer's enthusiasm, it is difficult to find a good word. He was a typical specimen of the offensive variety of University don; narrow-minded, formal, peevish, cold-blooded, and intolerably conceited. As Johnson says of 'Hermes' Harris, he was 'a prig, and a bad prig.' Even Warburton, it is said, could never talk to him freely. In his country vicarage he saw nobody, kept his curate at arm's length, and never gave an entertainment except on one occasion, when Warburton, who was staying with him, rebelled against the intolerable solitude.[128] As a bishop, he never drove a quarter of a mile without his episcopal coach and his servants in full liveries. His elevation to the bench was justified by his fame—for which there are some grounds—as an elegant writer of Addisonian English and a good critic of Horace. The virtue which he particularly affected was filial piety. After five years' acquaintance, his Christian humility led him to confide to Warburton, the son of a country attorney, that his own father was a farmer.[129] He was sufficiently amiable to speak in endearing terms of his mother; and, in a letter to Warburton, after touching upon certain presentation copies of one of his books, and on Sir John Dalrymple's newly published Memoirs, observes quite pathetically that the good woman 'almost literally fell asleep' about a fortnight before.[130] Warburton, though not a very lofty character, had, at least, a little more human nature in his composition.

5. The relations between the pair recall, in some degree, those between Johnson and Boswell. Warburton, however, is but a feeble-jointed and knock-kneed giant in comparison with the great lexicographer, and Hurd but a dry and barren counterpart to Boswell. The flattery in this case was reciprocal; and perhaps the great man pours out more mouth-filling

compliments than his satellite. If Hurd thinks that Warburton's memory will be endeared to the wise and the good for ever, Warburton takes Hurd to be one of the first men of the day, and holds him to be Addison's equal in 'correctness,' whilst far superior to him in strength of reasoning.[131] The two looked out with condescension upon Warburton's humbler jackals, and with superb contempt upon the rest of mankind. The general principle of their common creed is neatly expressed by Hurd, who observes that one 'hardly meets with anything else' than coxcombs in this world.[132] To which Warburton adds the comment, that 'nature never yet put one grain of gratitude or generosity into the composition of a coxcomb.'[133] The application of this maxim to particular cases shows that Horace Walpole is an insufferable coxcomb;[134] Johnson full of malignity, folly and insolence;[135] Garrick, a writer below Cibber, whose 'sense, whenever he deviates into it, is more like nonsense;'[136] Young, 'the finest writer of nonsense of any of this age;'[137] Smollett, a 'vagabond Scot,' who 'writes nonsense 10,000 strong;'[138] Priestly, 'a wretched fellow;'[139] and Voltaire, 'a scoundrel.'[140] Hurd carefully preserved this correspondence, and left it for publication after his death, hoping that the reader would forgive the 'playfulness of his' (Warburton's) 'wit,' in consideration of the faithful portraiture of character.

6. The mode in which these congenial spirits co-operated during their lives may be sufficiently illustrated by their quarrel with Jortin. Jortin, who had been on excellent terms with Warburton, mildly observed, in a 'Dissertation on the State of the Dead,' as described by Homer and Virgil, that Warburton's 'elegant conjecture' as to the meaning of the sixth book of the 'Æneid' (a conjecture chiefly remarkable as affording the occasion of one of Gibbon's first literary efforts) was not satisfactorily established. Hereupon Hurd published a pamphlet bitterly assailing Jortin for his audacity. Hurd's elaborate irony, as translated by a contemporary writer, amounted to presenting the following rules by which the conduct of all men should be regulated in presence of the great master:—

'You must not write on the same subject that he does. You

must not write against him. You must not glance at his arguments even without naming him, or so much as referring to him. You must not oppose his principles, though you let his arguments quite alone. If you find his reasonings ever so faulty, you must not presume to furnish him with better of your own, even though you approve and are desirous to support his conclusions. You must not pretend to help forward any of his arguments that happen to fall lame, and may seem to require your needful support. When you design him a compliment, you must express it in full form, and with all the circumstances of panegyrical approbation, without impertinently qualifying your civilities by assigning a reason why you think he deserves them; as this might possibly be taken for a hint that you know something of the matter he is writing about as well as himself. You must never call any of his discoveries by the name of conjectures, though you allow them their full proportion of elegance, learning, &c.; for you ought to know that this great genius never proposed anything to the judgment of the public (though ever so new and uncommon) with diffidence in his life.'[141]

7. The infringement of such rules as these was, in fact, all that Hurd could lay to Jortin's charge. Warburton welcomed the assistance of his jackal with a shout of delight. He knew of but one man from whose heart or whose pen so fine a piece of irony could come. Next to his pleasure in seeing himself so 'finely praised,' was his truly Christian pleasure 'in seeing Jortin mortified.'[142] And in a following letter he remarks that 'they must be dirty fellows indeed, who can think I have no reason to complain of Jortin's mean, low, ungrateful conduct towards me'[143]—that is to say, the conduct of openly expressing a difference of opinion as to a critical question. Jortin afterwards revenged himself upon Hurd's master by pointing out a blunder in the translation of a Latin phrase. Warburton, unable openly to deny the error, made a surly overture to Jortin, which was coldly accepted; but no real reconciliation followed. The two conspirators abused Jortin in private,[144] but did not continue open hostilities.

8. The almost incredible arrogance of which this is a specimen breathes in every page of Warburton's serious writings.

His style is too cumbrous to be effective; he has not the acuteness or the temper to aim at the joints in his opponent's armour; he is content to belabour them with huge clumsy blows, which make a noise, but do little mischief in proportion.[145] His epithets are mere random substitutes for profane oaths. When, for example, he calls the Moravian hymn-book 'a heap of blasphemous and beastly nonsense,'[146] or says of Grey's Commentary upon 'Hudibras,' that he hardly thinks that 'there ever appeared in any language so execrable a heap of nonsense,'[147] we do not feel that 'blasphemous and beastly' in the one case, and 'execrable' in the other, give a distinct definition of these rival 'heaps of nonsense.' He, therefore, hardly does as much mischief as he could have wished to 'the pestilent herd of libertine scribblers with which the island is overrun, whom I would hunt down as good King Edgar did his wolves, from the mighty author of 'Christianity as Old as the Creation,'' to the drinking blaspheming cobbler who wrote against ''Jesus and the Resurrection;'' '[148] or to those 'agents of public mischief, who not only accelerate our ruin, but accumulate our disgraces—wretches, the most contemptible for their parts, the most infernal for their manners.'[149] Amongst the contemptible, pestilent and infernal wretches, were men whose shoe-latchet he was not worthy to unloose; and it is difficult not to feel a foolish desire that Warburton could have had revealed to him the true relations between himself and his antagonists. Of Hume, for example, he says, in what is probably the feeblest of his works, for it is that which takes him furthest out of his depth, that he merely runs 'his usual philosophic course from knavery to nonsense;'[150] and he adds that Hume's 'great philosophic assertion of one of the master-wheels of superstition, labours with immovable nonsense.' Of a statement of Voltaire's about the Jewish hostility to the human race, he observes: 'I think it will not be easy to find, even in the dirtiest sink of freethinking, so much falsehood, absurdity, and malice heaped together in so few words.'[151] Hume and Voltaire have survived Warburton's attacks, and we may allow our natural resentment to drop. Time has avenged them sufficiently. I add, though with some reluctance, a

90

couple of illustrations of the lengths to which Warburton's 'playfulness of wit' could sometimes carry him. 'Even this choice piece of the first philosophy, his lordship's' (Boling-broke's) 'sacred pages, is ready,' he says, 'to be put to very different uses, according to the tempers in which they have found his few admirers on the one side, and the public on the other; like the china utensil in the Dunciad, which one hero used for a ——pot, and another carried home for his head-piece.'[152] And here is his retort to poor Dr. Stebbing, who conceived himself to have shown that a prophecy was equally relevant, whether Warburton's interpretation were or were not admitted. 'He hath shown it indeed,' snorts his antago-nist, 'as the Irishman showed his ——.'[153]

9. Warburton's confidence in his own invincibility was unsurpassable. Every now and then he pledges himself that some argument shall never again be regarded in the 'learned world' as anything but an ignorant prejudice; whilst a similar boast from an antagonist is declared to be worthy only of some 'wild conventicle of Methodists or Hutchinsonians.'[154] His confidence is so great that he ventures to take the danger-ous line of insisting upon the strength of the enemy's case. Nobody had thoroughly confuted Collins, until Warburton searched the matter to the bottom. Nay, it might be doubted whether the weight of argument was not, on the whole, against Christianity, till he turned the scale. For want of the master-key by which he unlocked all puzzles, 'the Mosaic dispensation had lain for some ages involved in obscurities, and the Christian had become subject to insuperable difficul-ties.'[155] The very conception of such an expedient, concealed from the eyes of all theologians till the middle of the eigh-teenth century, and now for the first time to provide an immovable basis for the superstructure of revealed religion, is a sufficient index of its inventor's religious insight. It con-firms the natural inference from the characteristics hitherto noted that Warburton is a worthless writer. And it is true that his writings are in substantive value below even the low level of the later theology of his age. He never seems to understand that the great question is one of facts, not of words. He is worth study solely as the most striking example of certain

tendencies embodied in contemporary thought, and exhibited by him upon an abnormal scale. Yet he flourished for a
time. 'He is, perhaps, the last man,' says Johnson, 'who has
written with a mind full of reading and reflection.' He
succeeded in impressing his contemporaries by sheer bulk;
and few cared to recognise the obvious fact that this colossus
was built up of rubbish. He resembles, in the width and
indiscriminate application of his learning, some of the great
writers of the preceding century. From an external glance he
might be taken to be the last of that great brotherhood. Many
men have spoken more to the purpose in a page than he has
done in many volumes; but it is worth while to consider what
were the conditions under which a man possessed of huge
brute force, though of no real acuteness, could blunder on so
gigantic a scale.

10. Warburton's strange passion for a paradox is admitted
by himself with a quaint complacency. After stating, for
example, that 'if the Scriptures have,' as Middleton had said,
every possible fault which can deform a language, 'this is so
far from proving such language not divinely inspired, that it
is one certain mark of its original;'[156] he winds up his demonstration by asserting that the Koran became to true believers
'as real and substantial a pattern of eloquence as any whatso-
ever;' and adds that this is a paradox, 'which, like many
others that I have had the odd fortune to advance, will
presently be seen to be only another name for truth.'[157] He is
never so proud as when he has hit upon some proposition so
ingeniously offensive to all parties, that, as he puts it, 'believers and unbelievers have concurred, by some blind chance
or other,' in objecting to it.[158] The Warburtonian paradox is
one of a class unfortunately too common. It is not the paradox
produced by the excessive acuteness which, seizing upon
some new aspect of a subject, fails properly to correlate its
conclusions with established principles. Warburton is sometimes paradoxical, as a deaf man writing upon music might
be paradoxical. He blunders into the strangest criticisms upon
Shakespeare or the Bible, from sheer absence of poetical or
spiritual insight. More often his paradoxes resemble those of

a pettifogging lawyer, content to strain the words of a statute into any meaning that may serve his turn, without the slightest regard to its spirit. The Bible is his Act of Parliament, and to him one argument is as good as another if it can be twisted into a syllogism with a text of Scripture for its premiss. He is fond of quoting Hobbes's inimitable maxim, that words are the counters of wise men and the money of fools. It is unfortunately applicable to his own practice. The fundamental though unconscious assumption of many people is, that reasoning is not a process of discovering, but of inventing, truth. Logic, they seem to think, is a mechanism by which new conclusions may be manufactured. Given a certain set of assumptions, there can in reality be only one right conclusion, and that conclusion may be that no certainty is obtainable. But many people fancy that a sufficiently skilful logician might distil truth out of the most unsatisfactory materials. They measure his skill by the length of the chain of reasoning; and fail to see that the best logician is often the man who pronounces the materials to be insufficient. Reasoning thus becomes a mere game of skill. A proper manipulation of the 'counters' will enable a good player to win a victory, where a bad one would suffer defeat. The sentiments, proper enough in a mere game of scholastic fence, are transferred to matters of scientific research. The clever dialectician who can puzzle his adversary is assumed to show the same qualities as the profound and accurate reasoner.

11. Such qualities become prominent only in a time when the desire for truth has grown weak; and the anxiety to attain a knowledge of facts is superseded by the curiosity excited by a display of dialectical fencing. At such a time, however, the writings of a Warburton have a certain incidental interest. He brings into startling relief the current opinions of the day. A man of genius is guided by an unconscious instinct which prevents him from obtruding the more offensive side of his doctrine. A Warburton, utterly wanting in logical tact, blurts out the absurdities which the judicious keep in the background. He splashes indiscriminately through thick and thin, and unintentionally reveals the errors of his allies. Indeed, we

may find in Warburton, in all their native absurdity, some arguments which still pass muster by the help of a little philosophical varnish.

12. The 'Divine Legation' is an attempt to support one gigantic paradox by a whole system of affiliated paradoxes. Warburton, as Bentley shrewdly said, was a man of 'monstrous appetite and bad digestion.' Johnson applied to him a couplet from Savage:—

Here learning, blinded first and then beguiled,
Looks dark as Ignorance, as Frenzy wild.

He has tumbled out his intellectual spoils into his ponderous pages with boundless prodigality. Starting with the professed intention of vindicating Moses, he diverges into all manner of subsidiary enquiries. He discourses upon the origin and nature of morality; he gives the true theory of the alliance of Church and State; he devotes many pages to an elucidation of the ancient mysteries; he discusses the origin of writing and the meaning of hieroglyphics; he investigates the chronology of Egypt; he indulges in an elaborate argument to determine the date of the Book of Job; he assails all freethinkers, orthodox divines, Jews, Turks, Socinians, classical scholars, antiquaries, and historians, who may happen to differ from any of his opinions. At every stage in the argument new vistas of controversy present themselves; and as every phenomenon in the universe is more or less connected with every other, Warburton finds abundant excuses for rambling from end to end of the whole field of human knowledge when an adversary is to be encountered, or a bit of reading to be illustrated, or, in short, any caprice to be gratified. It is not wonderful that a man pursuing so vast a plan, and stirring so many prejudices at every step, should have wearied of his task before it was completed, and have sunk into episcopal repose before the edifice received its crowning ornaments.

13. The position, as Warburton conceived it, was this. The deists had been pressing on with overweening confidence from their reliance upon a certain argument. They had made, so he assures us,[159] a great point of the supposed absence from the Old Testament of any distinct reference to a future

state of rewards and punishments. Apologists of Christianity had been put to awkward shifts, and had endeavoured by strained interpretations to relieve the Jewish creed from this imputation. Warburton proposes to discover a new move in the game (he maintains, in a characteristic passage, that there is as much room for new discoveries in religion, as for new discoveries in science)[160] by which the deists, with victory just in their grasp, may be stale-mated. He resolves to admit the very proposition for which they had contended, and to convert the admission into what his title characteristically describes as a 'demonstration' of the truth of the Mosaic religion. The demonstration—one, as he informs us, which falls 'very little short of mathematical certainty, and to which nothing but a mere physical possibility of the contrary can be opposed'[161]—is comprised in three very clear and simple propositions. The first is, that the doctrine of a future state of rewards and punishments is necessary to the well-being of society; the second, that the utility of this doctrine has been admitted by all mankind, and especially by the wisest and most learned nations of antiquity; the third, that this doctrine is not to be found in the Mosaic dispensation. The statement bears insincerity upon the very face of it. The reasoning is intended to be startling, and asserted to be obvious. Warburton boldly says that one would have thought that 'we might proceed directly to our conclusion that therefore the law of Moses is of divine original.'[162] Yet, as some persons may be stupid enough to miss the force of his argument, he draws it out more fully in elaborate syllogisms. Substantially they amount to the assertion that Moses would not have omitted a sanction which he knew to be essential had he not had a certainty of miraculous interference. The statement that he ventured into the desert without an adequate provision of food, might be urged as a proof that he reckoned upon a supply of quails and manna; and, similarly, the statement that he started as a legislator without so essential a spiritual provision as a belief in hell, is taken by Warburton to show that he reckoned upon a supernatural substitute for the terrors of the next world. We shall see directly what it was. Grotesque as the argument appears, and must have been intended to appear when thus bluntly stated, it is scarcely more than a caricature of a favourite method of arguing. Some apologists still venture to maintain that the Christian doctrine was revolting to the ordinary mind in order to prove that its success was miraculous. An admission that it suited the wants of the time may suggest that its growth was spontaneous. They, therefore, urge that human nature is revolted by a teaching of humility and purity, as Warburton declared it to be so corrupt that nothing but the fear of hell could check the progress of decay.

14. It will be enough to notice briefly the critical points of the strange system erected upon this doubtful foundation. The whole argument obviously rests upon the assumption that nothing but a belief in a future world can sustain the moral law. The facts, as stated by Warburton, would seem to confute the theory. If the Jewish economy, as he said, prospered, and the Jews, as he says, knew nothing of a future state, the obvious inference is that the belief is unnecessary to national prosperity. No, says Warburton, in substance; the facts contradict my theory; therefore, the facts were miraculous. This reliance upon the infallibility of an *a priori* argument, or rather of a round assertion, gives at once the key to his whole book. He attempts, indeed, to prove the doctrine —one sufficiently familiar to his contemporaries—though his proofs are as feeble as most of his speculative flights. He asserts in a great many words that men will not be virtuous unless they are paid for it. Neither a moral sense, nor a perfection of the fitness of things, will be sufficient motives without the obligation of a superior will. Nothing else can 'make actions moral, *i.e.* such as deserve reward and punishment.' This, of course, is the familiar theory of Waterland or Paley. But nobody can dispute the originality of Warburton's application. That Moses, being well acquainted with the importance of the belief, for the Moses of Warburton is a highly intelligent politician of the eighteenth century, should have omitted to preach it, is strange enough. But the paradox, pretty enough as it stands, is heightened by an appendix. The ancient philosophers, as Warburton tells us, generally disbelieved the doctrine, and yet preached it for its

utility. And thus we have the curious phenomenon that the one inspired teacher in the world neglected to preach, whilst all the false teachers systematically preached, the one vital doctrine of all morality, and in both cases acted in opposition to their real belief.

15. In seeking to account for the singular fact that a man of true, though coarse, intellectual vigour should have cheated himself into a state of mind so far resembling belief in this grotesque doctrine as to stake his reputation upon maintaining it, we come to the heart of Warburton's position. The best test of the civilisation of a race, it has been said, is the conception which it has formed of the Deity. The remark is applicable to others than savages. In one of his fierce assaults upon Bolingbroke, Warburton says, 'I should choose to have the clergy's God, though made of no better stuff than artificial theology (because this gives him both justice and goodness), rather than his Lordship's God, who has neither, although composed of the most refined materials of the first philosophy. In the meantime, I will not deny that he may be right in what he says, that men conceive of the Deity *more humano,* and that his Lordship's God and the clergy's God are equally faithful copies of themselves.'[163] Warburton's view of the Mosaic dispensation will enable us to form a tolerably adequate portrait of this Deity, formed of artificial theology, who was a 'faithful copy' of the Bishop of Gloucester. What logical grounds Warburton would have assigned for his belief is a question which matters very little; because the plain fact is that the conception in his mind did not really repose upon any philosophical argument whatever.

16. The God of Warburton, then, is, in the first place, the omnipresent legislator and chief justice. It is his function to sentence to condign punishment the Bolingbrokes, Spinozas, Tindals, and other offenders against morality; and to enact and to promulgate, from time to time, the laws by which his creatures, or any part of them, were to be bound. Now Warburton's hypothesis seems to imply a capriciousness in God's behaviour to the Jews for which it is difficult to account. A full explanation was to have been given in the last book of the 'Divine Legation;' but Warburton became too

weary to finish up his argument. Archdeacon Towne, one of Warburton's humble friends, was grieved at the omission, and could only make the rather lame apology that a system might be true and well founded, though objections to it never had been nor could be answered.[164] He admitted that adversaries would triumph, and even urge that the bishop was unable to answer the difficulties he had raised. We need not lament the absence of one more verbal distortion of logic. For some reason, unexplained or inexplicable, God had chosen to manage the Jews on a peculiar system, or, as Warburton calls it, by an extraordinary providence. The ordinary human being is punished or rewarded in the next world according to his deserts in this. But in the case of the Jew, each man received his full reward in the present life. The necessity of any belief in a future life, nay, it would seem, of a future life at all, was thus obviated. The proof of this strange proposition is everywhere. 'It would be absurd to quote particular texts when the whole Bible is one continued proof of it.' We can, indeed, dispense with any historical proof. It must have been so, 'for a people in society, without both a future state and an equal Providence' (that is, a Providence equally working in this world), 'could have no belief in the moral government of God,' and would have relapsed into a savage state. Therefore, to prove that the Jews did not believe in a future state, is to prove that they had an 'equal Providence.' The ordinary argument for a future state would break down if all crimes were sufficiently punished, and all virtues sufficiently rewarded, in this world. As the Jews did not believe, they cannot have been in presence of the facts which convince us. This is the superlative expression of the assumption that the Jewish history refers to a state of things outside of our ordinary experience. As Warburton says, in attacking Plutarch, 'we know' (though he did not) 'that all things' (in the Jewish history) 'were extraordinary, and nothing to be brought to example any more than to imitation.'[165] A singular sentiment, surely, for a sound divine! and yet a characteristic result of the tacit compromise by which the miraculous element was retained in the past and banished from the present.

17. The doctrine of an equal Providence required some corollaries to make it fit notorious facts. Thus, for example, it scarcely accounts at first sight for the punishment of children for their fathers' sins. But Warburton can always stop a gap by a new hypothesis. Though evildoers amongst the Jews met with temporal punishment, there are 'men of stronger complexions, superior to all fear of personal temporal evil.' The knowledge that an Almighty power would punish them—a knowledge which, according to Warburton, rested on the immediate testimony of their senses—would not restrain these desperate ruffians. They were, therefore, to be reached through the 'instinctive fondness of parents to their offspring.'[166] This punishment supplied, for such persons, the absent terrors of hell. That a man who would not be restrained by dread of Almighty vengeance should be controlled by fear of the consequences to his great-grandchildren, is a queer doctrine in Warburton's mouth; but the justice of the proceeding is still more questionable than its efficiency. Warburton defends it characteristically. God, he says, was here acting, not as the Almighty Governor of the universe, but as the civil governor of the Jews. In a theocracy sin must be treasonable. 'Now we know it to be the practice of all states to punish the sin of leze majesty in this manner. And to render it just, no more is required than that it was in the compact (as it certainly was here) on men's free entrance into society.'[167] He proceeds to defend the system more fully by appealing to the English laws of forfeiture for high treason. Warburton caps the worst absurdities of his fellows; but he is only expressing more articulately and systematically an argument familiar to them in some shape. God was often justified by showing that his conduct was conformable to the provisions of the British Constitution.

18. Other difficulties, of course, abound. What, for example, was to become in the next world of the Jews to whom a full recompense had been meted out in this? Bolingbroke made a great point of this objection, and Warburton blusters more than usual in the attempt to evade it. As to future punishments, he retreats under the usual subterfuge of admitting the fact to be mysterious, and then boasting of his

admission as though it were a solution of the difficulty. As to rewards, he says that he does not grudge the Jews the advantage of a double payment. To meet the case of men of the pre-Mosaic age, he invents a 'secret reprieve' (kept 'hid, indeed, from the early world,' and, it may be added, from all the predecessors of Warburton) 'passed along with the sentence of condemnation. So that they who never received their due in this world, would still be kept in existence till they had received it in the next; such being in no other sense sufferers by the administration of an unequal Providence, than in being ignorant of the reparation which attended them.' God, like some kings of previous ages, could agree to a treaty in public, and make a private reservation to break it when he thought fit.

19. This singular confusion between the attributes of the Deity and those of a constitutional monarch underlies all Warburton's argumentation. There is but one God, and Warburton is his attorney-general. Like other persons standing in that relation to earthly potentates, he finds the obligation to defend the policy of his government at all hazards not a little burdensome. Once, after a long argument destined to indicate the wisdom, purity, and justice of the Almighty, he asks pathetically: 'How can I hope to be heard in the defence of this conduct of the God of Israel, when even the believing part of those whom I oppose seem to pay so little attention to the reasoning of Jesus himself?'[168] The difficulty is increased by the complexity and variability of the system adopted in the government of the universe. The Almighty generally acts as a constitutional ruler, with a scrupulous regard for the exigencies of his position; he refrains from miracles, as such a king would refrain from bringing his personal influence to bear upon politics; but, in certain cases, for which it is difficult to assign any principle, he chose to govern as well as to reign, and produced a variety of complex relations, which it tasks all Warburton's skill to unravel. The Law of Nature, so often cited by the deists and their opponents, is the Common Law of the Universe, and like that of England, supposed to embody the perfection of human wisdom. The details were capable of being defined with mathematical

accuracy, and Warburton has drawn out some of its provisions with a startling minuteness. We are a little surprised, for example, to discover that 'an ESTABLISHED RELIGION with a TEST LAW is the universal voice of Nature.'[169] But we must leave Warburton's politics for the moment, to illustrate his religious application of the doctrine. The essence of all religion, as he frequently says, is a belief in the divine system of rewards and punishments—a proposition which he illustrates by St. Paul's words, containing the most concise statement of natural religion. God is a rewarder of those who seek him. He may reward here or hereafter; but 'piety and morality spring only from the belief that God is, and is a rewarder.'[170] The voice of nature, however, does not tell us that these rewards should be eternal. Warburton boldly asserts that the notion of eternal penalties, instead of being discoverable by, is absolutely revolting to the unassisted intellect; and that 'fancy, even when full plumed by vanity,'[171] could scarcely rise to the idea of infinite rewards. The law of nature may be enforced by some future penalties, but cannot define their amount; and the specifically Christian doctrine of immortality is rather repulsive than probable. When, therefore, the Almighty interferes by direct personal action, there arises a distinction between the law of nature and the statutes promulgated by the Divine Legislator.

20. The results are exceedingly complex. Mankind, for example, occupied a different legal position towards their Maker, in the periods before the Fall, and in the interval between the Fall and the appearance of Moses; and the divine prerogatives differed as they affected Jews and Gentiles. The great change took place when the Almighty 'took upon himself the office of supreme magistrate of the Jewish people.' Having resolved for some inscrutable reason to govern them by temporal instead of eternal punishments, there arose the difficulty as to their proper position in the world to come. God, says Warburton, 'proceeded on the most equitable grounds of civil government;' he became King of the Jews 'by free choice;' and he thus acquired certain privileges, as, for example, that of prosecuting idolaters as traitors. But as direct punishment, though supplemented by the sufferings

101

of posterity, became inadequate, he enacted a cumbrous ceremonial, destined to distract popular attention from the claims of pretenders, that is, of false gods. One Herman Witsius[172] had protested against attributing to God the 'tricks of crafty politicians;'[173] and Warburton admits that the wisdom displayed was identical in kind with 'what we call human policy,' though it differed in degree. He excuses it on the convenient theological ground, that God used his miraculous power as little as possible, though he is arguing that all Jewish history was one stupendous miracle.

21. Difficulties thicken. After a time, God appointed an 'under-agent or instrument;' the Jewish kings became his viceroys; and Warburton has to prove that the change did alter the essence of the form of government. David, he says, was called the man after God's own heart, because he 'seconded God's views in support of the theocracy.'[174] He was, in fact, like Lord Bute, a thoroughgoing king's friend. The Jews, badly as they behaved, could not withdraw from the covenant which occupied the place of the original compact in the theocracy; for it is against all principles of equity that one party to a contract should repudiate it at pleasure. God, therefore, retained his rights; but, in consequence of the misbehaviour of his subjects, declined to exercise them. Thus we have the curious result, that, whilst the theocracy existed *de jure*, it ceased to operate *de facto*. Penalties and rewards were no longer enacted in this world, and though no revelation had hitherto been made of a future life, prophets began to discover its existence. From this fact, amongst other things, we may determine the precise date of the Book of Job. The purpose of that book is to discuss the difficult problem suggested by the prosperity of the wicked and the adversity of the virtuous; and, as Warburton says, no satisfactory conclusion is reached. It must therefore have been written at the critical period when rewards and punishments ceased to be administered in this world, and the next world had not been discovered. Gradually, however, the new doctrine became clear, until the theocracy was finally abrogated, and the Almighty ceasing to be the 'family God of the race of Abraham,' or the 'tutelary Deity, gentilitial and local,' became

the constitutional governor of the universe, governing only through second causes, and directly interfering only upon critical occasions.

22. Man thus stands in the most varying relations to his Maker. Some of his claims depend upon positive law; others upon equity; sometimes he must stick to the terms of a particular bargain; sometimes he may go upon the general principles of the law of nature; immortality is a free gift (sometimes, it must be confessed, of very questionable benefit), and may therefore be granted subject to any regulations arbitrarily imposed by the giver. Some kind of future reward is a strict legal right, and must necessarily be granted on condition of repentance; persecution is lawful under a theocracy, and becomes intolerable under any other circumstances, where the law of nature imperatively demands a test law, but forbids any more stringent discouragement of dissent; eternal punishment is detestably cruel if judged by ordinary principles of reason, but quite justifiable if it has been made the subject of a revelation; and the Jews were governed by the Almighty on principles which to the human intellect appear to be simply eccentric, and which varied materially at different stages of their history, and were totally different from anything that has prevailed before or since. The lawyer's clerk had not forgotten his early training when he excogitated this amazing theory of the legislative organisation of the universe. The 'infamous' Spinoza warns his readers to be specially on their guard against confounding the power of God with that of human rulers or with human law.[175] Warburton illustrates the results of systematically disregarding this warning.

23. One other side of Warburton's teaching must be noticed. One of the most vehement of his polemical writings was directed against Wesley. In the course of it, he remarks that 'the power of working miracles, and not the conformity of Scripture doctrines to the truth, is the great criterion of a divine mission.'[176] Accordingly, we find that he has an intense affection for a miracle, tempered by a strong desire to show that any particular miracle has been misunderstood. Defending, for example, the miracle supposed to have been wrought

103

to defeat Julian's reconstruction of the Temple at Jerusalem, he argues valiantly for the truth of the main incident; but he is almost equally anxious to prove that some of the subsidiary incidents were not miraculous. It is stated that crosses appeared in the sky and on the garments of the spectators. Warburton produces some curious parallel instances, in which such crosses are said to have actually appeared in consequence of a thunderstorm, and of an eruption of Vesuvius. These he attributes to natural causes. 'The fathers,' he says, 'are so impatient to be at their favourite miracles, the crosses in the sky and on the garments, that they slip negligently over what ought principally to have been insisted on, the fiery eruption; and leave what was truly miraculous to run after an imaginary prodigy.'[177] The fathers who believe too much, and the infidels who believe too little, are equally censured, though it seems hard upon the fathers to condemn them for want of familiarity with events in the seventeenth century. Warburton's credulity is as capricious as his logic. He seems actually to have believed in an absurd prophecy uttered by one Arise Evans during the Commonwealth, though he admits Evans to have been a notorious rogue; and he inserted an interpretation of the prophecy in one of Jortin's works. But when poor Wesley was rash enough to publish those accounts of modern miracles with which his journals are so curiously stuffed, the episcopal wrath knew no bounds. That a man living in his own time, and that man an ecclesiastical rebel, should produce miracles to confirm his foolish fancies was intolerable. Some of Warburton's ridicule of the great religious leader might have been pardonable in a man who had not exaggerated the sphere of the miraculous beyond all other writers; but his arguments are curiously characteristic. Miracles, he says, are no longer required. The martyrs, in the dismal days of yore, might have wanted such a support; 'but now the profession of the Christian faith is attended with ease and honour; and the conviction which the weight of human testimony and the conclusions of human reason afford us of its truth is abundantly sufficient to support us in our religious perseverance.'[178] It is easy enough to be a Christian when a defence of Christianity is the direct road to a bishopric; but Wesleyans might smile at the quiet assumption that Warburton, rather than the Methodists, presented the closest analogy to the early martyrs of the faith.

24. The very plan of the treatise is significant. The treatise on the Doctrine of Grace is, like his other writings, ambidextrous. He is not happy unless he can be slaying the freethinker with one hand, and the enthusiast with the other. He therefore begins by assailing Middleton for his assertion that the gift of tongues was temporary. He maintains that, far from disappearing after its first manifestation, it lasted through the apostolic age. But, having overthrown this antagonist, he is equally vigorous against the other who goes upon diametrically opposite principles. He clutches at a text and tortures it after his own fashion. The decisive passage is the celebrated saying of St. Paul: 'Charity never faileth; but whether there be prophecies, they shall fail; whether there be tongues, they shall cease; whether there shall be knowledge, it shall vanish away.' After due manipulation, the meaning of this clause in the statute-book comes out as follows: 'The virtue of Charity is to accompany the Christian Church through all its stages here on earth; whereas the gifts of prophecy, of strange tongues, of supernatural knowledge, are only transitory graces bestowed upon the Church in its infirm and infant state, to manifest its divine birth, and to support it against the delusions of the powers of darkness.'[179] He explains in the same spirit the statement that 'when that which is perfect is come, that which is in part shall be done away;' perfection, it seems, having been attained at the end of the apostolic age; and he has thus the pleasure of administering a blow at one additional enemy, the Church of Rome, in whose pretences 'the blunder seems to be as glaring as the imposture.'[180] On such grounds, the man who held that the whole Jewish history was one continued miracle for many centuries, and who was willing to put faith in Arise Evans, denounced Wesley for his folly and impiety in believing that God might do in the eighteenth century what he had done in the first. Wesley succeeded where Warburton failed, just because his God—whether the true God or not—was at least a living God; whereas Warburton's had sunk into a mere heap of verbal formulas.

25. Was Warburton an honest man? Did he believe in the theories thus coarsely and ostentatiously maintained? That any man could 'believe' in them, in the sense in which belief means a force capable of governing action, may be pronounced impossible. We have not the right to say that Warburton did not believe that he believed, or, in other words, that he had not cheated himself before he cheated his followers. Disraeli maintains, in the 'Quarrels of Authors,' that Warburton was throughout guided by 'a secret principle;' this secret principle was 'invention;' in other words, apparently, a morbid love of paradoxical novelty. He points to Warburton's curious admiration for Bayle, a writer who, in Warburton's own language, 'struck into the province of paradox as an exercise for the restless vigour of his mind,' and was unable to overcome that 'last foible of superior geniuses, the temptation of honour, which the academic exercise of wit is conceived to bring to its professors.'[181] Certainly, Warburton is describing his own practice. The 'academic exercise of wit' employed upon the most important of all human enquiries, forms the staple of his books. But Warburton had not Bayle's acuteness. His paradoxes imply verbal dexterity, instead of logical power. We admire his impudence more than his intellectual audacity. Lowth speaks of Towne as shrinking behind Warburton's 'mighty Telamonian shield,'

> With seven thick folds o'ercast
> Of tough bull-hide; of solid brass the last.

That brazen defence sheltered Warburton in his life, and even enabled him to impose upon posterity. An admiring reviewer[182] did not shrink from declaring that, whilst Hooker, Stillingfleet, Chillingworth, Locke, Jeremy Taylor, and Swift, might have contributed the erudition, acuteness, imaginative power, and sarcastic wit of the 'Divine Legation,' Warburton alone could have amassed the materials into a comprehensive, consistent, and harmonious whole. We fairly stand aghast at such a saying, and are tempted to bow down before the colossal impudence which could thus find defenders beyond the grave. Indeed, Warburton's fame loomed so vast in the eyes of the ordinary reader, that his name is still at times quoted with respect, as though his alliance with any cause could be aught but an encumbrance.

26. Some insinuations have been thrown out that Warburton was really as unbelieving as he was certainly lax in his religious observances.[183] To us it matters little what degree of consciousness of the natural tendency of his arguments may have penetrated to the inner depths of his mind. The fact which, for my purpose, is alone interesting, is the bare circumstance that such a book as the 'Divine Legation' could ever have passed for a serious defence of Christianity. To explain, we must revert once more to the real problem which was vexing men's minds. How, it may be stated, could the God of the universe be also the Jehovah of the Jews, and the three persons of the Christian Trinity? How can we reconcile philosophy with the traditional creeds? Hume's answer is decisive. God is a name for our ignorance. The Jews were a semi-savage race, who invented a corresponding deity to account for unintelligible phenomena. The Christian Trinity is the creation of later philosophical speculation, strangely combined with an earlier traditional element. We have grown wiser, and know that we know nothing. Nature means the aggregate of sensible phenomena, and we cannot pierce behind them. Butler's answer is more hesitating in tone, but still rests upon an intelligible principle. We know little, indeed; we are lost in mysteries, if once we dare to enquire, and it is safer not to push enquiries too far. But, in the midst of the darkness, we may find a sufficient guide in the conscience, which bears with it evidence of divine origin. Natural religion describes the general order of the world as detected by reason acting under their guidance upon the materials supplied by experience. Revealed religion professes to describe the same general order on the direct authority of the Almighty. The coincidence of the two doctrines affords a strong presumption of the authenticity of the claims of revelation; and, therefore, of the identity of the God of revelation with the God of nature. The external evidences confirm the presumption thus based upon independent grounds. The dealings of Jehovah with the Jews, and of the Christian God with believers, are such as we might anticipate from a fair observation of nature, and are not such

as we should anticipate from the God of the deist. Nature, that is, rightly interrogated, confirms revelation and destroys Deism. We cannot find God either in nature or revelation, said Hume; we can dimly see God in both, said Butler, and the features are alike. The God of nature is unlike the God of revelation, said Warburton; but they are the same, because both are called God.

27. Warburton thus leaves the two conceptions as different as he found them. He does not seriously attempt to consider the reasons which should lead us to accept either, or prefer one to the other. He is content simply to bring them into contact, and welds them together by the help of words. Jehovah is as different as possible from the God of reason or from the God of Christianity. Certainly, says Warburton, God acts on different principles at different times. We cannot believe in miracles, said the deist; they are produced by 'enthusiasm' or imposture, as in the case of Wesley and Mahomet. Warburton fully agrees that there have been no miracles for the last sixteen centuries; but miracles were as abundant as you please in the preceding ages of the world. The Jewish history, said the deists, was incredible because it contradicted all that we know of human nature, and often offends our belief in the moral attributes of God. Warburton accepts the facts, but he explains them by assuming that God has changed in the course of centuries. He argues as if an orthodox advocate should now maintain against positivists that the world was once ruled by fetishes, afterwards by a number of gods, and finally by one Supreme God. It is a fundamental canon of all historical enquiry, and, indeed, of all science, that the laws now operative in the world have operated throughout the period under observation. A slow realisation of this doctrine was transforming our conceptions of past history. Warburton uses his human and capricious deity to evade it, and being perfectly satisfied with a verbal answer to any difficulty, imagines that, by accepting the worst consequences attributed to his creed, he is really answering them.

28. The phenomenon represented by the Warburtonians would be scarcely worth notice were it not for the imposing

bulk of their leader, and for the fact that his errors are but magnified reproductions of confusions common enough amongst less sophistical reasoners. They have their source in the same weakness—the unwillingness, characteristic of all the controversialists from Butler downwards, to face the final questions. Even the bare external plausibility of Warburton's logomachy vanishes when he is asked what he means by God, and why he believed in such a God as his theory demands. That was just the question which no writer, except Hume, dared to ask openly. It was, therefore, impossible to apply a real test to the various theories which justified God by lowering him to the level of humanity, or which filled a gap in the optimist's creed by an abstract phrase. The controversy had to go deeper, and to arouse stronger passions, before it could be cleared of the unreality which must beset every controversy in which both sides shrink from probing the dispute to the bottom. Meanwhile, such a braggart as Warburton could, for a time, impose upon the world, though keen thinkers sneered, and pious souls were revolted, at speculations as perplexed in logic as irreverent in temper.

2
English Literature and Society
in the Eighteenth Century

The deepest thinker is not really—though we often use the phrase—in advance of his day so much as in the line along which advance takes place. The greatest poet does not write for a future generation in the sense of not writing for his own; it is only that in giving the fullest utterance to its thoughts and showing the deepest insight into their significance, he is therefore the most perfect type of its general mental attitude, and his work is an embodiment of the thoughts which are common to men of all generations.

When the critic began to perceive that many forms of art might be equally legitimate under different conditions, his first proceeding was to classify them in different schools. English poets, for example, were arranged by Pope and Gray as followers of Chaucer, Spenser, Donne, Dryden, and so forth; and, in later days, we have such literary genera as are indicated by the names classic and romantic or realist and idealist, covering characteristic tendencies of the various historical groups. The fact that literary productions fall into schools is of course obvious, and suggests the problem as to the cause of their rise and decline. Bagehot treats the question in his *Physics and Politics*. Why, he asks, did there arise a special literary school in the reign of Queen Anne—'a marked

Reprinted from *English Literature and Society in the Eighteenth Century* (1907), chaps. 1 (abridged) and 2.

variety of human expression, producing what was then written and peculiar to it'? Some eminent writer, he replies, gets a start by a style congenial to the minds around him. Steele, a rough, vigorous, forward man, struck out the periodical essay; Addison, a wise, meditative man, improved and carried it to perfection. An unconscious mimicry is always producing countless echoes of an original writer. That, I take it, is undeniably true. Nobody can doubt that all authors are in some degree echoes, and that a vast majority are never anything else. But it does not answer why a particular form should be fruitful of echoes or, in Bagehot's words, be 'more congenial to the minds around.' Why did the *Spectator* suit one generation and the *Rambler* its successors? Are we incapable of giving any answer? Are changes in literary fashions enveloped in the same inscrutable mystery as changes in ladies' dresses? It is, and no doubt always will be, impossible to say why at one period garments should spread over a hoop and at another cling to the limbs. Is it equally impossible to say why the fashion of Pope should have been succeeded by the fashion of Wordsworth and Coleridge? If we were prepared to admit the doctrine of which I have spoken—the supreme importance of the individual—that would of course be all that could be said. Shakespeare's successors are explained as imitators of Shakespeare, and Shakespeare is explained by his 'genius' or, in other words, is inexplicable. If, on the other hand, Shakespeare's originality, whatever it may have been, was shown by his power of interpreting the thoughts of his own age, then we can learn something from studying the social and intellectual position of his contemporaries. Though the individual remains inexplicable, the general characteristics of the school to which he belongs may be tolerably intelligible; and some explanation is in fact suggested by such epithets, for example, as romantic and classical. For, whatever precisely they mean,—and I confess to my mind the question of what they mean is often a very difficult one,—they imply some general tendency which cannot be attributed to individual influence. When we endeavour to approach this problem of the rise and fall of literary schools, we see that it is a case of a phenomenon which is very often

111

noticed and which we are more ready to explain in proportion to the share of youthful audacity which we are fortunate enough to possess.

In every form of artistic production, in painting and architecture, for example, schools arise; each of which seems to embody some kind of principle, and develops and afterwards decays, according to some mysterious law. It may resemble the animal species which is, somehow or other, developed and then stamped out in the struggle of existence by the growth of a form more appropriate to the new order. The epic poem, shall we say? is like the 'monstrous efts,' as Tennyson unkindly calls them, which were no doubt very estimable creatures in their day, but have somehow been unable to adapt themselves to recent geological epochs. Why men could build cathedrals in the Middle Ages, and why their power was lost instead of steadily developing like the art of engineering, is a problem which has occupied many writers, and of which I shall not attempt to offer a solution. That is the difference between artistic and scientific progress. A truth once discovered remains true and may form the nucleus of an independently interesting body of truths. But a special form of art flourishes only during a limited period, and when it decays and is succeeded by others, we cannot say that there is necessarily progress, only that for some reason or other the environment has become uncongenial. It is, of course, tempting to infer from the decay of an art that there must be a corresponding decay in the vitality and morality of the race. Ruskin, for example, always assumed in his most brilliant and incisive, but not very conclusive, arguments that men ceased to paint good pictures simply because they ceased to be good men. He did not proceed to prove that the moral decline really took place, and still less to show why it took place. But, without attacking these large problems, I shall be content to say that I do not see that any such sweeping conclusions can be made as to the kind of changes in literary forms with which we shall be concerned. That there is a close relation between the literature and the general social condition of a nation is my own contention. But the relation is hardly of this simple kind. Nations, it seems to me, have got on remarkably

112

well, and made not only material but political and moral progress in the periods when they have written few books, and those bad ones; and, conversely, have produced some admirable literature while they were developing some very ugly tendencies. To say the truth, literature seems to me to be a kind of by-product. It occupies far too small a part in the whole activity of a nation, even of its intellectual activity, to serve as a complete indication of the many forces which are at work, or as an adequate moral barometer of the general moral state. The attempt to establish such a condition too closely, seems to me to lead to a good many very edifying but not the less fallacious conclusions.

The succession of literary species implies that some are always passing into the stage of 'survivals': and the most obvious course is to endeavour to associate them with the general philosophical movement. That suggests one obvious explanation of many literary developments. The great thriving times of literature have occurred when new intellectual horizons seemed to be suddenly opening upon the human intelligence; as when Bacon was taking his Pisgah sight of the promised land of science, and Shakespeare and Spenser were making new conquests in the world of the poetic imagination. A great intellectual shock was stimulating the parallel, though independent, outbursts of activity. The remark may suggest one reason for the decline as well as for the rise of the new genus. If, on the one hand, the man of genius is especially sensitive to the new ideas which are stirring the world, it is also necessary that he should be in sympathy with his hearers—that he should talk the language which they understand, and adopt the traditions, conventions, and symbols with which they are already more or less familiar. A generally accepted tradition is as essential as the impulse which comes from the influx of new ideas. But the happy balance which enables the new wine to be put into the old bottles is precarious and transitory. The new ideas as they develop may become paralysing to the imagery which they began by utilising. The legends of chivalry which Spenser turned to account became ridiculous in the next generation, and the mythology of Milton's great poem was incredible or

113

revolting to his successors. The machinery, in the old phrase, of a poet becomes obsolete, though when he used it, it had vitality enough to be a vehicle for his ideas. The imitative tendency described by Bagehot clearly tends to preserve the old, as much as to facilitate the adoption of a new form. In fact, to create a really original and new form seems to exceed the power of any individual, and the greatest men must desire to speak to their own contemporaries. It is only by degrees that the inadequacy of the traditional form makes itself felt, and its successor has to be worked out by a series of tentative experiments. When a new style has established itself its representatives hold that the orthodoxy of the previous period was a gross superstition: and those who were condemned as heretics were really prophets of the true faith, not yet revealed. However that may be, I am content at present to say that in fact the development of new literary types is discontinuous, and implies a compromise between the two conditions which in literature correspond to conservatism and radicalism. The conservative work is apt to become a mere survival: while the radical may include much that has the crudity of an imperfect application of new principles. Another point may be briefly indicated. The growth of new forms is obviously connected not only with the intellectual development but with the social and political state of the nation, and there comes into close connection with other departments of history. Authors, so far as I have noticed, generally write with a view to being read. Moreover, the reading class is at most times a very small part of the population. A philosopher, I take it, might think himself unusually popular if his name were known to a hundredth part of the population. But even poets and novelists might sometimes be surprised if they could realise the small impression they make upon the mass of the population. There is, you know, a story of how Thackeray, when at the height of his reputation he stood for Oxford, found that his name was unknown even to highly respectable constituents. The author of *Vanity Fair* they observed, was named John Bunyan. At the present day the number of readers has, I presume, enormously increased; but authors who can reach the lower strata of the great lower pyramid, which widens so rapidly at its base, are few indeed. The characteristics of a literature correspond to the national characteristics, as embodied in the characteristics of a very small minority of the nation. Two centuries ago the reading part of the nation was mainly confined to London and to certain classes of society. The most important changes which have taken place have been closely connected with the social changes which have entirely altered the limits of the reading class; and with the changes of belief which have been cause and effect of the most conspicuous political changes. That is too obvious to require any further exposition. Briefly, in talking of literary changes, considered as implied in the whole social development, I shall have, first, to take note of the main intellectual characteristics of the period; and secondly, what changes took place in the audience to which men of letters addressed themselves, and how the gradual extension of the reading class affected the development of the literature addressed to them.

I hope and believe that I have said nothing original. I have certainly only been attempting to express the views which are accepted, in their general outline at least, by historians, whether of the political or literary kind. They have often been applied very forcibly to the various literary developments, and, by way of preface to my own special topic, I will venture to recall one chapter of literary history which may serve to illustrate what I have already said, and which has a bearing upon what I shall have to say hereafter.

One of the topics upon which the newer methods of criticism first displayed their power was the school of the Elizabethan dramatists. Many of the earlier critics wrote like lovers or enthusiasts who exalted the merits of some of the old playwrights beyond our sober judgments, and were inclined to ignore the merits of other forms of the art. But we have come to recognise that the Elizabethans had their faults, and that the best apology for their weaknesses as well as the best explanation of their merits was to be found in a clearer appreciation of the whole conditions. It is impossible of course to overlook the connection between that great outburst of literary activity and the general movement of the time; of the period when many impulses were breaking up the old intellectual stagnation, and when the national spirit which took the great Queen for its representative was finding leaders in the Burleighs and Raleighs and Drakes. The connection is emphasised by the singular brevity of the literary efflorescence. Marlowe's *Tamburlaine* heralded its approach on the eve of the Spanish Armada: Shakespeare, to whom the lead speedily fell, had shown his highest power in *Henry IV.* and *Hamlet* before the accession of James I.: his great tragedies *Othello, Macbeth* and *Lear* were produced in the next two or three years; and by that time, Ben Jonson had done his best work. When Shakespeare retired in 1611, Chapman and Webster, two of the most brilliant of his rivals, had also done their best; and Fletcher inherited the dramatic throne. On his death in 1625, Massinger and Ford and other minor luminaries were still at work; but the great period had passed. It had begun with the repulse of the Armada and culminated some fifteen years later. If in some minor respects there may afterwards have been an advance, the spontaneous vigour had declined and deliberate attempts to be striking had taken the place of the old audacity. There can be no more remarkable instance of a curious phenomenon, of a volcanic outburst of literary energy which begins and reaches its highest intensity while a man is passing from youth to middle age, and then begins to decay and exhaust itself within a generation.

A popular view used to throw the responsibility upon the wicked Puritans who used their power to close the theatres. We entered the 'prison-house' of Puritanism says Matthew Arnold, I think, and stayed there for a couple of centuries. If so, the gaolers must have had some difficulty, for the Puritan (in the narrower sense, of course) has always been in a small and unpopular minority. But it is also plain that the decay had begun when the Puritan was the victim instead of the inflictor of persecution. When we note the synchronism between the political and the literary movement our conception of the true nature of the change has to be modified. The accession of James marks the time at which the struggle between the court and the popular party was beginning to develop itself: when the monarchy and its adherents cease to represent the strongest current of national feeling, and the bulk of the most vigorous and progressive classes have become alienated and are developing the conditions and passions which produced the civil war. The genuine Puritans are still an exception; they only form the left wing, the most thorough-going opponents of the court-policy; and their triumph afterwards is only due to the causes which in a revolution give the advantage to the uncompromising partisans, though their special creed is always regarded with aversion by a majority. But for the time, they are the van of the party which, for whatever reason, is gathering strength and embodying the main political and ecclesiastical impulses of the time. The stage, again, had been from the first essentially aristocratic: it depended upon the court and the nobility and their adherents, and was hostile both to the Puritans and to the whole class in which the Puritan found a congenial element. So long, as in Elizabeth's time, as the class which supported the stage also represented the strongest aspirations of the period, and a marked national sentiment, the drama could embody a marked national sentiment. When the unity was broken up and the court is opposed to the strongest current of political sentiment, the players still adhere to their patron. The drama comes to represent a tone of thought, a social stratum, which, instead of leading, is getting more and more opposed to the great bulk of the most vigorous elements of the society. The stage is ceasing to be a truly national organ, and begins to suit itself to the tastes of the unprincipled and servile courtiers, who, if they are not more immoral than their predecessors, are without the old heroic touch which ennobled even the audacious and unscrupulous adventurers of the Armada period. That is to say, the change is beginning which became palpable in the Restoration time, when the stage became simply the melancholy dependent upon the court of Charles II, and faithfully reflected the peculiar morality of the small circle over which it presided. Without taking into account this process by which the organ of the nation gradually became transformed into the organ of the class which was entirely alienated from the general body of the nation, it is, I think, impossible to understand clearly

117

the transformation of the drama. It illustrates the necessity of accounting for the literary movement, not only by intellectual and general causes, but by noting how special social developments radically alter the relation of any particular literary genus to the general national movement. I shall soon have to refer to the case again.

I have now only to say briefly what I propose to attempt in these lectures. The literary history, as I conceive it, is an account of one strand, so to speak, in a very complex tissue: it is connected with the intellectual and social development; it represents movements of thought which may sometimes check and be sometimes propitious to the existing forms of art; it is the utterance of a class which may represent, or fail to represent, the main national movement; it is affected more or less directly by all manner of religious, political, social, and economical changes; and it is dependent upon the occurrence of individual genius for which we cannot even profess to account. I propose to take the history of English literature in the eighteenth century. I do not aim at originality: I take for granted the ordinary critical judgments upon the great writers of whom so much has been said by judges certainly more competent than myself, and shall recall the same facts both of ordinary history and of the history of thought. What I hope is, that by bringing familiar facts together I may be able to bring out the nature of the connection between them; and, little as I can say that will be at all new, to illustrate one point of view, which, as I believe, it is desirable that literary histories should take into account more distinctly than they have generally done.

The first period of which I am to speak represents to the political historian the Avatar of Whiggism. The glorious revolution has decided the long struggle of the previous century; the main outlines of the British Constitution are irrevocably determined; the political system is in harmony with the great political forces, and the nation has settled, as Carlyle is fond of saying, with the centre of gravity lowest, and therefore in a position of stable equilibrium. For another century no organic change was attempted or desired. Parliament has become definitely the great driving-wheel of the political machinery; not, as a century before, an intrusive body acting spasmodically and hampering instead of regulating the executive power of the Crown. The last Stuart kings had still fancied that it might be reduced to impotence, and the illusion had been fostered by the loyalty which meant at least a fair unequivocal desire to hold to the old monarchical traditions. But, in fact, parliamentary control had been silently developing; the House of Commons had been getting the power of the purse more distinctly into its hands, and had taken very good care not to trust the Crown with the power of the sword. Charles II had been forced to depend on the help of the great French monarchy to maintain his authority at home; and when his successor turned out to be an anachronism, and found that the loyalty of the nation would not bear the strain of a policy hostile to the strongest national impulses, he was thrown off as an intolerable incubus. The system which had been growing up beneath the surface was now definitely put into shape and its fundamental principles embodied in legislation. The one thing still needed was to work out the system of party government, which meant that parliament should become an organised body with a corporate body, which the ministers of the Crown had first to consult and then to obey. The essential parts of the system had, in fact, been established by the end of Queen Anne's reign; though the change which had taken place in the system was not fully recognised because marked by the retention of the old forms. This, broadly speaking, meant the supremacy of the class which really controlled Parliament: of the aristocratic class, led by the peers but including the body of squires and landed gentlemen, and including also a growing infusion of 'moneyed' men, who represented the rising commercial and manufacturing interests. The division between Whig and Tory corresponded mainly to the division between the men who inclined mainly to the Church and squirearchy and those who inclined towards the mercantile and the dissenting interests. If the Tory professed zeal for the monarchy, he did not mean a monarchy as opposed to Parliament and therefore to his own dearest privileges. Even the

Jacobite movement was in great part personal, or meant dislike to Hanover with no preference for arbitrary power, while the actual monarchy was so far controlled by Parliament that the Whig had no desire to limit it further. It was a useful instrument, not an encumbrance.

We have to ask how these conditions affect the literary position. One point is clear. The relation between the political and the literary class was at this time closer than it had ever been. The alliance between them marks, in fact, a most conspicuous characteristic of the time. It was the one period, as authors repeat with a fond regret, in which literary merit was recognised by the distributors of state patronage. This gratifying phenomenon has, I think, been often a little misinterpreted, and I must consider briefly what it really meant. And first let us note how exclusively the literary society of the time was confined to London. The great town—it would be even now a great town—had half a million inhabitants. Macaulay, in his admirably graphic description of the England of the preceding period, points out what a chasm divided it from country districts; what miserable roads had to be traversed by the nobleman's chariot and four, or by the ponderous waggons or strings of pack-horses which supplied the wants of trade and of the humbler traveller; and how the squire only emerged at intervals to be jeered and jostled as an uncouth rustic in the streets of London. He was not a great buyer of books. There were, of course, libraries at Oxford and Cambridge, and here and there in the house of a rich prelate or of one of the great noblemen who were beginning to form some of the famous collections; but the squire was more than usually cultivated if Baker's *Chronicle* and Gwillim's *Heraldry* lay on the window-seat of his parlour, and one has often to wonder how the learned divines of the period managed to get the books from which they quote so freely in their discourses. Anyhow the author of the day must have felt that the circulation of his books must be mainly confined to London, and certainly in London alone could he meet with anything that could pass for literary society or an appreciative audience. We have superabundant descriptions of the audience and its meeting-places. One of the familiar features of the day, we know, was the number of coffee-houses. In 1657, we are told, the first coffee-house had been prosecuted as a nuisance. In 1708 there were three thousand coffee-houses; and each coffee-house had its habitual circle. There were coffee-houses frequented by merchants and stock-jobbers carrying on the game which suggested the new nickname bulls and bears: and coffee-houses where the talk was Whig and Tory, of the last election and change of ministry: and literary resorts such as the Grecian, where, as we are told, a fatal duel was provoked by a dispute over a Greek accent, in which, let us hope, it was the worst scholar who was killed; and Wills', where Pope as a boy went to look reverently at Dryden; and Buttons', where, at a later period, Addison met his little senate. Addison, according to Pope, spent five or six hours a day lounging at Buttons'; while Pope found the practice and the consequent consumption of wine too much for his health. Thackeray notices how the club and coffee-house 'boozing shortened the lives and enlarged the waist-coats of the men of those days.' The coffee-house implied the club, while the club meant simply an association for periodical gatherings. It was only by degrees that the body made a permanent lodgment in the house and became first the tenants of the landlord and then themselves the proprie-tors. The most famous show the approximation between the statesmen and the men of letters. There was the great Kit-cat Club, of which Tonson the bookseller was secretary; to which belonged noble dukes and all the Whig aristocracy, besides Congreve, Vanbrugh, Addison, Garth, and Steele. It not only brought Whigs together but showed its taste by giving a prize for good comedies. Swift, when he came into favour, helped to form the Brothers' Club, which was especially intended to direct patronage towards promising writers of the Tory persuasion. The institution, in modern slang, differ-entiated as time went on. The more aristocratic clubs became exclusive societies, occupying their own houses, more devoted to gambling than to literature; while the older type, repre-sented by Jonson's famous club, were composed of literary and professional classes.

The characteristic fraternisation of the politicians and the authors facilitated by this system leads to the critical point. When we speak of the nobility patronising literature, a reserve must be made. A list of some twenty or thirty names has been made out, including all the chief authors of the time, who received appointments of various kinds. But I can only find two, Congreve and Rowe, upon whom offices were bestowed simply as rewards for literary distinction; and both of them were sound Whigs, rewarded by their party, though not for party services. The typical patron of the day was Charles Montagu, Lord Halifax. As member of a noble family he came into Parliament, where he distinguished himself by his financial achievements in founding the Bank of England and reforming the currency, and became a peer and a member of the great Whig junto. At college he had been a chum of Prior, who joined him in a literary squib directed against Dryden, and, as he rose, he employed his friend in diplomacy. But the poetry by which Prior is known to us was of a later growth, and was clearly not the cause but the consequence of his preferment. At a later time, Halifax sent Addison abroad with the intention of employing him in a similar way; and it is plain that Addison was not—as the familiar but obviously distorted anecdote tells us—preferred on account of his brilliant Gazette in rhyme, but really in fulfilment of his patron's virtual pledge. Halifax has also the credit of bestowing office upon Newton and patronising Congreve. As poet and patron Halifax was carrying on a tradition. The aristocracy in Charles's days had been under the impression that poetry, or at least verse writing, was becoming an accomplishment for a nobleman. Pope's 'mob of gentlemen who wrote with ease,' Rochester and Buckingham, Dorset and Sedley, and the like, managed some very clever, if not very exalted, performances and were courted by the men of letters represented by Butler, Dryden, and Otway. As, indeed, the patrons were themselves hangers-on of a thoroughly corrupt court, seeking to rise by court intrigues, their patronage was apt to be degrading and involved the mean flattery of personal dependence. The change at the Revolution meant that the court no longer overshadowed society. The court, that is, was beginning to be superseded by the

town. The new race of statesmen were coming to depend
upon parliamentary influence instead of court favour. They
were comparatively, therefore, shining by their own light.
They were able to dispose of public appointments; places on
the various commissions which had been founded as parliament took control of the financial system—such as commissions for the wine-duties, for licensing hackney coaches, excise
duties, and so forth—besides some of the other places which
had formerly been the perquisites of the courtier. They could
reward personal dependants at the cost of the public; which
was convenient for both parties. Promising university students, like Prior and Addison, might be brought out under the
wing of the statesman, and no doubt literary merit, especially
in conjunction with the right politics, might recommend them
to such men as Halifax or Somers. The political power of the
press was meanwhile rapidly developing. Harley, Lord Oxford, was one of the first to appreciate its importance. He
employed Defoe and other humble writers who belonged to
Grub Street—that is, to professional journalism in its infancy
—as well as Swift, whose pamphlets struck the heaviest blow
at the Whigs in the last years of that period. Swift's first
writings, we may notice, were not a help but the main
hindrance to his preferment. The patronage of literature was
thus in great part political in its character. It represents the
first scheme by which the new class of parliamentary statesmen recruited their party from the rising talent, or rewarded
men for active or effective service. The speedy decay of the
system followed for obvious reasons. As party government
became organised, the patronage was used in a different
spirit. Offices had to be given to gratify members of parliament and their constituents, not to scholars who could write
odes on victories or epistles to secretaries of state. It was the
machinery for controlling votes. Meanwhile we need only
notice that the patronage of authors did not mean the patronage of learned divines or historians, but merely the patronage of men who could use their pens in political warfare,
or at most of men who produced the kind of literary work
appreciated in good society.

The 'town' was the environment of the wits who produced

123

the literature generally called after Queen Anne. We may call it the literary organ of the society. It was the society of London, or of the region served by the new penny-post, which included such remote villages as Paddington and Brompton. The city was large enough, as Addison observes, to include numerous 'nations,' each of them meeting at the various coffee-houses. The clubs at which the politicians and authors met each other represented the critical tribunals, when no such things as literary journals existed. It was at these that judgment was passed upon the last new poem or pamphlet, and the writer sought for their good opinion as he now desires a favourable review. The tribunal included the rewarders as well as the judges of merit; and there was plenty of temptation to stimulate their generosity by flattery. Still the relation means a great improvement on the preceding state of things. The aristocrat was no doubt conscious of his inherent dignity, but he was ready on occasion to hail Swift as 'Jonathan' and, in the case of so highly cultivated a specimen as Addison, to accept an author's marriage to a countess. The patrons did not exact the personal subservience of the preceding period; and there was a real recognition by the more powerful class of literary merit of a certain order. Such a method, however, had obvious defects. Men of the world have their characteristic weaknesses; and one, to go no further, is significant. The Club in England corresponded more or less to the Salon which at different times had had so great an influence upon French literature. It differed in the marked absence of feminine elements. The clubs meant essentially a society of bachelors, and the conversation, one infers, was not especially suited for ladies. The Englishman, gentle or simple, enjoyed himself over his pipe and his bottle and dismissed his womenkind to their bed. The one author of the time who speaks of the influence of women with really chivalrous appreciation is the generous Steele, with his famous phrase about Lady Elizabeth Hastings and a liberal education. The Clubs did not foster the affectation of Molière's *Précieuses;* but the general tone had a coarseness and occasional brutality which shows too clearly that they did not enter into the full meaning of Steele's most admirable saying.

To appreciate the spirit of this society we must take into account the political situation and the intellectual implication. The parliamentary statesman, no longer dependent upon court favour, had a more independent spirit and personal self-respect. He was fully aware of the fact that he represented a distinct step in political progress. His class had won a great struggle against arbitrary power and bigotry. England had become the land of free speech, of religious toleration, impartial justice, and constitutional order. It had shown its power by taking its place among the leading European states. The great monarchy before which the English court had trembled, and from which even patriots had taken bribes in the Restoration period, was met face to face in a long and doubtful struggle and thoroughly humbled in a war, in which an English General, in command of an English contingent, had won victories unprecedented in our history since the Middle Ages. Patriotic pride received a stimulus such as that which followed the defeat of the Armada and preceded the outburst of the Elizabethan literature. Those successes, too, had been won in the name of 'liberty'—a vague if magical word which I shall not seek to define at present. England, so sound Whigs at least sincerely believed, had become great because it had adopted and carried out the true Whig principles. The most intelligent Frenchmen of the coming generation admitted the claim; they looked upon England as the land both of liberty and philosophy, and tried to adopt for themselves the creed which had led to such triumphant results. One great name may tell us sufficiently what the principles were in the eyes of the cultivated classes, who regarded themselves and their own opinions with that complacency in which we are happily never deficient. Locke had laid down the fundamental outlines of the creed, philosophical, religious, and political, which was to dominate English thought for the next century. Locke was one of the most honourable, candid, and amiable of men, if metaphysicians have sometimes wondered at the success of his teaching. He had not the logical thoroughness and consistency which marks a Descartes or Spinoza, nor the singular subtlety which distinguishes Berkeley and Hume; nor the eloquence and imaginative power which gave to Bacon an authority greater than was due to his scientific requirements. He was a thoroughly modest, prosaic, tentative, and sometimes clumsy writer, who raises great questions without solving them or fully seeing the consequences of his own position. Leaving any explanation of his power to metaphysicians, I need only note the most conspicuous condition. Locke ruled the thought of his own and the coming period because he interpreted so completely the fundamental beliefs which had been worked out at his time. He ruled, that is, by obeying. Locke represents the very essence of the common sense of the intelligent classes. I do not ask whether his simplicity covered really profound thought or embodied superficial crudities; but it was most admirably adapted to the society of which I have been speaking. The excellent Addison, for example, who was no metaphysician, can adopt Locke when he wishes to give a philosophical air to his amiable lectures upon arts and morals. Locke's philosophy, that is, blends spontaneously with the ordinary language of all educated men. To the historian of philosophy the period is marked by the final disappearance of scholasticism. The scholastic philosophy had of course been challenged generations before. Bacon, Descartes, and Hobbes, however, in the preceding century had still treated it as the great incubus upon intellectual progress, and it was not yet exorcised from the universities. It had, however, passed from the sphere of living thought. This implies a series of correlative changes in the social and intellectual which are equally conspicuous in the literary order, and which I must note without attempting to inquire which are the ultimate or most fundamental causes of reciprocally related developments. The changed position of the Anglican church is sufficiently significant. In the time of Laud, the bishops in alliance with the Crown endeavoured to enforce the jurisdiction of the ecclesiastical courts upon the nation at large, and to suppress all nonconformity by law. Every subject of the king is also amenable to church discipline. By the

Revolution any attempt to enforce such discipline had become hopeless. The existence of nonconformist churches has to be recognised as a fact, though perhaps an unpleasant fact. The Dissenters can be worried by disqualifications of various kinds; but the claim to toleration, of Protestant sects at least, is admitted; and the persecution is political rather than ecclesiastical. They are not regarded as heretics, but as representing an interest which is opposed to the dominant class of the landed gentry. The Church as such has lost the power of discipline and is gradually falling under the power of the dominant aristocratic class. When Convocation tries to make itself troublesome, in a few years, it will be silenced and drop into impotence. Church-feeling indeed, is still strong, but the clergy have become thoroughly subservient, and during the century will be mere appendages to the nobility and squirearchy. The intellectual change is parallel. The great divines of the seventeenth century speak as members of a learned corporation condescending to instruct the laity. The hearers are supposed to listen to the voice (as Donne puts it) as from 'angels in the clouds.' They are experts, steeped in a special science, above the comprehension of the vulgar. They have been trained in the schools of theology and have been thoroughly drilled in the art of 'syllogising.' They are walking libraries with the ancient fathers at their finger-ends; they have studied Aquinas and Duns Scotus, and have shown their technical knowledge in controversies with the great Jesuits, Suarez and Bellarmine. They speak frankly, if not ostentatiously, as men of learning, and their sermons are overweighted with quotations, showing familiarity with the classics, and with the whole range of theological literature. Obviously the hearers are to be passive recipients not judges of the doctrine. But by the end of the century Tillotson has become the typical divine, whose authority was to be as marked in theology as that of Locke in philosophy. Tillotson has entirely abandoned any ostentatious show of learning. He addresses his hearers in language on a level with their capabilities, and assumes that they are not 'passive buckets to be pumped into' but reasonable men who have a right to be critics as well as disciples. It is taken for granted that the appeal must be to reason, and to the reason which has not gone through any special professional training. The audience, that is, to which the divine must address himself is one composed of the average laity who are quite competent to judge for themselves. That is the change that is meant when we are told that this was the period of the development of English prose. Dryden, one of its great masters, professed to have learned his style from Tillotson. The writer, that is, has to suit himself to the new audience which has grown up. He has to throw aside all the panoply of scholastic logic, the vast apparatus of professional learning, and the complex Latinised constructions, which, however admirable some of the effects produced, shows that the writer is thinking of well-read scholars, not of the ordinary man of the world. He has learned from Bacon and Descartes, perhaps, that his supposed science was useless lumber; and he has to speak to men who not only want plain language but are quite convinced that the pretensions of the old authority have been thoroughly exploded.

Politically, the change means toleration, for it is assumed that the vulgar can judge for themselves; intellectually, it means rationalism, that is, an appeal to the reason common to all men; and, in literature it means the hatred of pedantry and the acceptance of such literary forms as are thoroughly congenial and intelligible to the common sense of the new audience. The hatred of the pedantic is the characteristic sentiment of the time. When Berkeley looked forward to a new world in America, he described it as the Utopia

'Where men shall not impose for truth and sense
The pedantry of Courts and Schools.'

When he announced a metaphysical discovery he showed his understanding of the principle by making his exposition—strange as the proceeding appears to us—as short and as clear as the most admirable literary skill could contrive. That eccentric ambition dominates the writings of the times. In a purely literary direction it is illustrated by the famous but curiously rambling and equivocal controversy about the Ancients and Moderns begun in France by Perrault and Boileau.

In England the most familiar outcome was Swift's *Battle of the Books,* in which he struck out the famous phrase about sweetness and light, 'the two noblest of things'; which he illustrated by ridiculing Bentley's criticism and Dryden's poetry. I may take for granted the motives which induced that generation to accept as their models the great classical masterpieces, the study of which had played so important a part in the revival of letters and the new philosophy. I may perhaps note, in passing, that we do not always remember what classical literature meant to that generation. In the first place, the education of a gentleman meant nothing then except a certain drill in Greek and Latin—whereas now it includes a little dabbling in other branches of knowledge. In the next place, if a man had an appetite for literature, what else was he to read? Imagine every novel, poem, and essay written during the last two centuries to be obliterated—and further, the literature of the early seventeenth century and all that went before to be regarded as pedantic and obsolete, the field of study would be so limited that a man would be forced in spite of himself to read his *Homer* and *Virgil.* The vice of pedantry was not very accurately defined—sometimes it is the ancient, sometimes the modern, who appears to be pedantic. Still, as in the *Battle of the Books* controversy, the general opinion seems to be that the critic should have before him the great classical models, and regard the English literature of the seventeenth century as a collection of all possible errors of taste. When, at the end of this period, Swift with Pope formed the project of the Scriblerus Club, its aim was to be a joint-stock satire against all 'false tastes' in learning, art, and science. That was the characteristic conception of the most brilliant men of letters of the time.

Here, then, we have the general indication of the composition of the literary organ. It is made up of men of the world—'Wits' is their favourite self-designation, scholars and gentlemen, with rather more of the gentlemen than the scholars—living in the capital, which forms a kind of island of illumination amid the surrounding darkness of the agricultural country—including men of rank and others of sufficient social standing to receive them on friendly terms—

meeting at coffee-houses and in a kind of tacit confederation of clubs to compare notes and form the whole public opinion of the day. They are conscious that in them is concentrated the enlightenment of the period. The class to which they belong is socially and politically dominant—the advance guard of national progress. It has finally cast off the incubus of a retrograde political system; it has placed the nation in a position of unprecedented importance in Europe; and it is setting an example of ordered liberty to the whole civilised world. It has forced the Church and the priesthood to abandon the old claim to spiritual supremacy. It has, in the intellectual sphere, crushed the old authority which embodied superstition, antiquated prejudice, and a sham system of professional knowledge, which was upheld by a close corporation. It believes in reason—meaning the principles which are evident to the ordinary common sense of men at its own level. It believes in what it calls the Religion of Nature—the plain demonstrable truths obvious to every intelligent person. With Locke for its spokesman, and Newton as a living proof of its scientific capacity, it holds that England is the favoured nation marked out as the land of liberty, philosophy, common sense, toleration, and intellectual excellence. And with certain reserves, it will be taken at its own valuation by foreigners who are still in darkness and deplorably given to slavery, to say nothing of wooden shoes and the consumption of frogs. Let us now consider the literary result.

I may begin by recalling a famous controversy which seems to illustrate very significantly some of the characteristic tendencies of the day. The stage, when really flourishing, might be expected to show most conspicuously the relations between authors and the society. The dramatist may be writing for all time; but if he is to fill a theatre, he must clearly adapt himself to the tastes of the living and the present. During the first half of the period of which I am now speaking, Dryden was still the dictator of the literary world; and Dryden had adopted Congreve as his heir, and abandoned to him the province of the drama—Congreve, though he ceased to write, was recognised during his life as the great man of letters to whom Addison, Swift, and Pope agreed in paying respect, and indisputably the leading writer of English Comedy. When the comic drama was unsparingly denounced by Collier, Congreve defended himself and his friends. In the judgment of contemporaries the pedantic parson won a complete triumph over the most brilliant of wits. Although Congreve's early abandonment of his career was not caused by Collier's attack alone, it was probably due in part to the general sentiment to which Collier gave utterance. I will ask what is implied as a matter of fact in regard to the social and literary characteristics of the time. The Shakespearian drama had behind it a general national impulse. With Fletcher, it began to represent a court already out of harmony with the strongest currents of national feeling. Dryden, in a familiar passage, gives the reason of the change from his own point of view. Two plays of Beaumont and Fletcher, he says in an often quoted passage, were acted (about 1668) for one of Shakespeare or Jonson. His explanation is remarkable. It was because the later dramatists 'understood the conversation of gentlemen much better,' whose wild 'debaucheries and quickness of wit no poet can ever paint as they have done.' In a later essay he explains that the greater refinement was due to the influence of the court. Charles II, familiar with the most brilliant courts of Europe, had roused us from barbarism and rebellion, and taught us to 'mix our solidity' with 'the air and gaiety of our neighbours'! I need not cavil at the phrases 'refinement' and 'gentleman.' If those words can be fairly applied to the courtiers whose 'wild debaucheries' disgusted Evelyn and startled even the respectable Pepys, they may no doubt be applied to the stage and the dramatic persons. The rake, or 'wild gallant,' had made his first appearance in Fletcher, and had shown himself more nakedly after the Restoration. This is the so-called reaction so often set down to the account of the unlucky Puritans. The degradation, says Macaulay, was the 'effect of the prevalence of Puritanism under the Commonwealth.' The attempt to make a 'nation of saints' inevitably produced a nation of scoffers. In what sense, in the first place, was there a 'reaction' at all? The Puritans had suppressed the stage when it was already far gone in decay because it no longer satisfied the great bulk of the nation. The reaction does not imply that the drama regained its old position. When the rule of the saints or pharisees was broken down, the stage did not become again a national organ. A very small minority of the people can ever have seen a performance. There were, we must remember, only two theatres under Charles II, and there was a difficulty in supporting even two. Both depended almost exclusively on the patronage of the court and the courtiers. From the theatre, therefore, we can only argue directly to the small circle of the rowdy debauchees who gathered round the new king. It certainly may be true, but it was not proved from their behaviour, that the national morality deteriorated, and in fact I think nothing is more difficult than to form any trustworthy estimate of the state of morality in a whole nation, confidently as such estimates are often put forward. What may be fairly inferred, is that a certain class, who had got from under the rule of the Puritan, was now free from legal restraint and took advantage of the odium excited by pharisaical strictness, to indulge in the greater license which suited the taste of their patrons. The result is sufficiently shown when we see so great a man as Dryden pander to the lowest tastes, and guilty of obscenities of which he was himself ashamed, which would be now inexcusable in the lowest public haunts. The comedy, as it appears to us, must have been written by blackguards for blackguards. When Congreve became Dryden's heir he inherited the established tradition. Under the new order the 'town' had become supreme; and Congreve wrote to meet the taste of the class which was gaining in self-respect and independence. He tells us in the dedication of his best play, *The Way of the World,* that his taste had been refined in the company of the Earl of Montagu. The claim is no doubt justifiable. So Horace Walpole remarks that Vanbrugh wrote so well because he was familiar with the conversation of the best circles. The social influences were favourable to the undeniable literary merits, to the force and point in which Congreve's dialogue is still superior to that of any English rival, the vigour of Vanbrugh and the vivacity of their chief ally, Farquhar. Moreover, although their moral code is anything but strict, these writers did not descend to some of the depths often sounded by Dryden and Wycherly. The new spirit might seem to be passing on with more literary vitality into the old forms. And yet the consequence, or certainly the sequel to Collier's attack, was the decay of the stage in every sense, from which there was no recovery till the time of Goldsmith and Sheridan.

This is the phenomenon which we have to consider;—let us listen for a moment to the 'distinguished critics' who have denounced or defended the comedy of the time. Macaulay gives as a test of the morality of the Restoration stage that on it, for the first time, marriage becomes the topic of ridicule. We are supposed to sympathise with the adulterer, not with the deceived husband—a fault, he says, which stains no play written before the Civil War. Addison had already suggested this test in the *Spectator*, and proceeds to lament that 'the multitudes are shut out from this noble "diversion" by the immorality of the lessons inculcated.' Lamb, indulging in ingenious paradox, admires Congreve for 'excluding from his scenes (with one exception) any pretensions to goodness or good feeling whatever.' Congreve, he says, spreads a 'privation of moral light' over his characters, and therefore we can admire them without compunction. We are in an artificial world where we can drop our moral prejudices for the time being. Hazlitt more daringly takes a different position and asserts that one of Wycherly's coarsest plays is 'worth ten sermons'—which perhaps does not imply with him any high estimate of moral efficacy. There is, however, this much of truth, I take it, in Hazlitt's contention. Lamb's theory of the non-morality of the dramatic world will not stand examination. The comedy was in one sense thoroughly 'realistic'; and I am inclined to say, that in that lay its chief merit. There is some value in any truthful representation, even of vice and brutality. There would certainly be no difficulty in finding flesh and blood originals for the rakes and the fine ladies in the memoirs of Grammont or the diaries of Pepys. The moral atmosphere is precisely that of the dissolute court of Charles II, and the 'privation of moral light' required is a delicate way of expressing its characteristic feeling. In the worst performances we have not got to any unreal region, but are

133

breathing for the time the atmosphere of the lowest resorts, where reference to pure or generous sentiment would undoubtedly have been received with a guffaw, and coarse cynicism be regarded as the only form of comic insight. At any rate the audiences for which Congreve wrote had just so much of the old leaven that we can quite understand why they were regarded as wicked by a majority of the middle classes. The doctrine that all playgoing was wicked was naturally confirmed, and the dramatists retorted by ridiculing all that their enemies thought respectable. Congreve was, I fancy, a man of better morality than his characters, only forced to pander to the tastes of the rake who had composed the dominant element of his audience. He writes not for mere blackguards, but for the fine gentleman, who affects premature knowledge of the world, professes to be more cynical than he really is, and shows his acuteness by deriding hypocrisy and pharisaic humbug in every claim to virtue. He dwells upon the seamy side of life, and if critics, attracted by his undeniable brilliance, have found his heroines charming, to me it seems that they are the kind of young women whom, if I adopted his moral code, I should think most desirable wives—for my friends.

Though realistic in one sense, we may grant to Lamb that such comedy becomes 'artificial,' and so far Lamb is right, because it supposes a state of things such as happily was abnormal except in a small circle. The plots have to be made up of impossible intrigues, and imply a distorted theory of life. Marriage after all is not really ridiculous, and to see it continuously from this point of view is to have a false picture of realities. Life is not made up of dodges worthy of card-sharpers—and the whole mechanism becomes silly and disgusting. If comedy is to represent a full and fair portrait of life, the dramatist ought surely, in spite of Lamb, to find some space for generous and refined feeling. There, indeed, is a difficulty. The easiest way to be witty is to be cynical. It is difficult, though desirable, to combine good feeling with the comic spirit. The humourist has to expose the contrasts of life, to unmask hypocrisy, and to show selfishness lurking under multitudinous disguises. That, on Hazlitt's showing, was the preaching of Wycherly. I can't think that it was the impression made upon Wycherly's readers. Such comedy may be taken as satire; which was the excuse that Fielding afterwards made for his own performances. But I cannot believe that the actual audiences went to see vice exposed, or used Lamb's ingenious device of disbelieving in the reality. They simply liked brutal and immoral sentiment, spiced, if possible, with art. We may inquire whether there may not be a comedy which is enjoyable by the refined and virtuous, and in which the intrusion of good feeling does not jar upon us as a discord. An answer may be suggested by pointing to Molière, and has been admirably set forth in Mr. George Meredith's essay on the 'Comic Spirit.' There are, after all, ridiculous things in the world, even from the refined and virtuous point of view. The saint, it is true, is apt to lose his temper and become too serious for such a treatment of life-problems. Still the sane intellect which sees things as they are can find a sphere within which it is fair and possible to apply ridicule to affectation and even to vice, and without simply taking the seat of the scorner or substituting a coarse laugh for a delicate smile. A hearty laugh, let us hope, is possible even for a fairly good man. Mr. Meredith's essay indicates the conditions under which the artist may appeal to such a cultivated and refined humour. The higher comedy, he says, can only be the fruit of a polished society which can supply both the model and the audience. Where the art of social intercourse has been carried to a high pitch, where men have learned to be at once courteous and incisive, to admire urbanity, and therefore really good feeling, and to take a true estimate of the real values of life, a high comedy which can produce irony without coarseness, expose shams without advocating brutality, becomes for the first time possible. It must be admitted that the condition is also very rarely fulfilled.

This, I take it, is the real difficulty. The desirable thing, one may say, would have been to introduce a more refined and human art and to get rid of the coarser elements. The excellent Steele tried the experiment. But he had still to work upon the old lines, which would not lend themselves to the new purpose. His passages of moral exhortation would not supply the salt of the old cynical brutalities; they had a painful tendency to become insipid and sentimental, if not maudlin; and only illustrated the difficulty of using a literary tradition which developed spontaneously for one purpose to adapt itself to a wholly different aim. He produced at best not a new genus but an awkward hybrid. But behind this was the greater difficulty that a superior literature would have required a social elaboration, the growth of a class which could appreciate and present appropriate types. Now even the good society for which Congreve wrote had its merits, but certainly its refinement left much to be desired. One condition, as Mr. Meredith again remarks, of the finer comedy is such an equality of the sexes as may admit the refining influence of women. The women of the Restoration time hardly exerted a refining influence. They adopted the ingenious compromise of going to the play, but going in masks. That is, they tacitly implied that the brutality was necessary, and they submitted to what they could not openly approve. Throughout the eighteenth century a contempt for women was still too characteristic of the aristocratic character. Nor was there any marked improvement in the tastes of the playgoing classes. The plays denounced by Collier continued to hold the stage, though more or less expurgated, throughout the century. Comedy did not become decent. In 1729 Arthur Bedford carried on Collier's assault in a 'Remonstrance against the horrid blasphemies and improprieties which are still used in the English playhouses,' and collected seven thousand immoral sentiments from the plays (chiefly) of the last four years. I have not verified his statements. The inference, however, seems to be clear. Collier's attack could not reform the stage. The evolution took the form of degeneration. He could, indeed, give utterance to the disapproval of the stage in general, which we call Puritanical, though it was by no means confined to Puritans or even to Protestants. Bossuet could denounce the stage as well as Collier. Collier was himself a Tory and a High Churchman, as was William Law, of the *Serious Call*, who also denounced the stage. The sentiment was, in fact, that of the respectable middle classes

136

in general. The effect was to strengthen the prejudice which held that playgoing was immoral in itself, and that an actor deserved to be treated as a 'vagrant'—the class to which he legally belonged. During the next half-century, at least, that was the prevailing opinion among the solid middle-class section of society.

The denunciations of Collier and his allies certainly effected a reform, but at a heavy price. They did not elevate the stage or create a better type, but encouraged old prejudices against the theatre generally; the theatre was left more and more to a section of the 'town,' and to the section which was not too particular about decency. When Congreve retired, and Vanbrugh took to architecture, and Farquhar died, no adequate successors appeared. The production of comedies was left to inferior writers, to Mrs. Centlivre, and Colley Cibber, and Fielding in his unripe days, and they were forced by the disfavour into which their art had fallen to become less forcible rather than to become more refined. When a preacher denounces the wicked, his sermons seem to be thrown away because the wicked don't come to church. Collier could not convert his antagonists; he could only make them more timid and careful to avoid giving palpable offence. But he could express the growing sentiment which made the drama an object of general suspicion and dislike, and induced the ablest writers to turn to other methods for winning the favour of a larger public.

The natural result, in fact, was the development of a new kind of literature, which was the most characteristic innovation of the period. The literary class of which I have hitherto spoken reflected the opinions of the upper social stratum. Beneath it was the class generally known as Grub Street. Grub Street had arisen at the time of the great civil struggle. War naturally generates journalism; it had struggled on through the Restoration and taken a fresh start at the Revolution and the final disappearance of the licensing system. The daily newspaper—meaning a small sheet written by a single author (editors as yet were not)—appeared at the opening of the eighteenth century. Now for Grub Street the wit of the higher class had nothing but dislike. The 'hackney author,'

137

as Dunton called him, in his curious *Life and Errors,* was a mere huckster, who could scarcely be said as yet to belong to a profession. A Tutchin or Defoe might be pilloried, or flogged, or lose his ears, without causing a touch of compassion from men like Swift, who would have disdained to call themselves brother authors. Yet politicians were finding him useful. He was the victim of one party, and might be bribed or employed as a spy by the other. The history of Defoe and his painful struggles between his conscience and his need of living, sufficiently indicates the result; Charles Leslie, the gallant nonjuror, for example, or Abel Boyer, the industrious annalist, or the laborious but cantankerous Oldmixon, were keeping their heads above water by journalism, almost exclusively, of course, political. Defoe showed a genius for the art, and his mastery of vigorous vernacular was hardly rivalled until the time of Paine and Cobbett. At any rate, it was plain that a market was now arising for periodical literature which might give a scanty support to a class below the seat of patrons. It was at this point that the versatile, speculative, and impecunious Steele hit upon his famous discovery. The aim of the *Tatler,* started in April 1709, was marked out with great accuracy from the first. Its purpose is to contain discourses upon all manner of topics—*quicquid agunt homines,* as his first motto put it—which had been inadequately treated in the daily papers. It is supposed to be written in the various coffee-houses, and it is suited to all classes, even including women, whose taste, he observes, is to be caught by the title. The *Tatler,* as we know, led to the *Spectator,* and Addison's co-operation, cordially acknowledged by his friend, was a main cause of its unprecedented success. The *Spectator* became the model for at least three generations of writers. The number of imitations is countless: Fielding, Johnson, Goldsmith, and many men of less fame tried to repeat the success; persons of quality, such as Chesterfield and Horace Walpole, condescended to write papers for the *World*—the 'Bow of Ulysses,' as it was called, in which they could test their strength. Even in the nineteenth century Hazlitt and Leigh Hunt carried on the form; as indeed, in a modified shape, many later essayists have aimed at a substantially similar achievement. To have contributed three or four articles was, as in the case of the excellent Henry Grove (a name, of course, familiar to all of you), to have graduated with honours in literature. Johnson exhorted the literary aspirant to give his days and nights to the study of Addison; and the *Spectator* was the most indispensable set of volumes upon the shelves of every library where the young ladies described by Miss Burney and Miss Austen were permitted to indulge a growing taste for literature. I fear that young people of the present day discover, if they try the experiment, that their curiosity is easily satisfied. This singular success, however, shows that the new form satisfied a real need. Addison's genius must, of course, count for much in the immediate result; but it was plainly a case where genius takes up the function for which it is best suited, and in which it is most fully recognised. When we read him now we are struck by one fact. He claims in the name of the *Spectator* to be a censor of manners and morals; and though he veils his pretensions under delicate irony, the claim is perfectly serious at bottom. He is really seeking to improve and educate his readers. He aims his gentle ridicule at social affectations and frivolities; and sometimes, though avoiding ponderous satire, at the grosser forms of vice. He is not afraid of laying down an aesthetic theory. In a once famous series of papers on the Imagination, he speaks with all the authority of a recognised critic in discussing the merits of Chevy Chase or of *Paradise Lost;* and in a series of Saturday papers he preaches lay-sermons—which were probably preferred by many readers to the official discourses of the following day. They contain those striking poems (too few) which led Thackeray to say that he could hardly fancy a 'human intellect thrilling with a purer love and admiration than Joseph Addison's.' Now, spite of the real charm which every lover of delicate humour and exquisite urbanity must find in Addison, I fancy that the *Spectator* has come to mean for us chiefly Sir Roger de Coverley. It is curious, and perhaps painful, to note how very small a proportion of the whole is devoted to that most admirable achievement; and to reflect how little life there is in much that in kindness of feeling and grace of style is equally charming. One cause is obvious. When Addison talks of psychology or æsthetics or ethics (not to speak of his criticism of epic poetry or the drama), he must of course be obsolete in substance; but, moreover, he is obviously superficial. A man who would speak upon such topics now must be a grave philosopher, who has digested libraries of philosophy. Addison, of course, is the most modest of men; he has not the slightest suspicion that he is going beyond his tether; and that is just what makes his unconscious audacity remarkable. He fully shares the characteristic belief of the day, that the abstract problems are soluble by common sense, when polished by academic culture and aided by a fine taste. It is a case of *sancta simplicitas;* of the charming, because perfectly unconscious, self-sufficiency with which the Wit, rejecting pedantry as the source of all evil, thinks himself obviously entitled to lay down the law as theologian, politician, and philosopher. His audience are evidently ready to accept him as an authority, and are flattered by being treated as capable of reason, not offended by any assumption of their intellectual inferiority.

With whatever shortcomings, Addison, and in their degree Steele and his other followers, represent the stage at which the literary organ begins to be influenced by the demands of a new class of readers. Addison feels the dignity of his vocation and has a certain air of gentle condescension, especially when addressing ladies who cannot even translate his mottoes. He is a genuine prophet of what we now describe as Culture, and his exquisite urbanity and delicacy qualify him to be a worthy expositor of the doctrines, though his outlook is necessarily limited. He is therefore implicitly trying to solve the problem which could not be adequately dealt with on the stage; to set forth a view of the world and human nature which shall be thoroughly refined and noble, and yet imply a full appreciation of the humorous aspects of life. The inimitable Sir Roger embodies the true comic spirit; though Addison's own attempt at comedy was not successful.

One obvious characteristic of this generation is the didacticism which is apt to worry us. Poets, as well as philosophers and preachers, are terribly argumentative. Fielding's remark (through Parson Adams), that some things in Steele's comedies are almost as good as a sermon, applies to a much wider range of literature. One is tempted by way of explanation to ascribe this to a primitive and ultimate instinct of the race. Englishmen—including of course Scotsmen—have a passion for sermons, even when they are half ashamed of it; and the British Essay, which flourished so long, was in fact a lay sermon. We must briefly notice that the particular form of this didactic tendency is a natural expression of the contemporary rationalism. The metaphysician of the time identifies emotions and passions with intellectual affirmations, and all action is a product of logic. In any case we have to do with a period in which the old concrete imagery has lost its hold upon the more intelligent classes, and instead of an imaginative symbolism we have a system of abstract reasoning. Diagrams take the place of concrete pictures: and instead of a Milton justifying the ways of Providence by the revealed history, we have a Blackmore arguing with Lucretius, and are soon to have a Pope expounding a metaphysical system in the *Essay on Man*. Sir Roger represents a happy exception to this method and points to the new development. Addison is anticipating the method of later novelists, who incarnate their ideals in flesh and blood. This, and the minor character sketches which are introduced incidentally, imply a feeling after a less didactic method. As yet the sermon is in the foreground, and the characters are dismissed as soon as they have illustrated the preacher's doctrine. Such a method was congenial to the Wit. He was, or aspired to be, a keen man of the world; deeply interested in the characteristics of the new social order; in the eccentricities displayed at clubs, or on the Stock Exchange, or in the political struggles; he is putting in shape the practical philosophy implied in the conversations at clubs and coffee-houses; he delights in discussing such psychological problems as were suggested by the worldly wisdom of Rochefoucauld, and he appreciates clever character sketches such as those of La Bruyére. Both writers were favourites in England. But he has become heartily tired of the old romance, and has not yet discovered how to combine the interest of direct observation of man with a thoroughly concrete form of presentation.

The periodical essay represents the most successful innovation of the day; and, as I have suggested, because it represents the mode by which the most cultivated writer could be brought into effective relation with the genuine interests of the largest audience. Other writers used it less skilfully, or had other ways of delivering their message to mankind. Swift, for example, had already shown his peculiar vein. He gives a different, though equally characteristic, side of the intellectual attitude of the Wit. In the *Battle of the Books* he had assumed the pedantry of the scholar; in the *Tale of a Tub* with amazing audacity he fell foul of the pedantry of divines. His blows, as it seemed to the Archbishops, struck theology in general; he put that right by pouring out scorn upon Deists and all who were silly enough to believe that the vulgar could reason; and then in his first political writings began to expose the corrupt and selfish nature of politicians—though at present only of Whig politicians. Swift is one of the most impressive of all literary figures, and I will not even touch upon his personal peculiarities. I will only remark that in one respect he agrees with his friend Addison. He emphasises, of course, the aspect over which Addison passes lightly; he scorns fools too heartily to treat them tenderly and do justice to the pathetic side of even human folly. But he too believes in culture —though he may despair of its dissemination. He did his best, during his brief period of power, to direct patronage towards men of letters, even to Whigs; and tried, happily without success, to found an English Academy. His zeal was genuine, though it expressed itself by scorn for dunces and hostility to Grub Street. He illustrates one little peculiarity of the Wit. In the society of the clubs there was a natural tendency to form minor cliques of the truly initiated, who looked with sovereign contempt upon the hackney author. One little indication is the love of mystifications, or what were entitled 'bites.' All the Wits, as we know, combined to tease the unlucky fortune-teller, Partridge, and to maintain that their prediction of his death had been verified, though he absurdly pretended to be still alive. So Swift tells us in the journal to Stella how he had circulated a lie about a man who had been hanged coming to life again, and how footmen are sent out to inquire into its success. He made a hit by writing a sham account of Prior's mission to Paris supposed to come from a French valet. The inner circle chuckled over such performances, which would be impossible when their monopoly of information had been broken up. A similar satisfaction was given by the various burlesques and more or less ingenious fables which were to be fully appreciated by the inner circle; such as the tasteless narrative of Dennis's frenzy by which Pope professed to be punishing his victim for an attack upon Addison: or to such squibs as Arbuthnot's *John Bull*—a parable which gives the Tory view in a form fitted for the intelligent. The Wits, that is, form an inner circle, who like to speak with an affectation of obscurity even if the meaning be tolerably transparent, and show that they are behind the scenes by occasionally circulating bits of sham news. They like to form a kind of select upper stratum, which most fully believes in its own intellectual eminence, and shows a contempt for its inferiors by burlesque and rough sarcasm.

It is not difficult (especially when we know the result) to guess at the canons of taste which will pass muster in such regions. Enthusiastical politicians of recent days have been much given to denouncing modern clubs, where everybody is a cynic and unable to appreciate the great ideas which stir the masses. It may be so; my own acquaintance with club life, though not very extensive, does not convince me that every member of a London club is a Mephistopheles; but I will admit that a certain excess of hard worldly wisdom may be generated in such resorts; and we find many conspicuous traces of that tendency in the clubs of Queen Anne's reign. Few of them have Addison's gentleness or his perception of the finer side of human nature. It was by a rare combination of qualities that he was enabled to write like an accomplished man of the world, and yet to introduce the emotional element without any jarring discord. The literary reformers of a later day denounce the men of this period as 'artificial'! a phrase the antithesis of which is 'natural.' Without asking at present what is meant by the implied distinction—an inquiry which is beset by whole systems of equivocations—I may just observe that in this generation the appeal to Nature was as common and emphatic as in any later time. The leaders of thought believe in reason, and reason sets forth the Religion of Nature and assumes that the Law of Nature is the basis of political theory. The corresponding literary theory is that Art must be subordinate to Nature. The critics' rules, as Pope says in the poem which most fully expresses the general doctrine,

> 'Are Nature still, but Nature methodised;
> Nature, like Liberty, is but restrained
> By the same laws which first herself ordained.'

The Nature thus 'methodised' was the nature of the Wit himself; the set of instincts and prejudices which to him seemed to be so normal that they must be natural. Their standards of taste, if artificial to us, were spontaneous, not fictitious; the Wits were not wearing a mask, but were exhibiting their genuine selves with perfect simplicity. Now one characteristic of the Wit is always a fear of ridicule. Above all things he dreads making a fool of himself. The old lyric, for example, which came so spontaneously to the Elizabethan poet or dramatist, and of which echoes are still to be found in the Restoration, has decayed, or rather, has been transformed. When you have written a genuine bit of love-poetry, the last place, I take it, in which you think of seeking the applause of a congenial audience, would be the smoking-room of your club: but that is the nearest approach to the critical tribunal of Queen Anne's day. It is necessary to smuggle in poetry and passion in disguise, and conciliate possible laughter by stating plainly that you anticipate the ridicule yourself. In other words you write society verses like Prior, temper sentiment by wit, and if you do not express vehement passion, turn out elegant verses, salted by an irony which is a tacit apology perhaps for some genuine feeling. The old pastoral had become hopelessly absurd because Thyrsis and Lycidas have become extravagant and 'unnatural.' The form might be adopted for practice in versification; but when Ambrose Phillips took it a little too seriously, Pope, whose own performances were not much better, came down on him for his want of sincerity, and Gay showed what could be still made of the form by introducing real rustics and turning it into a burlesque. Then, as Johnson puts it, the 'effect of reality and truth became conspicuous, even when the intention was to show them grovelling and degraded.' *The Rape of the Lock* is the masterpiece, as often noticed, of an unconscious allegory. The sylph, who was introduced with such curious felicity, is to be punished if he fails to do his duty, by imprisonment in a lady's toilet apparatus.

'Gums and pomatums shall his flight restrain,
While clogged he beats his silver wings in vain.'

Delicate fancy and real poetical fancy may be turned to account; but under the mask of the mock-heroic. We can be poetical still, it seems to say, only we must never forget that to be poetical in deadly earnest is to run the risk of being absurd. Even a Wit is pacified when he is thus dexterously coaxed into poetry disguised as mere playful exaggeration, and feels quite safe in following the fortune of a game of cards in place of a sanguinary Homeric battle. Ariel is still alive, but he adopts the costume of the period to apologise for his eccentricities. Poetry thus understood may either give a charm to the trivial or fall into mere burlesque; and though Pope's achievement is an undeniable triumph, there are blots in an otherwise wonderful performance which show an uncomfortable concession to the coarser tastes of his audience.

I will not dwell further upon a tolerably obvious theme. I must pass to the more serious literature. The Wit had not the smallest notion that his attitude disqualified him for succession in the loftiest poetical endeavour. He thinks that his critical keenness will enable him to surpass the old models. He wishes, in the familiar phrase, to be 'correct'; to avoid the gross faults of taste which disfigured the old Gothic barbarism of his forefathers. That for him is the very meaning of reason and nature. He will write tragedies which must get rid of the brutalities, the extravagance, the audacious mixture of farce and tragedy which was still attractive to the vulgar. He has, indeed, a kind of lurking regard for the rough vigour of the Shakespearian epoch; his patriotic prejudices pluck at him at intervals, and suggest that Marlborough's countrymen ought not quite to accept the yoke of the French Academy. When Ambrose Phillips produced the *Distrest Mother*—adapted from Racine—all Addison's little society was enthusiastic. Steele stated in the Prologue that the play was meant to combine French correctness with British force, and praised it in the *Spectator* because it was 'everywhere Nature.' The town, he pointed out, would be able to admire the passions 'within the rules of decency, honour, and good breeding.' The performance was soon followed by *Cato,* unquestionably, as Johnson still declares, 'the noblest production of Addison's genius.' It presents at any rate the closest conformity to the French model; and falls into comic results, as old Dennis pointed out, from the so-called Unity of Place, and consequent necessity of transacting all manner of affairs, love-making to Cato's daughter, and conspiring against Cato himself, in Cato's own hall. Such tragedy, however, refused to take root. Cato, as I think no one can deny, is a good specimen of Addison's style, but, except a few proverbial phrases, it is dead. The obvious cause, no doubt, is that the British public liked to see battle, murder, and sudden death, and, in spite of Addison's arguments, enjoyed a mixture of tragic and comic. Shakespeare, though not yet an idol, had still a hold upon the stage, and was beginning to be imitated by Rowe and to attract the attention of commentators. The sturdy Briton would not be seduced to the foreign model. The attempt to refine tragedy was as hopeless as the attempt to moralise comedy. This points to the process by which the Wit becomes 'artificial.' He has a profound conviction, surely not altogether wrong, that a tragedy ought to be a work of art. The artist must observe certain rules; though I need not ask whether he was right in thinking that these rules were represented by the accepted interpreters of the teaching of Nature. What he did not perceive was that another essential condition was absent; namely, that the tragic mood should correspond to his own 'nature.' The tragic art can, like other arts, only flourish when it embodies spontaneously the emotions and convictions of the spectator; when the dramatist is satisfying a genuine demand, and is himself ready to see in human life the conflict of great passions and the scene of impressive catastrophes. Then the theatre becomes naturally the mirror upon which the imagery can be projected. But the society to which Addison and his fellows belonged was a society of good, commonplace, sensible people, who were fighting each other by pamphlets instead of by swords; who played a game in which they staked not life and death but a comfortable competency; who did not even cut off the head of a fallen minister, who no longer believed in great statesmen of heroic proportions rising above the vulgar herd; and who had a very hearty contempt for romantic extravagance. A society in which common sense is regarded as the cardinal intellectual virtue does not naturally suggest the great tragic themes. Cato is obviously contrived, not inspired; and the dramatist is thinking of obeying the rules of good taste, instead of having them already incorporated in his thought. This comes out in one chief monument in the literary movement, I mean Pope's *Homer*. Pope, as we know, made himself independent by that performance. The method of publication is significant. He had no interest in the general sale, which was large enough to make his publisher's fortune. The publisher meanwhile supplied him gratuitously with the copies for which the subscribers paid him six guineas apiece. That means that he received a kind of commission from the upper class to execute the translation. The list of his subscribers seems to be almost a directory to the upper circle of the day; every person of quality has felt himself bound to promote so laudable an undertaking; the patron had been superseded by a kind of joint-stock body of collective patronage. The Duke of Buckingham, one of its accepted mouthpieces, had said in verse in his *Essay on Poetry* that if you once read Homer, everything else will be 'mean and poor.'

> 'Verse will seem prose; yet often in him look
> And you will hardly need another book.'

That was the correct profession of faith. Yet as a good many Wits found Greek an obstacle, a translation was needed. Chapman had become barbarous; Hobbes and Ogilvie were hopelessly flat; and Pope was therefore handsomely paid to produce a book which was to be the standard of the poetical taste. Pope was thus the chosen representative of the literary spirit. It is needless to point out that Pope's *Iliad* is not Homer's. That was admitted from the first. When we read in a speech of Agamemnon exhorting the Greeks to abandon the siege,

> 'Love, duty, safety summon us away;
> 'Tis Nature's voice, and Nature we obey,'

we hardly require to be told that we are not listening to Homer's Agamemnon but to an Agamemnon in a full-bottomed wig. Yet Pope's Homer had a success unparalleled by any other translation of profane poetry; for the rest of the century it was taken to be a masterpiece; it has been the book from which Byron and many clever lads first learned to enjoy what they at least took for Homer; and, as Mrs. Gallup has discovered, it was used by Bacon at the beginning of the seventeenth century, and by somebody at the beginning of the twentieth. That it has very high literary merits can, I think, be denied by no unprejudiced reader, but I have only to do with one point. Pope had the advantage—I take it to be an advantage—of having a certain style prescribed for him by the literary tradition inherited from Dryden. A certain diction and measure had to be adopted, and the language to be run into an accepted mould. The mould was no doubt conventional, and corresponded to a temporary phase of sentiment. Like the costume of the period, it strikes us now as 'artificial' because it was at the time so natural. It was worked out by the courtly and aristocratic class, and was fitted to give a certain dignity and lucidity, and to guard against mere greatness and triviality of utterance. At any rate it saved Pope from one enormous difficulty. The modern translator is aware that Homer lived a long time ago in a very different state of intellectual and social development, and yet feels bound to reproduce the impressions made upon the ancient Greek.

The translator has to be an accurate scholar and to give the right shade of meaning for every phrase, while he has also to approximate to the metrical effect. The conclusion seems to be that the only language into which Homer could be adequately translated would be Greek, and that you must then use the words of the original. The actual result is that the translator is cramped by his fetters; that his use of archaic words savours of affectation, and that, at best, he has to emphasise the fact that his sentiments are fictitious. Pope had no trouble of that kind. He aims at giving something equivalent to Homer, not Homer himself, and therefore at something really practical. He has the same advantage as a man who accepts a living style of architecture or painting; he can exert all his powers of forcible expression in a form which will be thoroughly understood by his audience, and which saves him, though at a certain cost, from the difficulties of trying to reproduce the characteristics which are really incongruous.

There are disadvantages. In his time the learned M. Bossu was the accepted authority upon the canons of criticism. Buckingham says he had explained the 'mighty magic' of Homer. One doctrine of his was that an epic poet first thinks of a moral and then invents a fable to illustrate it. The theory struck Addison as a little overstated, but it is an exaggeration of the prevalent view. According to Pope Homer's great merit was his 'invention'—and by this he sometimes appears to imply that Homer had even invented the epic poem. Poetry was, it seems, at a 'low pitch' in Greece in Homer's time, as indeed were other arts and sciences. Homer, wishing to instruct his countrymen in all kinds of topics, devised the epic poem: made use of the popular mythology to supply what in the technical language was called his 'machinery'; converted the legends into philosophical allegory, and introduced 'strokes of knowledge from his whole circle of arts and sciences.' This 'circle' includes for example geography, rhetoric, and history; and the whole poem is intended to inculcate the political moral that many evils sprang from the want of union among the Greeks. Not a doubt of it! Homer was in the sphere of poetry what Lycurgus was supposed to be in the field of legislation. He had at a single bound created poetry

149

and made it a vehicle of philosophy, politics, and ethics. Upon this showing the epic poem is a form of art which does not grow out of the historical conditions of the period; but it is a permanent form of art, as good for the eighteenth century as for the heroic age of Greece; it may be adopted as a model, only requiring certain additional ornaments and refinements to adapt it to the taste of a more enlightened period. Yet, at the same time, Pope could clearly perceive some of the absurd consequences of M. Bossu's view. He ridiculed that authority very keenly in the 'Recipe to make an Epic Poem' which first appeared in the *Guardian,* while he was at work upon his own translation. Bossu's rules, he says, will enable us to make epic poems without genius or reading; and he proceeds to show how you are to work your 'machines,' and introduce your allegories and descriptions, and extract your moral out of the fable at leisure, 'only making it sure that you strain it sufficiently.'

That was the point. The enlightened critic sees that the work of art embodies certain abstract rules; which may, and probably will—if he be a man of powerful intellectual power, —be rational, and suggest instructive canons. But, as Pope sees, it does not follow that the inverse process is feasible; that is, that you construct your poem simply by applying the rules. To be a good cricketer you must apply certain rules of dynamics; but it does not follow that a sound knowledge of dynamics will enable you to play good cricket. Pope sees that something more than an acceptance of M. Bossu's or Aristotle's canons is requisite for the writer of a good epic poem. The something more, according to him, appears to be learning and genius. It is certainly true that at least genius must be one requisite. But then, there is the further point. Will the epic poem, which was the product of certain remote social and intellectual conditions, serve to express the thoughts and emotions of a totally different age? Considering the difference between Achilles and Marlborough, or the bards of the heroic age and the wits who frequented clubs and coffee-houses under Queen Anne, it was at least important to ask whether Homer and Pope—taking them to be alike in genius —would not find it necessary to adopt radically different forms. That is for us so obvious a suggestion that one wonders at the tacit assumption of its irrelevance. Pope, indeed, by taking the *Iliad* for a framework, a ready-made fabric which he could embroider with his own tastes, managed to construct a singularly spirited work, full of good rhetoric and not infrequently rising to real poetical excellence. But it did not follow that an original production on the same lines would have been possible. Some years later, Young complained of Pope for being imitative, and said that if he had dared to be original, he might have produced a modern epic as good as the *Iliad* instead of a mere translation. That is not quite credible. Pope himself tried an epic poem too, which happily came to nothing; but a similar ambition led to such works as Glover's *Leonidas* and *The Epigoniad* of the Scottish Homer Wilkie. English poets as a rule seem to have suffered at some period of their lives from this malady and contemplated Arthuriads; but the constructional epic died, I take it, with Southey's respectable poems.

We may consider, then, that any literary form, the drama, the epic poem, the essay, and so forth, is comparable to a species in natural history. It has, one may say, a certain organic principle which determines the possible modes of development. But the line along which it will actually develop depends upon the character and constitution of the literary class which turns it to account, for the utterance of its own ideas; and depends also upon the correspondence of those ideas with the most vital and powerful intellectual currents of the time. The literary class of Queen Anne's day was admirably qualified for certain formations: the Wits leading the 'town,' and forming a small circle accepting certain canons of taste, could express with admirable clearness and honesty the judgment of bright common sense; the ideas which commend themselves to the man of the world, and to a rationalism which was the embodiment of common sense. They produced a literature, which in virtue of its sincerity and harmonious development within certain limits could pass for some time as a golden age. The aversion to pedantry limited its capacity for the highest poetical creation, and made the imagination subservient to the prosaic understanding. The comedy had come to adapt itself to the tastes of the class which, instead of representing the national movement, was composed of the more disreputable part of the town. The society unable to develop it in the direction of refinement left it to second-rate writers. It became enervated instead of elevated. The epic and the tragic poetry, ceasing to reflect the really powerful impulses of the day, were left to the connoisseur and dilettante man of taste, and though they could write with force and dignity when renovating or imitating older masterpieces, such literature became effete and hopelessly artificial. It was at best a display of technical skill, and could not correspond to the strongest passions and conditions of the time. The invention of the periodical essay, meanwhile, indicated what was a condition of permanent vitality. There, at least, the Wit was appealing to a wide and growing circle of readers, and could utter the real living thoughts and impulses of the time. The problem for the coming period was therefore marked out. The man of letters had to develop a living literature by becoming a representative of the ideas which really interested the whole cultivated classes, instead of writing merely for the exquisite critic, or still less for the regenerating and obnoxious section of society. That indeed, I take it, is the general problem of literature; but I shall have to trace the way in which its solution was attempted in the next period.

3
Thoughts on Criticism, by a Critic

Perhaps the most offensive type of human being in the present day is the young gentleman of brilliant abilities and high moral character who has just taken a good degree. It is his faith that the University is the centre of the universe, and its honours the most conclusive testimonials to genius. His seniors appear to him to be old fogies; his juniors mere children; and women, whatever his theories as to their possible elevation, fitted at present for no better task than the skilful flattery of youthful genius. He is at the true social apex. He is half-afraid, it may be, of men of the world and women of society; but his fear masks itself under a priggish self-satisfaction. A few years in a wider circle will knock the nonsense out of him, unless he is destined to ripen into one of those scholastic pedants now fortunately rarer than of old. But meanwhile it happens that a large part of the critical staff of the nation is formed by fresh recruits from this class of society. The young writer, with the bloom of his achievements still fresh, is prepared to sit in judgment with equal confidence upon the last new novel or theory of the universe. The aim of much University teaching is to produce that kind of readiness which tells in a competitive examination, and is equally applicable to the composition of a smart review. In the schools, a lad of twenty-two is ready with a neat summary

Reprinted from *Cornhill Magazine*, 1876.

of any branch of human knowledge. When he issues into the world, he is prepared to deal with the ripest thinkers of the day, as he dealt with the most eminent philosophers of old. In three hours he can give a history of philosophy from Plato to Hegel. Why waste more time upon Mill or Hamilton?

That much contemporary criticisms represent the views of such writers, will, I think, be admitted by most readers of periodical literature. It is a favourite belief of many sufferers under the critical lash, that it represents scarcely anything else. When an author has spent years, or even months, in elaborating an argument or accumulating knowledge, it is rather annoying to see himself tried and sentenced within a week from his appearance in the world. His critic, it seems, can merely have glanced over his pages, taken down a label at random from some appropriate pigeon-hole, and affixed it with a magisterial air of supercilious contempt. *Là voilà le chameau!* as Mr. Lewes' French philosopher remarks, when composing the natural history of the animal on the strength of half-an-hour in the Jardin des Plantes. The poor history or philosophy, the darling of its author's heart, so long patiently meditated, so delicately and carefully prepared, associated with so much labour, anxiety, and forethought, is put in its proper place as rapidly as Professor Owen could assign a ticket to a fossil tooth. It is not strange if the victim condemns his judge as an ignorant prig, and is tormented by an impotent longing for retaliation. But experience has probably taught him that to argue with a critic in his own columns is like drawing a badger in its den. You may be the strongest outside, but within you have to rush upon a sharp cagework of defensive teeth with your own hands tied. Silence, with as much dignity as may be, is his only course.

All criticism, one may say, is annoying. A wise man should never read criticisms of his own work. It is invariably a painful process; for all blame is obviously unfair, and praise as certainly comes in the wrong place. Moreover, it is a bad habit to be always looking in a glass, and especially in a mirror apt to distort and magnify. If a man is conscious that he has done his best, he should let his work take its chance with such indifference as he can command. Its success will be in the long run what it deserves, or, which comes to much the same thing, will be determined by a tribunal from which there is no appeal. All that criticism does is slightly to retard or hasten the decision, but scarcely to influence it. Every attack is an advertisement, and few authors nowadays have any difficulty in finding the circle really congenial to them. That circle once reached, an author should be satisfied. It may gain him much pecuniary profit but little real influence or fame when he comes to be forced upon those who don't spontaneously care for him. Now, the true author should, of course, be as indifferent to money as to insincere praise, and he is pretty certain to get all that he can really claim, namely, a sufficient hearing. Therefore, authors should burn unread all reviews of themselves, and possess their souls in peace.

Nobody, of course, will take this advice; but at least one may hope that a sense of decency will prevent authors and their admirers from howling too noisily under the lash. Why should the heaven-born poet shriek and rant because his earthborn critic does not do him justice? A true poet is the apostle of a new creed. He reveals hitherto unnoticed aspects of truth or beauty; his originality measures at once his genius and his chance of being misunderstood. It is his special prerogative to give form and colour to the latent thoughts and emotions of his time, and those whom he interprets to themselves will be grateful. But the utterance necessarily shocks all who cling from pedantry or from conservatism to the good old conventions. Their resistance is in proportion to the vigour of his attack, and he should hail their reproaches as compliments in disguise. Bacon or Locke had no right to be angry because the representatives of old scholasticism resented their attacks; nor Wordsworth nor Keats, because the admirers of Pope objected to the new forms of poetry. Wordsworth, with his sublime self-complacency, took hostile criticism as an unconscious confession of stupidity, and declared contemporary unpopularity to be a mark of true genius. The friends of Keats howled, and have been more or less howling ever since, because the old walls of convention did not fall down of themselves to welcome their assailants. Byron's contempt for the soul which let itself be snuffed out by an article is more to the purpose than Shelley's unmanly wailing over the supposed murder. The *Adonais* is an exquisite poem, but to read it with pleasure one must put the facts out of sight.

> Our Adonais hath drunk poison, oh!
> What deaf and viperous murderer could crown
> Life's early cup with such a draught of woe!

Beautiful! but a rather overstrained statement of the fact that Keats had been cut up in the *Quarterly Review*. On the theory that poetry and manliness are incompatible, that a poet is and ought to be a fragile being, ready to

> Die of a rose in aromatic pain,

the expressions may be justified. Otherwise Keats's death—if it had really been caused by the review—would certainly provoke nothing but pitying contempt. He that goes to war should count the cost; and one who will break the slumbers of mankind by new strains of poetic fervour must reckon upon the probability that many of the slumberers will resent the intrusion by a growl or an execration. Poets have a prescriptive right to be a thin-skinned race; but even they should not be guilty of the ineffable meanness of prostrating themselves before reviewers to receive sentence of life or death. What have these dwellers in the upper sphere to do with the hasty guesses of newspapers? What would a Shakespeare, or a Milton, or a Wordsworth, have said to such wailings? After all, what does it matter? Take it at the worst, and suppose yourself to be crushed for ever by a column of contemptuous language. Will the universe be much the worse for it? Can't we rub along tolerably without another volume or two of graceful rhymes? Is it anything but a preposterous vanity which generates the fancy that a rebuff to your ambition is an event in the world's history? If you are but a bubble, pray burst and hold your tongue. The great wheels of the world will grind on, and your shrieks be lost in the more serious chorus of genuine suffering. Whilst millions are starving in soul and body, we can't afford to waste many tears because a poet's toes have been trampled in the crush.

Though criticism may have far less power than our fears and our vanities assign to it, it has its importance; and at a time when all literature is becoming more critical, it is worth while to consider some of the principles which should guide it. We should, if possible, spare needless pangs even to a childish vanity, and we should anxiously promote the growth of a critical spirit such as raises instead of depressing the standard of literary excellence. The historian and the man of science can count upon fairly intelligent and scholarlike critics. Even if they be a little arrogant and prejudiced, they have one great advantage. There is a definite code of accepted principles. A mistake is clearly a mistake; and if the critic and his victim disagree, they have a definite issue and a settled method for decision. The judge may give a wrong decision, but he is administering a recognised code. We can apply scales and balances, and measure the work done with something like arithmetical accuracy.

In aesthetic questions the case is different. There is no available or recognised standard of merit. The ultimate appeal seems to lie to individual taste. I like Wordsworth, you like Pope—which is right? Are both right, or neither, or is it merely a matter of individual taste, as insoluble as a dispute between a man who prefers burgundy and one who prefers claret? The question would be answered if there were ever a science of aesthetics. At present we have got no further towards that consummation than in some other so-called sciences; we have invented a sounding name and a number of technical phrases, and are hopelessly at a loss for any accepted principles. We can, therefore, talk the most delicious jargon with all the airs of profound philosophy, but we cannot convince anyone who differs from us. The result is unfortunate, and oddly illustrates a popular confusion of ideas. There is surely no harm in a man's announcing his individual taste, if he expressly admits that he is not prescribing to the tastes of others. If I say that I dislike Shakespeare, I announce a fact, creditable or otherwise, of which I am the sole judge. So long as I am sincere, I am no more to be blamed than if I announced myself to be blind or deaf, or expressed an aversion to champagne. But, in practice, nobody is allowed to announce his own taste without being suspected of making it into a universal rule. It is a curious experiment, for example, to say openly that you don't care for music. Many men of good moral character have shared the distaste, and it may mean no more than some trifling physical defect. A thickness in the drum of the ear is not disgraceful, but it makes you necessarily incapable of appreciating Beethoven. One who avows his incapacity is simply revealing the melancholy fact that he is shut out from one great source of innocent pleasure. But no arguments will convince an ordinary hearer that your confession does not carry with it a declaration of belief that delight in music is contemptible and possibly immoral. To disavow so illogical a conclusion is hopeless. Experience, we must presume, has made it into an axiom that a man always hates and despises, and regards as a fit object for universal contempt and hatred, whatever he does not understand.

This is the first great stumbling-block in aesthetic criticism. Both readers and writers confound the enunciation of their own taste with the enunciation of universal and correct principles of taste. There is an instructive story in *Don Quixote* which is much to the purpose. Sancho Panza had two uncles who had an unrivalled taste in wine. One of them asserted that a certain butt of wine had a twang of leather; another detected, with equal confidence, a slight flavour of iron. The assistants laughed; but the laugh was the other way when the butt was drunk out and an old key with a leather thong detected at the bottom. Which things are an allegory. The skilled critic detects a flavour of vulgarity, of foreign style, or of what not, in a new writer. The mob of readers protests or acquiesces. Possibly at some future time the truth is discovered. The critic's palate was vitiated by prejudice, or some biographical fact turns up which justifies his appreciation; or, though no overt fact can be adduced, the coincidence of opinion of other qualified judges or the verdict of posterity confirms or refutes the verdict. We must wait, however, till the butt is drunk out, till time or accident has revealed the truth, and the judge himself has undergone judgment. And meanwhile we have, in the last resort, nothing but an individual expression of opinion, to be valued according to our appreciation of the writer's skill.

We know further that the best of critics is the one who makes fewest mistakes. We laugh at the familiar instances of our ancestors' blindness; but we ourselves are surely not infallible. We plume ourselves on detecting the errors of so many able men; but the very boast should make us modest. Will not the twentieth century laugh at the nineteenth? Will not our grandchildren send some of our modern idols to the dust heaps, and drag out works of genius from the neglect in which we so undeservedly left them? No man's fame, it is said, is secure till he has lived through a century. His children are awed by his reputation; his grandchildren are prejudiced by a reaction; only a third generation pronounces with tolerable impartiality on one so far removed from the daily conflict of opinion. In a century or so, we can see what a man has really done. We can measure the force of his blows. We can see, without reference to our personal likes or dislikes, how far he has moulded the thoughts of his race and become a source of spiritual power. That is a question of facts, as much as any historical question, and criticism which takes it properly into account may claim to be in some sense scientific. To anticipate the verdict of posterity is the great task of the true critic, which is accomplished by about one man in a generation.

The nature of the difficulty is obvious. The critic has to be a prophet without inspiration. The one fact given him is that he is affected in a particular way by a given work of art; the fact to be inferred is, that the work of art indicates such and such qualities in its author, and will produce such and such an effect upon the world. No definite mode of procedure is possible. It is a question of tact and instinctive appreciation; it is not to be settled by logic, but by what Dr. Newman calls the "illative sense"; the solution of the problem is to be felt out, not reasoned out, and the feeling is necessarily modified by the "personal equation," by that particular modification of the critic's own faculties, which cause him to see things in a light more or less peculiar to himself. He is disgusted by a certain poem; perhaps he

159

dislikes the author, or the author's religious or political school; or he is out of humour, or tried by overwork, or unconsciously biassed by a desire to point some pet moral of his own, or simply to find some excuse for a brilliant article. If he has succeeded in eliminating these disturbing influences, the problem is still intricate. Grant that the author disgusts me, and, further, that I can put my finger on the precise cause of disgust, and discover it to be some tone of sentiment which, in my opinion, is immoral or morbid; how can I be sure, first, that I am right, and, next, that the disgust should be equally felt by my descendants? The greatest errors of judgment have been founded on perfectly correct appreciations. Burke was undeniably right in the opinion that Rousseau's sentiment was often morbid, immoral, and revolutionary. He was wrong in inferring that these blemishes deprived Rousseau's work of all permanent value, so that under the vanity and the disease there was not a deep vein of true and noble passion. Every great writer of the present day is regarded in a similar spirit by the section opposed to him in sentiment, and yet it may be held by the charitable that even the most deadly antagonism is consistent with real co-operation. When we read the great works of a past epoch with due absence of prejudice, we are always astonished by the degree in which those who struck most fiercely really shared the ideas of their opponents.

A critic, it has been inferred, should in all cases speak for himself alone. He is, or ought to be, an infallible judge of his own likes or dislikes; he cannot dictate to his neighbour. For this reason, it has been suggested, all anonymous criticism is bad. A man who calls himself "we" naturally takes airs which the singular "I" would avoid. Whatever the general principles upon this subject, I do not much believe in the remedy. Anonymous criticism may be less responsible, but it is more independent. Why should I not condemn a man's work without telling him that I personally hold him to be a fool? Why should literary differences be embittered by personal feeling? If every man knew his judge, would not the practical result be an increase of bitterness in some cases and adulation in others? The mask may at times conceal an assassin, but it discourages flattery and softens antipathy. I fancy that a man, unjust enough to let his personal feelings colour his criticisms, generally likes to be known to his victim. Spite loses half its flavour when it is forced to be anonymous. Whatever the cause, the open critic differs from his anonymous rival by nothing but a trifling addition of pretentiousness, dogmatism, and severity. A writer is perhaps more modest the first time he has to give his name; but by the twentieth he has rubbed off that amiable weakness. Publicity hardens and generates conceit more decorously than privacy encourages laxity. The most ferocious denunciation, and the most arrogant dogmatism, have, I think, been shown by men whose names were known to everybody, if not actually published.

The fact, however, remains, that after all a criticism is only an expression of individual feeling. The universal formula might be: I, A. B., declare that you, C. D., are a weariness to me, or the reverse. The moral is, that a critic should speak of his author as one gentleman of another, or as a gentleman of a lady; the case being, of course, excepted when the author is palpably not a lady or gentleman, but a male or female blackguard. This maxim may be infringed by brutality or by dogmatism. The slashing reviewer seems to forget that he and his victim are both human beings, and bound by the ordinary decencies of life. The really pathetic case is, not when the heaven-born poet is misunderstood, but when some humble scribbler is scarified by the thoughtless critic. It is not a crime to be stupid, and to be forced to write for bread. Literature is a poor but a fairly honest profession. A widow with a family on her hands, a harmless governess, a clerk disabled by disease, has a pen, ink, and paper, can spell, and write grammar. With that slender provision, he or she tries to eke out a scanty living by some poor little novel. It is, of course, silly and commonplace. It is a third-rate imitation of an inferior author. It will go to the wastepaper heap, in any case, before the year is out, and the only wonder is that it has found a publisher. If the brilliant young prig could see the wretched author in the flesh, and realise the pangs of fear and suspense that have gone to the little venture, he would feel sheer pity, and his hand be attracted to his pockets. But when he sees only the book, and his pen is nearer than his purse, he proceeds to make fun of the miserable sufferer, and sprinkles two columns with sparkling epigrams with the sense of doing a virtuous action. Since the days of the *Dunciad,* it has been clear that nothing is so cruel as a wit. Wits have invented the opposite maxim. Take it for a rule, says Pope, with some truth,

No creature smarts so little as a fool.

But even a fool has his natural feelings as clearly as Shylock. When Macaulay jumped upon poor ''Satan'' Montgomery, and hacked and hewed and slashed him till he had not a whole bone in his body, he tried to prove that the example was demanded in the interests of literature. Surely, Macaulay was deluding himself, and the interest really consulted was his own reputation for smartness. *Satan* (I speak of the poem so-called) would have been dead long ago if Macaulay had never written; and the art of puffery could surely not have been more vigorous.

Such weapons should be kept for immoral writings or for successful imposture. There they are fair enough; and there is not the least danger that, confined to that application, they will rust from disuse. Stupidity enthroned in high places justifies the keenest ridicule. Stupidity on its knees scarcely requires the lash. Some amiable persons seem, indeed, to hold that the lash can never be required. They believe in sympathetic criticism. They would praise the good and leave the bad to decay of itself. The doctrine, however taking, is not more moral, and perhaps is more deleterious than the opposite. No man, says the excellent maxim, has ever been written down except by himself. Hostile criticism gives pain, but does not inflict vital wounds. Many writers, on the other hand, have been spoilt by indiscriminate praise. The temptation to become an imitator of oneself, is the most insidious of all to which an author is exposed. When a man has discovered his true power he should use it, but he should not use it to repeat his old feats in cold blood. The distinction is not always easy to urge, but it is of vital importance. The works of

162

the greatest writers, of the Shakespeares and Goethes, show a process of continuous development. The later display the same faculties as the earlier, but ripened and differently applied. The works of second-rate authors are often like a series of echoes. Each is a feeble repetition of the original which won the reputation. The flattery, now too common, makes this malady commoner than of old. A good writer, like a king, can do no wrong. Wonderful! admirable! faultless! is the cry; give us more of the same, and make it as much the same as possible. Is it wonderful that the poor man's head is turned, and his hold upon the ablest judges weakens whilst his circulation increases.

The mischief is intensified when a couple of sympathetic critics get together. They become the nucleus of a clique, and develop into a mutual admiration society. They form a literary sect, with its pet idols and its sacred canons of taste. They are the first persons to whom art has revealed its true secrets. Other cliques have flourished and laid down laws, and passed away; theirs will be eternal. The outside world may sneer, the members of the clique will only draw closer the curtain which excludes the profane vulgar from their meetings. As a rule, such a body contains one or two men of genuine ability, and has some ground for its self-praise, though not so unassailable a ground as it fancies. But genius condemned to live in such a vapour-bath of perpetually steaming incense, becomes soft of fibre and loses its productive power. It owes more than it would admit to the great world outside, which ridicules its pretensions and is perhaps blind even to its genuine merits. Addison was not the better for giving laws to a little senate; but Addison fortunately mixed in wider circles, and was not always exposed to the adulation of Tickell and "namby-pamby" Philips. Every man should try to form a circle of friends, lest he should be bewildered and isolated in the confused rush of a multitudinous society; but the circle should, so to speak, be constantly aërated by outside elements, or it will generate a mental valetudinarianism. The critic, who can speak the truth and speak out, is therefore of infinite service in keeping the atmosphere healthy.

A critic, then, should speak without fear or favour, so long as he can speak with the courtesy of a gentleman. He should give his opinion for what it is worth, neither more nor less. As the opinion of an individual, it should not be dogmatic; but as the opinion of a presumably cultivated individual, it should give at least a strong presumption as to that definitive verdict which can only be passed by posterity. The first difficulty which he will meet is to know what his opinion really is. No one who has not frankly questioned himself can appreciate the difficulty of performing this apparently simple feat. Every man who has read much has obscured his mind with whole masses of unconscious prejudice. An accomplished critic will declare a book to be fascinating of which he cannot read a page without a yawn, or a sheet without slumber. He will denounce as trashy and foolish a book which rivets his attention for hours. This is the one great advantage of the mob above the connoisseur. The vulgar have bad taste, but it is a sincere taste. They can't be persuaded to read except by real liking; and in some rare cases, where good qualities are accidentally offensive to the prevailing school of criticism, the cultivated reader will reject what is really excellent. The first point, therefore, is to have the rare courage of admitting your own feelings.

> In poets as true genius is but rare,
> True taste as seldom is the critic's share,

as Pope says; and chiefly for this reason. In all our array of critics, there are scarely half-a-dozen whose opinions are really valuable, and simply because there are scarcely so many whose opinions are their own. In ninety-nine cases out of a hundred, a so-called critique is a second-hand repetition of what the critic takes for the orthodox view. Whenever we see the expression of genuine feeling, we recognise a valuable contribution to our knowledge. That, for example, is the secret of the singular excellence of Lamb's too scanty fragments of criticism. He only spoke of what he really loved, and therefore almost every sentence he wrote is worth a volume of conventional discussion. He blundered at times; but his worst blunders are worth more than other men's second-hand judgments. Spontaneity is as valuable in the parasitic variety of literature as in the body of literature itself, and even more rare. Could we once distinguish between our own tastes and the taste which we adopt at second-hand, we should have at least materials for sound judgment.

This vivacity and originality of feeling is the first qualification of a critic. Without it no man's judgment is worth having. Almost any judgment really springing from it has a certain value. But the bare fact that an aversion or a liking exists requires interpretation. To find the law by which the antipathy is regulated is to discover the qualities of the antagonistic elements. A good critic can hardly express his feelings without implicitly laying down a principle. When (to take a case at random) Lamb says of certain scenes in Middleton, that the "insipid levelling morality to which the modern stage is tied down, would not admit of such admirable passions," as fill the passages in question, he preaches a doctrine, sound or unsound, of great importance. He says, that is, that certain rules of modern decorum are aesthetically injurious and ethically erroneous. The particular rules infringed are to be discovered from the special instance, and the fact that a man with Lamb's idiosyncrasies denounced them must be taken into account when we would apply them as canons of judgment. The judgments of good critics upon a number of such problems thus form a body of doctrine analogous to what is known to jurists as case-law. The rule for our guidance is not explicitly stated, but it is to be inferred from a number of particular instances, by carefully estimating their resemblance to the fresh instance and assigning due weight to the authority of the various judges.

As competent literary judges are rare, and their decisions conflicting, the task of extricating the general rule is difficult or rather impossible. No general rules perhaps can be laid down with absolute confidence. But the analogy may suggest the mode in which we may hope gradually to approximate to general rules, and to find grounds for reasonable certainty in special cases. Though no single critic is infallible, we may assume that the *vox populi* is infallible if strictly confined to its proper sphere. When many generations have been influenced by an individual, we have demonstrative evidence that he must have been a man of extraordinary power. It is an indisputable fact that Homer and Æschylus delighted all intelligent readers for over 2,000 years. To explain that fact by any other theory than the theory that the authors possessed extraordinary genius is impossible. A man, therefore, who flies in the face of the verdict of generations is self-condemned. The probability that his blindness indicates a defect in his eyesight is incomparably greater than the probability that all other eyes have been somehow under an illusion. The argument applies to less colossal reputations. Not only a critic of the last century who could see nothing in Dante, but a critic in the present who thinks Pope a mere fool, or Voltaire a mere buffoon, puts himself out of court. Let him by all means confess his want of perception if it be necessary; but do not let him go on to criticise men in regard to whom he suffers from a kind of colour-blindness. My palate refuses to distinguish between claret and burgundy, but I never set myself up for a judge of wine.

It may be added that the power of swaying the imaginations of many generations indicates more than mere force. It is a safe indication of some true merit. No religion thrives which does not embody—along with whatever errors—the deepest and most permanent emotions of mankind. No art retains its interest for posterity which does not give permanent expression to something more than the temporary tastes, and, moreover, to something more than the vicious and morbid propensities of mankind. To justify this maxim would lead us too far; but I venture to assume that it could be justified by a sufficient induction. All great writers have their weaknesses; but their true power rests upon their utterance of the ennobling and health-giving emotions.

This doctrine is accepted even too unreservedly by most critics of the past. A slavish care for established reputation is more common than a rash defiance. The way, for example, in which Shakespeare's faults have been idolised along with his surpassing merits is simply a disgrace to literature. Were I writing for students of old authors, I would exhort them rather to attend to the limitations of the doctrine than to the doctrine itself. We are too apt to confound the qualities by which a man has succeeded with those in spite of which he has succeeded. The application of the doctrine to the living is, however, a more pressing problem. Our aim, I have said, is to anticipate the verdict of posterity, and we cannot anticipate infallibly. We cannot even lay down absolute rules of a scientific character. All that we can do is to proceed in a scientific spirit, which may therefore be favourable to the discovery of such rules in the future. If doomed to continual blunders, our blunders may form landmarks for the future, and not be simple exhibitions of profitless folly and prejudice.

The critic who gives a matured expression of his tastes lays down a principle. He should proceed to apply an obvious test. Will his principle fit in with the accepted verdict as to the great men of the past? A simple attention to this rule would dissipate a vast amount of foolish criticism. There has been, for example, a great outcry against a vice known as sensationalism. In one sense, the outcry justifies itself. People have been shocked by overdoses of horror and crime; and the art which has shocked them must be in some sense bad. But when critics proceed to lay down canons which would suppress all literature more exciting than Miss Austen's novels, they are surely forgetting one or two obvious facts. Canons are calmly propounded which would condemn all Greek tragedy, which would condemn Dante, and Milton, and Shakespeare, and the whole school of early English dramatists, and some of Scott's finest novels, to say nothing of Byron, or of Balzac, or Victor Hugo. The simple fact that a poem or a novel deals with crime and suffering cannot be enough to condemn it, or we should be doomed to a diet of bread and butter for all future time. The true question is as to the right mode of dealing with such subjects, and the critic who would condemn all dealing with them is really betraying his cause. He is trying to force an impracticable code upon mankind, and is allowing the true culprits to associate their cause with better men. Moreover, he is talking nonsense.

To keep steadily in mind the verdict of the past, not to break a painted window in anxiety to smash the insect which is crawling over it, is thus the great safeguard of a critic. A more difficult problem is the degree of respect due to modern opinion. The widest popularity may certainly be gained by absolute demerits. We need not give examples of modern charlatans, whose fame has not yet gone to its own place. There are plenty of older examples. The false wit of Cowley and the strained epigrams of Young, the pompous sentimentalism of Hervey, the tinsel of Tom Moore, all won a share of popularity in their own day, which rivalled or eclipsed the fame of Milton and Pope, and Addison and Wordsworth. In two of these cases the fame was partly due to religious associations which superseded a purely literary judgment. On the other hand, there is a measure of fame which seems sufficiently to anticipate the verdict of posterity. There is perhaps more than one living writer of whom it may be confidently asserted that his influence over the most thoughtful of his contemporaries has been won by such palpable services to truth and lofty sentiment, and has been so independent of the aid of adventitious circumstances, that his fame is as secure, though not as accurately measured, as it will be a century hence. To treat such men with insolence is as monstrous as to insult their predecessors. The burden of proof at least is upon the assailant, and he is bound to explain not merely the cause of his antipathy, but to explain the phenomenon which, on his showing, ought not to exist. A summary *tant pis pour les faits* will not bring him off, tempting as the method may be. When a spiritual movement has acquired a certain impetus and volume, its leader must be a great man. To admit that a mere charlatan can move the world, is to hold with the housemaid that a plate breaks of itself, or, with the Tories in Queen Anne's time, that Marlborough won his battles by sheer cowardice.

How to distinguish between the true and the sham influence is indeed a question not strictly soluble. It is enough to suggest that any man of true force has a sure instinct for recognising force elsewhere. The blindness of patriotic or party rage may sometimes encourage a Frenchman to laugh at Moltke's strategy, or an English politician of one party to call the Pitt or Fox of his opponents an idiot. No man, swayed by such passions, can criticise to any purpose; and the best safeguard against the resulting errors is a constant application of the doctrine that every spiritual impulse requires an adequate moral explanation as well as a physical. Some people are fond of ascribing the success of their antagonists to chance or to diabolic influence. They would be wise if they would remember that either phrase, when analysed, is equivalent to the simple confession of ignorance. It means that the source of evil is in some sphere entirely outside our means of investigation. It is to abandon the problem, whilst masking our ignorance under an abusive epithet. Opponents may be justified if they take language of this kind as a panegyric in disguise.

There is, it is true, a weak side in the appeals often made to critical candour. Politicians sometimes denounce the bigotry of Liberals. The men who pride themselves upon their tolerance are often, it is said, the most dogmatic. But such denunciations, if often just, are apt to confound two very different things. Liberality imposes the duty of giving fair play to our opponents in action as in logic, but it does not command us to have no opinions at all. It is most desirable that every principle should be fully and fairly discussed, but it is certainly not desirable that no principles should ever be definitively established. The pure indifferentist naturally hates faith of all kinds, and tries to impute intolerance to any believer who carries faith into practice. There is, in short, a road to toleration which leads through pure scepticism; if every doctrine is equally true and equally false, there is no reason for ever being in a passion. That is not a desirable solution of the problem. It is very difficult to hold my own opinions and to respect all sincere dissentients—to believe that my doctrines are true and important, and yet to refuse to advance them by unworthy methods. But the only true Liberal is the man who can accomplish that feat, and the tolerance made out of pure incredulity is a mere mockery of the genuine virtue.

The fact that candid people dispute conclusions which seem to me evident is not always a reason for admitting even a scruple of doubt. There are cases in which it may even confirm them. A truth is fully established when it not only explains certain phenomena, but explains the source of erroneous conceptions of the phenomena. The true theory of astronomy shows why false theories were inevitably plausible at certain periods. No doctrine can be quite satisfactory till it helps us to see why other people do not see it. When that is clearly intelligible, the very errors confirm the true theory. In matters of taste there is a similar canon. There are undoubtedly bad tastes as well as good. There are tastes, that is, which imply stupidity, or craving for coarse excitement, or incapacity for distinguishing between rant and true rhetoric, between empty pomp of language and genuine richness and force of imagination. There are tastes which imply a thoroughly corrupt nature, and others which imply vulgarity and coarseness. To admit that all tastes are equally good is to fall into an aesthetic scepticism as erroneous as the philosophical scepticism which should make morality or political principles matters of arbitrary convention. A critic who is tolerant in the sense of admitting this indifference abnegates his true function; for the one great service which a critic can render is to keep vice, vulgarity, or stupidity at bay. He cannot supply genius; but he can preserve the prestige of genius by revealing to duller minds the difference between good work and its imitation.

The sense in which a critic should be liberal is marked out by this consideration. The existence of any artistic school, however much he dislikes its tendency, is a phenomenon to be explained and not to be denounced until it is explained. If it has a wide popularity, or includes many able men, there is a strong presumption that it corresponds in some way to a real want of the time. It embodies a widespread, and presumably, therefore, not a purely objectionable emotional impulse. It proves, at the lowest, that rival forms of expression do not satisfy the wants of contemporaries, and are so far defective. Even if it be, in the critic's eye, a purely reactionary movement, the existence of a reaction proves that something is wanting in that against which it reacts. Some element of feeling is inadequately represented, and therefore the objectionable movement indicates a want, if it does not suggest the true remedy. It may be that, in some cases, the critic will be forced to say that, after taking such considerations into account, he can yet see nothing more in his antagonist than the embodiment of a purely morbid tendency. They represent a disease in the social order which requires caustic and the knife. When a man has deliberately formed such an opinion, he should express it frankly, though as temperately as may be; but it will probably be admitted that such cases are very rare, and that a man who has the power of seeing through his neighbours' eyes will generally discover that they catch at least a distorted aspect of some truths not so clearly revealed to their opponents.

By keeping such rules in mind, the critic will certainly not become infallible. He will not discover any simple mechanical test for the accurate measurement of literary genius. Nor will he or a whole generation of critics succeed in making an exact science out of an art which must always depend upon natural delicacy of perception. But he will be working in the right direction, and undergoing a wholesome discipline. If he does not discover any rigidly correct formulae, he will be helping towards the establishment of sound methods; and though he will not store his mind with authoritative dogmas, he will encourage the right temper for approaching a most delicate task. In many cases, indeed, the task is easy enough. It would be affectation to deny that there are a good many books which may be summarily classified as rubbish, without much risk of real injustice, though sentence need not be passed in harsh language. But to judge of any serious work requires, besides the natural faculty, possessed by very few, an amount of habitual labour to look from strange points of view which is almost equally rare. There are many poems, for example, which can hardly be criticised to effect till the critic knows them by heart, and a man cannot be expected to do that who has to pronounce judgment within a week. In that case, all that can be recommended is a certain modesty in expression and diffidence in forming opinions which is not universal amongst our authoritative critics.

4

Hours in a Library

Dr. Johnson's Writings

A book appeared not long ago of which it was the professed object to give to the modern generation of lazy readers the pith of Boswell's immortal biography. I shall, for sufficient reasons, refrain from discussing the merits of the performance. One remark, indeed, may be made in passing. The circle of readers to whom such a book is welcome must, of necessity, be limited. To the true lovers of Boswell it is, to say the least, superfluous; the gentlest omissions will always mangle some people's favourite passages, and additions, whatever skill they may display, necessarily injure that dramatic vivacity which is one of the great charms of the original. The most discreet of cicerones is an intruder when we open our old favourite, and, without further magic, retire into that delicious nook of eighteenth-century society. Upon those, again, who cannot appreciate the infinite humour of the original, the mere exclusion of the less lively pages will be thrown away. There remains only that narrow margin of readers whose appetites, languid but not extinct, can be titillated by the promise that they shall not have the trouble of making their own selection. Let us wish them good digestions, and, in spite of modern changes of fashion, more robust taste for the future. I would still hope

Reprinted from *Hours in a Library*, vol. 2 (1876).

that to many readers Boswell has been what he has certainly been to some, the first writer who gave them a love of English literature, and the most charming of all companions long after the bloom of novelty has departed. I subscribe most cheerfully to Mr. Lewes's statement that he estimates his acquaintances according to their estimate of Boswell. A man, indeed, may be a good Christian and an excellent father of a family, without loving Johnson or Boswell, for a sense of humour is not one of the primary virtues. But Boswell's is one of the very few books which, after many years of familiarity, will still provoke a hearty laugh even in the solitude of a study; and the laughter is of that kind which does one good.

I do not wish, however, to pronounce one more eulogy upon an old friend, but to say a few words on a question which he sometimes suggests. Macaulay's well-known but provoking essay is more than usually lavish in overstrained paradoxes. He has explicitly declared that Boswell wrote one of the most charming of books because he was one of the greatest of fools. And his remarks suggest, if they do not implicitly assert, that Johnson wrote some of the most unreadable of books, although, if not because, he possessed one of the most vigorous intellects of the time. Carlyle has given a sufficient explanation of the first paradox; but the second may justify a little further inquiry. As a general rule, the talk of a great man is the reflection of his books. Nothing is so false as the common saying that the presence of a distinguished writer is generally disappointing. It exemplifies a very common delusion. People are so impressed by the disparity which sometimes occurs, that they take the exception for the rule. It is, of course, true that a man's verbal utterances may differ materially from his written utterances. He may, like Addison, be shy in company; he may, like many retired students, be slow in collecting his thoughts; or he may, like Goldsmith, be over-anxious to shine at all hazards. But a patient observer will even then detect the essential identity under superficial differences; and in the majority of cases, as in that of Macaulay himself, the talking and the writing are palpably and almost absurdly similar. The whole art of criticism consists in learning to know the human being who is partially revealed to us

173

in his spoken or his written words. Whatever the means of communication, the problem is the same. The two methods of inquiry may supplement each other; but their substantial agreement is the test of their accuracy. If Johnson, as a writer, appears to us to be a mere windbag and manufacturer of sesquipedalian verbiage, whilst, as a talker, he appears to be one of the most genuine and deeply feeling of men, we may be sure that our analysis has been somewhere defective. The discrepancy is, of course, partly explained by the faults of Johnson's style; but the explanation only removes the difficulty a degree further. "The style is the man" is a very excellent aphorism, though some eminent writers have lately pointed out that Buffon's original remark was *le style c'est de l'homme.* That only proves that, like many other good sayings, it has been polished and brought to perfection by the process of attrition in numerous minds, instead of being struck out at a blow by a solitary thinker. From a purely logical point of view, Buffon may be correct; but the very essence of an aphorism is that slight exaggeration which makes it more biting whilst less rigidly accurate. According to Buffon, the style might belong to a man as an acquisition rather than to natural growth. There are parasitical writers who, in the old phrase, have "formed their style" by the imitation of accepted models, and who have, therefore, possessed it only by right of appropriation. Boswell has a discussion as to the writers who may have served Johnson in this capacity. But, in fact, Johnson, like all other men of strong idiosyncrasy, formed his style as he formed his legs. The peculiarities of his limbs were in some degree the result of conscious efforts in walking, swimming, and "buffeting with his books." This development was doubtless more fully determined by the constitution which he brought into the world, and the circumstances under which he was brought up. And even that queer Johnsonese, which Macaulay supposes him to have adopted in accordance with a more definite literary theory, will probably appear to be the natural expression of certain innate tendencies, and of the mental atmosphere which he breathed from youth. To appreciate fairly the strangely cumbrous form of his written speech, we must penetrate more deeply than may at first sight seem necessary beneath the outer rind of this literary Behemoth. The difficulty of such spiritual dissection is, indeed, very great; but some little light may be thrown upon the subject by following out such indications as we possess.

The talking Johnson is sufficiently familiar to us. So far as Boswell needs an interpreter, Carlyle has done all that can be done. He has concentrated and explained what is diffused, and often unconsciously indicated in Boswell's pages. When reading Boswell, we are half ashamed of his power over our sympathies. It is like turning over a portfolio of sketches, caricatured, inadequate, and each giving only some imperfect aspect of the original. Macaulay's smart paradoxes only increase our perplexity by throwing the superficial contrasts into stronger relief. Carlyle, with true imaginative insight, gives us at once the essence of Johnson; he brings before our eyes the luminous body of which we have previously been conscious only by a series of imperfect images refracted through a number of distorting media. To render such a service effectually is the highest triumph of criticism; and it would be impertinent to say again in feebler language what Carlyle has expressed so forcibly. We may, however, recall certain general conclusions by way of preface to the problem which he has not expressly considered, how far Johnson succeeded in expressing himself through his writings.

The world, as Carlyle sees it, is composed, we all know, of two classes: there are ''the dull millions, who, as a dull flock, roll hither and thither, whithersoever they are led,'' and there are a few superior natures who can see and can will. There are, in other words, the heroes, and those whose highest wisdom is to be hero-worshippers. Johnson's glory is that he belonged to the sacred band, though he could not claim within it the highest, or even a very high, rank. In the current dialect, therefore, he was ''nowise a clothes-horse or patent digester, but a genuine man.'' Whatever the accuracy of the general doctrine, or of certain corollaries which are drawn from it, the application to Johnson explains one main condition of his power. Persons of colourless imagination may hold—nor will we dispute their verdict—that Carlyle overcharges his lights and shades, and brings his heroes into too startling a contrast with the vulgar herd. Yet it is undeniable that the great bulk of mankind are transmitters rather than originators of spiritual force. Most of us are necessarily condemned to express our thoughts in formulas which we have learnt from others and can but slightly tinge with our feeble personality. Nor, as a rule, are we even consistent disciples of any one school of thought. What we call our opinions are mere bundles of incoherent formulae, arbitrarily stitched together because our reasoning faculties are too dull to make inconsistency painful. Of the vast piles of books which load our libraries, ninety-nine hundredths and more are but printed echoes: and it is the rarest of pleasures to say, Here is a distinct record of impressions at first hand. We commonplace beings are hurried along in the crowd, living from hand to mouth on such slices of material and spiritual food as happen to drift in our direction, with little more power of taking an independent course, or of forming any general theory, than the polyps which are carried along by an oceanic current. Ask any man what he thinks of the world in which he is placed: whether, for example, it is on the whole a scene of happiness or misery, and he will either answer by some cut-and-dried fragments of what was once wisdom, or he will confine himself to a few incoherent details. He had a good dinner to-day and a bad toothache yesterday, and a family affliction or blessing the day before. But he is as incapable of summing up his impressions as an infant of performing an operation in the differential calculus. It is as rare as it is refreshing to find a man who can stand on his own legs and be conscious of his own feelings, who is sturdy enough to react as well as to transmit action, and lofty enough to raise himself above the hurrying crowd and have some distinct belief as to whence it is coming and whither it is going. Now Johnson, as one of the sturdiest of mankind, had the power due to a very distinct sentiment, if not to a very clear theory, about the world in which he lived. It had buffeted him severely enough, and he had formed a decisive estimate of its value. He was no man to be put off with mere phrases in place of opinions, or to accept doctrines which were not capable of expressing genuine emotion. To this it must be added that his emotions were as deep and tender as they were genuine. How sacred was his love

176

for his old and ugly wife; how warm his sympathy wherever it could be effective; how manly the self-respect with which he guarded his dignity through all the temptations of Grub Street, need not be once more pointed out. Perhaps, however, it is worth while to notice the extreme rarity of such qualities. Many people, we think, love their fathers. Fortunately, that is true; but in how many people is filial affection strong enough to overpower the dread of eccentricity? How many men would have been capable of doing penance in Uttoxeter market years after their father's death for a long-past act of disobedience? Most of us, again, would have a temporary emotion of pity for an outcast lying helplessly in the street. We should call the police, or send her in a cab to the workhouse, or, at least, write to the *Times* to denounce the defective arrangements of public charity. But it is perhaps better not to ask how many good Samaritans would take her on their shoulders to their own homes, care for her wants, and put her into a better way of life.

In the lives of most eminent men we find much good feeling and honourable conduct; but it is an exception, even in the case of good men, when we find that a life has been shaped by other than the ordinary conventions, or that emotions have dared to overflow the well-worn channels of respectability. The love which we feel for Johnson is due to the fact that the pivots upon which his life turned are invariably noble motives, and not mere obedience to custom. More than one modern writer has expressed a fraternal affection for Addison, and it is justified by the kindly humour which breathes through his "Essays." But what anecdote of that most decorous and successful person touches our hearts or has the heroic ring of Johnson's wrestlings with adverse fortune? Addison showed how a Christian could die—when his life has run smoothly through pleasant places, secretaryships of state, and marriages with countesses, and when nothing—except a few overdoses of port wine—has shaken his nerves or ruffled his temper. A far deeper emotion rises at the deathbed of the rugged old pilgrim, who has fought his way to peace in spite of troubles within and without, who has been jeered in Vanity Fair and has descended into the Valley of the Shadow of Death, and escaped with pain and difficulty from the clutches of Giant

Despair. When the last feelings of such a man are tender, solemn, and simple, we feel ourselves in a higher presence than that of an amiable gentleman who simply died, as he lived, with consummate decorum.

On turning, however, from Johnson's life to his writings, from Boswell to the "Rambler," it must be admitted that the shock is trying to our nerves. The "Rambler" has, indeed, high merits. The impression which it made upon his own generation proves the fact; for the reputation, however temporary, was not won by a concession to the fashions of the day, but to the influence of a strong judgment uttering itself through uncouth forms. The melancholy which colours its pages is the melancholy of a noble nature. The tone of thought reminds us of Bishop Butler, whose writings, defaced by a style even more tiresome, though less pompous than Johnson's, have owed their enduring reputation to a philosophical acuteness in which Johnson was certainly very deficient. Both of these great men, however, impress us by their deep sense of the evils under which humanity suffers, and their rejection of the superficial optimism of the day. Butler's sadness, undoubtedly, is that of a recluse, and Johnson's that of a man of the world; but the sentiment is fundamentally the same. It may be added, too, that here, as elsewhere, Johnson speaks with the sincerity of a man drawing upon his own experience. He announces himself as a scholar thrust out upon the world rather by necessity than choice; and a large proportion of the papers dwell upon the various sufferings of the literary class. Nobody could speak more feelingly of those sufferings, as no one had a closer personal acquaintance with them. But allowing to Johnson whatever credit is due to the man who performs one more variation on the old theme, *Vanitas vanitatum*, we must in candour admit that the "Rambler" has the one unpardonable fault: it is unreadable.

What an amazing turn it shows for commonplaces! That life is short, that marriages from mercenary motives produce unhappiness, that different men are virtuous in different degrees, that advice is generally ineffectual, that adversity has its uses, that fame is liable to suffer from detraction;—these and a host of other such maxims are of the kind upon which no genius and no depth of feeling can confer a momentary interest. Here and there, indeed, the pompous utterance invests them with an unlucky air of absurdity. "Let no man from this time," is the comment in one of his stories, "suffer his felicity to depend on the death of his aunt." Every actor, of course, uses the same dialect. A gay young gentleman tell us that he used to amuse his companions by giving them notice of his friends' oddities. "Every man," he says, "has some habitual contortion of body, or established mode of expression, which never fails to excite mirth if it be pointed out to notice. By premonition of these particularities, I secured our pleasantry." The feminine characters, Flirtillas, and Cleoras, and Euphelias, and Penthesileas, are, if possible, still more grotesque. Macaulay remarks that he wears the petticoat with as ill a grace as Falstaff himself. The reader, he thinks, will cry out with Sir Hugh, "I like not when a 'oman has a great peard! I spy a great peard under her muffler." Oddly enough Johnson gives the very same quotation; and goes on to warn his supposed correspondents that Phyllis must send no more letters from the Horse Guards; and that Belinda must "resign her pretensions to female elegance till she has lived three weeks without hearing the politics of Button's Coffee House." The Doctor was probably sensible enough of his own defects. And yet there is a still more wearisome set of articles. In emulation of the precedent set by Addison, Johnson indulges in the dreariest of allegories. Criticism, we are told, was the eldest daughter of Labour and Truth, but at last resigned in favour of Time, and left Prejudice and False Taste to reign in company with Fraud and Mischief. Then we have the genealogy of Wit and Learning, and of Satire, the Son of Wit and Malice, and an account of their various quarrels, and the decision of Jupiter. Neither are the histories of such semi-allegorical personages as Almamoulin, the son of Nouradin, or of Anningait and Ayut, the Greenland lovers, much more refreshing to modern readers. That Johnson possessed humour of no mean order, we know from Boswell; but no critic could have divined his power from the clumsy gambols in which he occasionally recreates himself. Perhaps his happiest effort is a dissertation upon the advantage of living in garrets; but the humour struggles and gasps dreadfully under the weight of words. "There are," he says, "some who would continue blockheads" (the Alpine Club was not yet founded), "even on the summit of the Andes or the Peak of Teneriffe. But let not any man be considered as unimprovable till this potent remedy has been tried; for perhaps he was found to be great only in a garret, as the joiner of Aretaeus was rational in no other place but his own shop."

How could a man of real power write such unendurable stuff? Or how, indeed, could any man come to embody his thoughts in the style of which one other sentence will be a sufficient example? As it is afterwards nearly repeated, it may be supposed to have struck his fancy. The remarks of the philosophers who denounce temerity are, he says, "too just to be disputed and too salutary to be rejected; but there is likewise some danger lest timorous prudence should be inculcated till courage and enterprise are wholly repressed and the mind congested in perpetual inactivity by the fatal influence of frigorifick wisdom." Is there not some danger, we ask, that the mind will be benumbed into perpetual torpidity by the influence of this soporific sapience? It is still true, however, that this Johnsonese, so often burlesqued and ridiculed, was, as far as we can judge, a genuine product. Macaulay says that it is more offensive than the mannerism of Milton or Burke, because it is a mannerism adopted on principle and sustained by constant effort. Facts do not confirm the theory. Milton's prose style seems to be the result of a conscious effort to run English into classical moulds. Burke's mannerism does not appear in his early writings, and we can trace its development from the imitation of Bolingbroke to the last declamation against the Revolution. But Johnson seems to have written Johnsonese from his cradle. In his first original composition, the preface to Father Lobo's "Abyssinia," the style is as distinctive as in the "Rambler." The Parliamentary reports in the "Gentleman's Magazine" make Pitt and Fox[1] express sentiments which are probably their own in language which is as unmistakably Johnson's. It is clear that his style, good or bad, was the same from his earliest efforts. It is only in his last book, the "Lives of the Poets," that the mannerism, though equally marked, is so far subdued as to be tolerable. What he himself called his habit of using "too big words and too many of them" was no affectation, but as much the result of his special idiosyncrasy as his queer gruntings and twitchings. Sir Joshua Reynolds indeed maintained, and we may believe so attentive an observer, that his strange physical contortions were the result of bad habit, not of actual disease. Johnson, he said, could sit as still as other people when his attention was called to it. And possibly, if he had tried, he might have avoided the fault of making "little fishes talk like whales." But how did the bad habits arise? According to Boswell, Johnson professed to have "formed his style" partly upon Sir W. Temple, and on "Chambers's Proposal for his Dictionary." The statement was obviously misinterpreted: but there is a glimmering of truth in the theory that the "style was formed"—so far as those words have any meaning—on the "giants of the seventeenth century," and especially upon Sir Thomas Browne. Johnson's taste, in fact, had led him to the study of writers in many ways congenial to him. His favourite book, as we know, was Burton's "Anatomy of Melancholy." The pedantry of the older school did not repel him; the weighty thought rightly attracted him; and the more complex structure of sentence was perhaps a pleasant contrast to an ear saturated with the Gallicised neatness of Addison and Pope. Unluckily, the secret of the old majestic cadence was hopelessly lost. Johnson, though spiritually akin to the giants, was the firmest ally and subject of the dwarfish dynasty which supplanted them. The very faculty of hearing seems to change in obedience to some mysterious law at different stages of intellectual development; and that which to one generation is delicious music is to another a mere droning of bagpipes or the grinding of monotonous barrel-organs.

Assuming that a man can find perfect satisfaction in the versification of the "Essay on Man," we can understand his saying of "Lycidas," that "the diction is harsh, the rhymes uncertain, and the numbers unpleasing." In one of the "Ramblers" we are informed that the accent in blank verse ought properly to rest upon every second syllable throughout the whole line. A little variety must, he admits, be allowed to avoid satiety; but all lines which do not go in the steady

181

jog-trot of alternate beats as regularly as the piston of a steam engine, are more or less defective. This simple-minded system naturally makes wild work with the poetry of the "mighty-mouthed inventor of harmonies." Milton's harsh cadences are indeed excused on the odd ground that he who was "vindicating the ways of God to man" might have been condemned for "lavishing much of his attention upon syllables and sounds." Moreover, the poor man did his best by introducing sounding proper names, even when they "added little music to his poem:" an example of this feeble though well-meant expedient being the passage about the moon, which—

> The Tuscan artist views
> At evening, from the top of Fiesole
> Or in Valdarno, to descry new lands, &c.

This profanity passed at the time for orthodoxy. But the misfortune was, that Johnson, unhesitatingly subscribing to the rules of Queen Anne's critics, is always instinctively feeling after the grander effects of the old school. Nature prompts him to the stateliness of Milton, whilst art orders him to deal out long and short syllables alternately, and to make them up in parcels of ten, and then tie the parcels together in pairs by the help of a rhyme. The natural utterance of a man of strong perceptions, but of unwieldly intellect, of a melancholy temperament, and capable of very deep, but not vivacious emotions, would be in stately and elaborate phrases. His style was not more distinctly a work of art than the style of Browne or Milton, but, unluckily, it was a work of bad art. He had the misfortune, not so rare as it may sound, to be born in the wrong century; and is, therefore, a giant in fetters; the amplitude of stride is still there, but it is checked into mechanical regularity. A similar phenomenon is observable in other writers of the time. The blank verse of Young, for example, is generally set to Pope's tune with the omission of the rhymes, whilst Thomson, revolting more or less consciously against the canons of his time, too often falls into mere pompous mouthing. Shaftesbury, in the previous generation, trying to write poetical prose, becomes as pedantic as Johnson, though in a different style; and Gibbon's mannerism is a familiar example of a similar escape from a monotonous simplicity into awkward complexity. Such writers are like men who have been chilled by what Johnson would call the "frigorifick" influence of the classicism of their fathers, and whose numbed limbs move stiffly and awkwardly in a first attempt to regain the old liberty. The form, too, of the "Rambler" is unfortunate. Johnson has always Addison before his eyes; to whom it was formerly the fashion to compare him for the same excellent reason which has recently suggested comparisons between Dickens and Thackeray—namely, that their works were published in the same external shape. Unluckily, Johnson gave too much excuse for the comparison by really imitating Addison. He has to make allegories, and to give lively sketches of feminine peculiarities, and to ridicule social foibles of which he was, at most, a distant observer. The inevitable consequence is, that though here and there we catch a glimpse of the genuine man, we are, generally, too much provoked by the awkwardness of his costume to be capable of enjoying, or even reading him.

In many of his writings, however, Johnson manages, almost entirely, to throw off these impediments. In his deep capacity for sympathy and reverence, we recognise some of the elements that go to the making of a poet. He is always a man of intuitions rather than of discursive intellect; often keen of vision, though wanting in analytical power. For poetry, indeed, as it is often understood now, or even as it was understood by Pope, he had little enough qualification. He had not the intellectual vivacity implied in the marvellously neat workmanship of Pope, and still less the delight in all natural and artistic beauty which we generally take to be essential to poetic excellence. His contempt for "Lycidas" is sufficiently significant upon that head. Still more characteristic is the incapacity to understand Spenser, which comes out incidentally in his remarks upon some of those imitations, which even in the middle of the eighteenth century showed that sensibility to the purest form of poetry was not by any means extinct amongst us. But there is a poetry, though we sometimes seem to forget it, which is the natural expression of deep moral sentiment; and of this Johnson has written enough to reveal very genuine power. The touching verses upon the death of Levett are almost as pathetic as Cowper; and fragments of the two imitations of Juvenal have struck deep enough to be not quite forgotten. We still quote the lines about pointing a moral and adorning a tale, which conclude a really noble passage. We are too often reminded of his melancholy musings over the

> Fears of the brave and follies of the wise,

and a few of the concluding lines of the "Vanity of Human Wishes," in which he answers the question whether man must of necessity

> Roll darkling down the torrent of his fate,

in helplessness and ignorance, may have something of a familiar ring. We are to give thanks, he says,

> For love, which scarce collective man can fill;
> For patience, sovereign o'er transmuted ill;
> For faith, that, panting for a happier seat,
> Counts death kind nature's signal for retreat;
> These goods for men, the laws of heaven ordain,
> These goods He grants, who grants the power to gain,
> With these celestial wisdom calms the mind,
> And makes the happiness she does not find.

These lines, and many others which might be quoted, are noble in expression, as well as lofty and tender in feeling. Johnson, like Wordsworth, or even more deeply than Wordsworth, had felt all the "heavy and the weary weight of all this unintelligible world;" and, though he stumbles a little in the narrow limits of his versification, he bears himself nobly, and manages to put his heart into his poetry. Coleridge's paraphrase of the well-known lines, "Let observation with extensive observation, observe mankind from China to Peru," would prevent us from saying that he had thrown off his verbiage. He has not the felicity of Goldsmith's "Traveller," though he wrote one of the best couplets in that admirable poem; but his ponderous lines show genuine vigour, and can be excluded from poetry only by the help of an arbitrary classification.

The fullest expression, however, of Johnson's feeling is undoubtedly to be found in "Rasselas." The inevitable comparison with Voltaire's "Candide," which, by an odd coincidence, appeared almost simultaneously, suggests some curious reflections. The resemblance between the moral of the two books is so strong that, as Johnson remarked, it would have been difficult not to suppose that one had given a hint to the other but for the chronological difficulty. The contrast, indeed, is as marked as the likeness. "Candide" is not adapted for family reading, whereas "Rasselas" might be a text-book for young ladies studying English in a convent. "Candide" is a marvel of clearness and vivacity; whereas to read "Rasselas" is about as exhilarating as to wade knee-deep through a sandy desert. Voltaire and Johnson, however, the great sceptic and the last of the true old Tories, coincide pretty well in their view of the world, and in the remedy which they suggest. The world is, they agree, full of misery, and the optimism which would deny the reality of the misery is childish. *Il faut cultiver notre jardin* is the last word of "Candide," and Johnson's teaching, both here and elsewhere, may be summed up in the words "Work, and don't whine." It need not be considered here, nor, perhaps, is it quite plain, what speculative conclusions Voltaire meant to be drawn from his teaching. The peculiarity of Johnson is, that he is apparently indifferent to any such conclusion. A dogmatic assertion, that the world is on the whole a scene of misery, may be pressed into the service of different philosophies. Johnson asserted the opinion resolutely, both in writing and in conversation, but apparently never troubled himself with any inferences but such as have a directly practical tendency. He was no "speculatist"—a word which now strikes us as having an American twang, but which was familiar to the lexicographer. His only excursion to the borders of such regions was in the very forcible review of Soane Jenyns, who had made a jaunty attempt to explain the origin of evil by the help of a few of Pope's epigrams. Johnson's sledge-hammer smashes his flimsy platitudes to pieces with an energy too good for such a foe. For speculation, properly so called, there was no need. The review, like "Rasselas," is simply a vigorous protest against the popular attempt to make things pleasant by a feeble dilution of the most watery kind of popular teaching. He has no trouble in remarking that the evils of poverty are not alleviated by calling it "want of riches," and that there is a poverty which involves want of necessaries. The offered consolation, indeed, came rather awkwardly from the elegant country gentleman to the poor scholar who had just known by experience what it was to live upon fourpence-halfpenny a day. Johnson resolutely looks facts in the face, and calls ugly things by their right names. Men, he tells us over and over again, are wretched, and there is no use in denying it. This doctrine appears in his familiar talk, and even in the papers which he meant to be light reading. He begins the prologue to a comedy with the words—

> Pressed with the load of life, the weary mind
> Surveys the general toil of human kind.

In the "Life of Savage" he makes the common remark that the lives of many of the greatest teachers of mankind have been miserable. The explanation to which he inclines is that they have not been more miserable than their neighbours, but that their misery has been more conspicuous. His melancholy view of life may have been caused simply by his unfortunate constitution; for everybody sees in the disease of his own liver a disorder of the universe; but it was also intensified by the natural reaction of a powerful nature against the fluent optimism of the time, which expressed itself in Pope's aphorism, Whatever is, is right. The strongest men of the time revolted against that attempt to cure a deep-seated disease by a few fine speeches. The form taken by Johnson's revolt is characteristic. His nature was too tender and too manly to incline to Swift's misanthropy. Men might be wretched, but he would not therefore revile them as filthy Yahoos. He was too reverent and cared too little for abstract thought to share the scepticism of Voltaire. In this miserable world the one worthy object of ambition is to do one's duty, and the one consolation deserving the name is to be found in religion. That Johnson's religious opinions sometimes took the form of rather grotesque superstition may be true; and it is easy enough to ridicule some of its manifestations. He took the creed of his day without much examination of the evidence upon which its dogmas rested; but a writer must be thoughtless indeed who should be more inclined to laugh at his superficial oddities, than to admire the reverent spirit and the brave self-respect with which he struggled through a painful life. The protest of "Rasselas" against optimism is therefore widely different from the protest of Voltaire. The deep and genuine feeling of the Frenchman is concealed under smart assaults upon the dogmas of popular theology; the Englishman desires to impress upon us the futility of all human enjoyments, with a view to deepen the solemnity of our habitual tone of thought. It is true, indeed, that the evil is dwelt upon more forcibly than the remedy. The book is all the more impressive. We are almost appalled by the gloomy strength which sees so forcibly the misery of the world and rejects so unequivocally all the palliatives of sentiment and philosophy. The melancholy is intensified by the ponderous style, which suggests a man weary of a heavy burden. The air seems to be filled with what Johnson once called "inspissated gloom." "Rasselas," one may say, has a narrow escape of being a great book, though it is ill calculated for the hasty readers of to-day. Indeed, the defects are serious enough. The class of writing to which it belongs demands a certain dramatic picturesqueness to point the moral effectively. Not only the long-winded sentences, but the slow evolution of thought and the deliberation with which he works out his pictures of misery, makes the general effect dull beside such books as "Candide" or "Gulliver's Travels." A touch of epigrammatic exaggeration is very much needed; and yet anybody who has the courage to read it through will admit that Johnson is not an unworthy guide into those gloomy regions of imagination which we all visit sometimes, and which it is as well to visit in good company.

After his fashion, Johnson is a fair representative of Greatheart. His melancholy is distinguished from that of feebler men by the strength of the conviction that "it will do no good to whine." We know his view of the great prophet of the Revolutionary school. "Rousseau," he said, to Boswell's astonishment, "is a very bad man. I would sooner sign a sentence for his transportation than that of any felon who has gone from the Old Bailey these many years. Yes, I should like to have him work in the plantations." That is a fine specimen of the good Johnsonese prejudices of which we hear so much; and, of course, it is easy to infer that Johnson was an ignorant bigot, who had not in any degree taken the measure of the great moving forces of his time. Nothing, indeed, can be truer than that Johnson cared very little for the new gospel of the rights of man. His truly British contempt for all such fancies ("for anything I see," he once said, "foreigners are fools") is one of his strongest characteristics. Now, Rousseau and his like took a view of the world as it was quite as melancholy as Johnson's. They inferred that it ought to be turned upside down, assured that the millennium would begin as soon as a few revolutionary dogmas were accepted. All their remedies appeared to the excellent Doctor as so much of that cant of which it was a man's first duty to clear his mind. The evils of life were far too deeply seated to be caused or cured by kings or demagogues. One of the most popular commonplaces of the day was the mischief of luxury. That we were all on the highroad to ruin on account of our wealth, our corruption, and the growth of the national debt, was the text of any number of political agitators. The whole of this talk was, to his mind, so much whining and cant. Luxury did no harm, and the mass of the people, as indeed was in one sense obvious enough, had only too little of it. The pet "state of nature" of theorists was a silly figment. The genuine savage was little better than an animal; and a savage woman, whose contempt for civilised life had prompted her to escape to the forest, was simply a "speaking cat." The natural equality of mankind was mere moonshine. So far is it from being true, he says, that no two people can be together for half an hour without one acquiring an evident superiority over the other. Subordination is an essential element of human happiness. A Whig stinks in his nostrils because to his eye modern Whiggism is "a negation of all principles." As he said of Priestley's writings, it unsettles everything and settles nothing. "He is a cursed Whig, a *bottomless* Whig as they all are now," was his description apparently of Burke. Order, in fact, is a vital necessity; what particular form it may take matters comparatively little; and therefore all revolutionary dogmas were chimerical as an attack upon the inevitable conditions of life, and mischievous so far as productive of useless discontent. We need not ask what mixture of truth and falsehood there may be in these principles. Of course, a Radical, or even a respectable Whig, like Macaulay, who believed in the magical efficacy of the British Constitution, might shriek or laugh at such doctrine. Johnson's political pamphlets, besides the defects natural to a writer who was only a politician by accident, advocate the most retrograde doctrines. Nobody at the present day thinks that the Stamp Act was an admirable or justifiable measure; or would approve of telling the Americans that they ought to have been grateful for their long exemption instead of indignant at the imposition. "We do not put a calf into the plough; we wait till he is an ox"—was not a judicious taunt. He was utterly wrong; and, if everybody who is utterly wrong in a political controversy deserves unmixed contempt, there is no more to be said for him. We might indeed argue that Johnson was in some ways entitled to the sympathy of enlightened people. His hatred of the Americans was complicated by his hatred of slave-owners. He anticipated Lincoln in proposing the emancipation of the negroes as a military measure. His uniform hatred for the slave trade scandalised poor Boswell, who held that its abolition would be equivalent to "shutting the gates of mercy on mankind." His language about the blundering tyranny of the English rule in Ireland would satisfy Mr. Froude, though he would hardly have loved a Home Ruler. He denounces the frequency of capital punishment and the harshness of imprisonment for debt, and he invokes a compassionate treatment of the outcasts of our streets as warmly as the more sentimental Goldsmith. His conservatism may be at times obtuse, but it is never of the cynical variety. He hates cruelty and injustice as righteously as he hates anarchy. Indeed, Johnson's contempt for mouthing agitators of the Wilkes and Junius variety is one which may be shared by most thinkers who would not accept his principles. There is a vigorous passage in the "False Alarm" which is scarcely unjust to the patriots of the day. He describes the mode in which petitions are generally got up. They are sent from town to town, and the people flock to see what is to be sent to the King. "One man signs because he hates the Papists; another because he has vowed destruction to the turnpikes; one because it will vex the parson; another because he owes his landlord nothing; one because he is rich; another because he is poor; one to show that he is not afraid, another to show that he can write." The people, he thinks, are as well off as they are likely to be under any form of government; and grievances about general warrants or the rights of juries in libel cases are not really felt so long as they have enough to eat and drink and wear. The error, we may probably say, was less in the contempt for a very shallow agitation than in the want of perception that deeper causes of discontent were accumulating in the background. Wilkes in himself was a worthless demagogue; but Wilkes was the straw carried by the rising tide of revolutionary sentiment, to which Johnson was entirely blind. Yet whatever we may think of his political philosophy, the value of these solid sturdy prejudices is undeniable. To the fact that Johnson was the typical representative of a large class of Englishmen, we owe it that the Society of Rights did not develop into a Jacobin Club. The fine phrases on which Frenchmen became intoxicated never turned the heads of men impervious to abstract theories and incapable of dropping substances for shadows. There are evils in each temperament; but it is as well that some men should carry into politics that rooted contempt for whining which lay so deep in Johnson's nature. He scorned the sickliness of the Rousseau school as, in spite of his constitutional melancholy, he scorned valetudinarianism whether of the bodily or the spiritual order. He saw evil enough in the world to be heartily, at times too roughly, impatient of all fine ladies who made a luxury of grief or of demagogues who shrieked about theoretical grievances which did not sensibly affect the happiness of one man in a thousand. The lady would not have time to nurse her sorrows if she had been a washerwoman; the grievances with which the demagogues yelled themselves hoarse could hardly be distinguished amidst the sorrows of the vast majority condemned to keep starvation at bay by unceasing labour. His incapacity for speculation makes his pamphlets worthless besides Burke's philosophical discourses; but the treatment, if wrong and defective on the theoretical side, is never contemptible. Here, as elsewhere, he judges by his intuitive aversions. He rejects too hastily whatever seems insipid or ill-flavoured to his spiritual appetite. Like all the shrewd and sensible part of mankind, he condemns as mere moonshine what may be really the first faint dawn of a new daylight. But then his intuitions are noble, and his fundamental belief is the vital importance of order, of religion, and of morality, coupled with a profound conviction, surely not erroneous, that the chief sources of human suffering lie far deeper than any of the remedies proposed by constitution-mongers and fluent theorists. The literary version of these prejudices or principles is given most explicitly in the "Lives of the Poets"—the book which is now the most readable of Johnson's performances, and which most frequently recalls his conversational style. Indeed, it is a thoroughly admirable book, and but for one or two defects might enjoy a much more decided popularity. It is full of shrewd sense and righteous as well as keen estimates of men and things. The "Life of Savage," written in earlier times, is the best existing portrait of that large class of authors who, in Johnson's phrase, "hung loose upon society" in the days of the Georges. The Lives of Pope, Dryden, and others have scarcely been superseded, though much fuller information has since come to light; and they are all well worth reading. But the criticism, like the politics, is woefully out of date. Johnson's division between the shams and the realities deserves all respect in both cases, but in both cases he puts many things on the wrong side of the dividing line. His hearty contempt for sham pastorals and sham love-poetry will be probably shared by modern readers. "Who will hear of sheep and goats and myrtle bowers and purling rivulets through five acts? Such scenes please barbarians in the dawn of literature, and children in the dawn of life, but will be for the most part thrown away as men grow wise and nations grow learned." But elsewhere he blunders into terrible misapprehensions. Where he errs by simply repeating the accepted rules of the Pope school, he for once talks mere second-hand nonsense. But his independent judgments are interesting even when erroneous. His unlucky assault upon "Lycidas," already noticed, is generally dismissed with a pitying shrug of the shoulders. "Among the flocks and copses and flowers appear the heathen deities; Jove and Phœbus, Neptune and Æolus, with a long train of mythological imagery, such as a college easily supplies. Nothing can less display knowledge, or less exercise invention, than to tell how a shepherd has lost his companions, and must now feed his flocks alone; how one god asks another god what has become of Lycidas, and how neither god can tell. He who thus grieves can excite no sympathy; he who thus praises will confer no honour."

Of course every tyro in criticism has his answer ready; he can discourse about the æsthetic tendencies of the *Renaissance* period, and explain the necessity of placing one's self at a writer's point of view, and entering into the spirit of the time. He will add, perhaps, that "Lycidas" is a test of poetical feeling, and that he who does not appreciate its exquisite melody has no music in his soul. The same writer who will tell us all this, and doubtless with perfect truth, would probably have adopted Pope or Johnson's theory with equal confidence if he had lived in the last century. "Lycidas" repelled Johnson by incongruities which, from his point of view, were certainly offensive. Most modern readers, I will venture to suggest, feel the same annoyances, though they have not the courage to avow them freely. If poetry is to be judged exclusively by the simplicity and force with which it expresses sincere emotion, "Lycidas" would hardly convince us of Milton's profound sorrow for the death of King, and must be condemned accordingly. To the purely pictorial or musical effects of a poem Johnson was nearly blind; but that need not suggest a doubt as to the sincerity of his love for the poetry which came within the range of his own sympathies. Every critic is in effect criticising himself as well as his author; and I confess that to my mind an obviously sincere record of impressions, however one-sided they may be, is infinitely refreshing, as revealing at least the honesty of the writer. The ordinary run of criticism generally implies nothing but the extreme desire of the author to show that he is open to the very last new literary fashion. I should welcome a good assault upon Shakespeare which was not prompted by a love of singularity; and there are half-a-dozen popular idols —I have not the courage to name them—a genuine attack upon whom I could witness with entire equanimity, not to say some complacency. If Johnson's blunder in this case implied sheer stupidity, one can only say that honest stupidity is a much better thing than clever insincerity or fluent repetition of second-hand dogmas. But, in fact, this dislike of "Lycidas," and a good many instances of critical incapacity might be added, is merely a misapplication of a very sound principle. The hatred of cant and humbug and affectation of all vanity is a most salutary ingredient even in poetical criticism. Johnson, with his natural ignorance of that historical method, the exaltation of which threatens to become a part of our contemporary cant, made the pardonable blunder of supposing that what would have been gross affectation in Gray must have been affectation in Milton. His ear had been too much corrupted by the contemporary school to enable him to recognise beauties which would even have shone through some conscious affectation. He had the rare courage —for, even then, Milton was one of the tabooed poets—to say what he thought as forcibly as he could say it; and he has suffered the natural punishment of plain speaking. It must, of course, be admitted that a book embodying such principles is doomed to become more or less obsolete, like his political pamphlets. And yet, as significant of the writer's own character, as containing many passages of sound judgment, expressed in forcible language, it is still, if not a great book, really impressive within the limits of its capacity.

After this imperfect survey of Johnson's writings, it only remains to be noticed that all the most prominent peculiarities are the very same which give interest to his spoken utterances. The doctrine is the same, though the preacher's manner has changed. His melancholy is not so heavy-eyed and depressing in his talk, for we catch him at moments of excitement; but it is there, and sometimes breaks out emphatically and unexpectedly. The prospect of death often clouds his mind, and he bursts into tears when he thinks of his past sufferings. His hearty love of truth, and uncompromising hatred of cant in all its innumerable transmutations, prompt half his most characteristic sayings. His queer prejudices take a humorous form, and give a delightful zest to his conversation. His contempt for abstract speculation comes out when he vanquishes Berkeley, not with a grin, but by ''striking his foot with mighty force against a large stone.'' His arguments, indeed, never seem to have owed much to such logic as implies systematic and continuous thought. He scarcely waits till his pistol misses fire to knock you down with the butt-end. The merit of his best sayings is not that they compress an argument into a phrase, but that they are vivid expressions of an intuitive judgment. In other words, they are always humorous rather than witty. He holds his own belief with so vigorous a grasp that all argumentative devices for loosening it seem to be thrown away. As Boswell says, he is through your body in an instant without any preliminary parade; he gives a deadly lunge, but cares little for skill of fence. ''We know we are free and there's an end of it,'' is his characteristic summary of a perplexed bit of metaphysics; and he would evidently have no patience to wander through the labyrinths in which men like Jonathan Edwards delighted to perplex themselves. We should have been glad to see a fuller report of one of those conversations in which Burke ''wound into a subject like a serpent,'' and contrast his method with Johnson's downright hitting. Boswell had not the power, even if he had the will, to give an adequate account of such a ''wit combat.''

That such a mind should express itself most forcibly in speech is intelligible enough. Conversation was to him not merely a contest, but a means of escape from himself. ''I may be cracking my joke,'' he said to Boswell, ''and cursing the sun: Sun, how I hate thy beams?'' The phrase sounds exaggerated, but it was apparently his settled conviction that the only remedy for melancholy, except indeed the religious remedy, was in hard work or in the rapture of conversational strife. His little circle of friends called forth his humour as the House of Commons excited Chatham's eloquence; and both of them were inclined to mouth too much when deprived of the necessary stimulus. Chatham's set speeches were as pompous as Johnson's deliberate writing. Johnson and Chatham resemble the chemical bodies which acquire entirely new properties when raised beyond a certain degree of temperature. Indeed, we frequently meet touches of the conversational Johnson in his controversial writing. "Taxation no Tyranny'' is at moments almost as pithy as Swift, though the style is never so simple. The celebrated Letter to Chesterfield, and the letter in which he tells MacPherson that he will not be "deterred from detecting what he thinks a cheat by the menaces of a ruffian,'' are as good specimens of the smashing repartee as anything in Boswell's reports. Nor, indeed, does his pomposity sink to mere verbiage so often as might be supposed. It is by no means easy to translate his ponderous phrases into simple words without losing some of their meaning. The structure of the sentences is compact, though they are too elaborately balanced and stuffed with superfluous antitheses. The language might be simpler, but it is not a mere sham aggregation of words. His written style, however faulty in other respects, is neither slipshod nor ambiguous, and passes into his conversational style by imperceptible degrees. The radical identity is intelligible, though the superficial contrast is certainly curious. We may perhaps say that his century, unfavourable to him as a writer, gave just what he required for talking. If, as is sometimes said, the art of conversation is disappearing, it is because society has become too large and diffuse. The good talker, as indeed the good artist of every kind, depends upon the tacit co-operation of the social medium. The chorus, as Johnson has himself shown very well in one of the "Ramblers,'' is quite as essential as the main performer. Nobody talks well in London, because everybody has constantly to meet a fresh set of interlocutors, and is as much put out as a musician who has to be always learning a new instrument. A literary dictator has ceased to be a possibility, so far as direct personal influence is concerned. In the club, Johnson knew how every blow would tell, and in the rapid thrust and parry dropped the heavy style which muffled his utterances in print. He had to deal with concrete illustrations, instead of expanding into platitudinous generalities. The obsolete theories which impair the value of his criticism and his politics, become amusing in the form of pithy sayings, though they weary us when asserted in formal expositions. His greatest literary effort, the "Dictionary," has of necessity become antiquated in use, and, in spite of the intellectual vigour indicated, can hardly be commended for popular reading. And thus but for the inimitable Boswell, it must be admitted that Johnson would probably have sunk very deeply into oblivion. A few good sayings would have been preserved by Mrs. Thrale and others, or have been handed down by tradition, and doubtless assigned in process of time to Sidney Smith and other conversational celebrities. A few couplets from the "Vanity of Human Wishes" would not yet have been submerged, and curious readers would have recognised the power of "Rasselas," and been delighted with some shrewd touches in the "Lives of the Poets." But with all desire to magnify critical insight, it must be admitted that that man would have shown singular penetration, and been regarded as an eccentric commentator, who had divined the humour and the fervour of mind which lay hid in the remains of the huge lexicographer. And yet when we have once recognised his power, we can see it everywhere indicated in his writings, though by an unfortunate fatality the style or the substance was always so deeply affected by the faults of the time, that the product is never thoroughly sound. His tenacious conservatism caused him to cling to decaying materials for the want of anything better, and he has suffered the natural penalty. He was a great force half wasted, so far as literature was concerned, because the fashionable costume of the day hampered the free exercises of his powers, and because the only creeds to which he could attach himself were in the phase of decline and inanition. A century earlier or later he might have succeeded in expressing himself through books as well as through his talk; but it is not given to us to choose the time of our birth, and some very awkward consequences follow.

Wordsworth's Ethics

Under every poetry, it has been said, there lies a philosophy. Rather, it may almost be said, every poetry is a philosophy. The poet and the philosopher live in the same world and are interested in the same truths. What is the nature of man and the world in which he lives, and what, in consequence, should be our conduct? These are the great problems, the answers to which may take a religious, a poetical, a philosophical, or an artistic form. The difference is that the poet has intuitions, while the philosopher gives demonstrations; that the thought which in one mind is converted into emotion, is in the other resolved into logic; and that a symbolic representation of the idea is substituted for a direct expression. The normal relation is exhibited in the case of the anatomist and the sculptor. The artist intuitively recognises the most perfect form; the man of science analyses the structural relations by which it is produced. Though the two provinces are concentric, they are not coincident. The reasoner is interested in many details which have no immediate significance for the man of feeling; and the poetic insight, on the other hand, is capable of recognising subtle harmonies and discords of which our crude instruments of weighing and measuring are incapable of revealing the secret. But the connection is so close that the greatest works of either kind seem to have a double nature. A philosophy may, like Spinoza's, be apparelled in the most technical and abstruse panoply of logic, and yet the total impression may stimulate a religious sentiment as effectively as any poetic or theosophic mysticism. Or a great imaginative work, like Shakespeare's, may present us with the most vivid concrete symbols, and yet suggest, as forcibly as the formal demonstrations of a metaphysician, the idealist conviction that the visible and tangible

197

world is a dream-woven tissue covering infinite and inscrutable mysteries. In each case the highest intellectual faculty manifests itself in the vigour with which certain profound conceptions of the world and life have been grasped and assimilated. In each case that man is greatest who soars habitually to the highest regions and gazes most steadily upon the widest horizons of time and space. The logical consistency which frames all dogmas into a consistent whole, is but another aspect of the imaginative power which harmonises the strongest and subtlest emotions excited.

The task, indeed, of deducing the philosophy from the poetry, of inferring what a man thinks from what he feels, may at times perplex the acutest critic. Nor, if it were satisfactorily accomplished, could we infer that the best philosopher is also the best poet. Absolute incapacity for poetical expression may be combined with the highest philosophic power. All that can safely be said is that a man's thoughts, whether embodied in symbols or worked out in syllogisms, are more valuable in proportion as they indicate greater philosophical insight; and therefore that, *ceteris paribus,* that man is the greater poet whose imagination is most transfused with reason; who has the deepest truths to proclaim as well as the strongest feelings to utter.

Some theorists implicitly deny this principle by holding substantially that the poet's function is simply the utterance of a particular mood, and that, if he utters it forcibly and delicately, we have no more to ask. Even so, we should not admit that the thoughts suggested to a wise man by a prospect of death and eternity are of just equal value, if equally well expressed, with the thoughts suggested to a fool by the contemplation of a good dinner. But, in practice, the utterance of emotions can hardly be dissociated from the assertion of principles. Psychologists have shown, ever since the days of Berkeley, that when a man describes (as he thinks) a mere sensation, and says, for example, "I see a house," he is really recording the result of a complex logical process. A great painter and the dullest observer may have the same impressions of coloured blotches upon their retina. The great man infers the true nature of the objects which produce his sensations, and can therefore represent the objects accurately. The other sees only with his eyes, and can therefore represent nothing. There is thus a logic implied even in the simplest observation, and one which can be tested by mathematical rules as distinctly as a proposition in geometry.

When we have to find a language for our emotions instead of our sensations, we generally express the result of an incomparably more complex set of intellectual operations. The poet, in uttering his joy or sadness, often implies, in the very form of his language, a whole philosophy of life or of the universe. The explanation is given at the end of Shakespeare's familiar passage about the poet's eye:—

> Such tricks hath strong imagination,
> That, if it would but apprehend some joy,
> It comprehends some bringer of that joy;
> Or in the night, imagining some fear,
> How easy is a bush supposed a bear!

The *ap*prehension of the passion, as Shakespeare logically says, is a *com*prehension of its cause. The imagination reasons. The bare faculty of sight involves thought and feeling. The symbol which the fancy spontaneously constructs, implies a whole world of truth or error, of superstitious beliefs or sound philosophy. The poetry holds a number of intellectual dogmas in solution; and it is precisely due to these general dogmas, which are true and important for us as well as for the poet, that his power over our sympathies is due. If his philosophy has no power in it, his emotions lose their hold upon our minds, or interest us only as antiquarians and lovers of the picturesque. But in the briefest poems of a true thinker we read the essence of the life-long reflections of a passionate and intellectual nature. Fears and hopes common to all thoughtful men have been coined into a single phrase. Even in cases where no definite conviction is expressed or even implied, and the poem is simply, like music, an indefinite utterance of a certain state of the emotions, we may discover an intellectual element. The rational and the emotional nature have such intricate relations that one cannot exist in great richness and force without justifying an inference as to the other. From a single phrase, as from a single gesture, we can often go far to divining the character of a man's thoughts and feelings. We know more of a man from five minutes' talk than from pages of what is called "psychological analysis." From a passing expression on the face, itself the result of variations so minute as to defy all analysis, we instinctively frame judgments as to a man's temperament and habitual modes of thought and conduct. Indeed, such judgments, if erroneous, determine us only too exclusively in the most important relations of life.

Now the highest poetry is that which expresses the richest, most powerful, and most susceptible emotional nature, and the most versatile, penetrative, and subtle intellect. Such qualities may be stamped upon trifling work. The great artist can express his power within the limits of a coin or a gem. The great poet will reveal his character through a sonnet or a song. Shakespeare, or Milton, or Burns, or Wordsworth can express his whole mode of feeling within a few lines. An ill-balanced nature reveals itself by a discord, as an illogical mind by a fallacy. A man need not compose an epic on a system of philosophy to write himself down an ass. And, inversely, a great mind and a noble nature may show itself by impalpable but recognisable signs within the "sonnet's scanty plot of ground." Once more, the highest poetry must be that which expresses not only the richest but the healthiest nature. Disease means an absence or a want of balance of certain faculties, and therefore leads to false reasoning or emotional discord. The defect of character betrays itself in some erroneous mode of thought or baseness of sentiment. And since morality means obedience to those rules which are most essential to the spiritual health, vicious feeling indicates some morbid tendency, and is so far destructive of the poetical faculty. An immoral sentiment is the sign either of a false judgment of the world and of human nature, or of a defect in the emotional nature which shows itself by a discord or an indecorum, and leads to a cynicism or indecency which offends the reason through the taste. What is called immorality does not indeed always imply such defects. Sound moral intuitions may be opposed to the narrow code prevalent at the time; or a protest against puritanical or ascetic perversions of the standard may hurry the poet into attacks upon true principles. And, again, the keen sensibility which makes a man a poet, undoubtedly exposes him to certain types of disease. He is more likely than his thick-skinned neighbour to be vexed by evil, and to be drawn into distorted views of life by an excess of sympathy or indignation. Injudicious admirers prize the disease instead of the strength from which it springs; and value the cynicism or the despair instead of the contempt for heartless commonplace or the desire for better things with which it was unfortunately connected. A strong moral sentiment has a great value, even when forced into an unnatural alliance. Nay, even when it is, so to speak, inverted, it often receives a kind of paradoxical value from its efficacy against some opposite form of error. It is only a complete absence of the moral faculty which is irredeemably bad. The poet in whom it does not exist is condemned to the lower sphere, and can only deal with the deepest feelings on penalty of shocking us by indecency or profanity. A man who can revel in "Epicurus' stye" without even the indirect homage to purity of remorse and bitterness, can do nothing but gratify our lowest passions. They, perhaps, have their place, and the man who is content with such utterances may not be utterly worthless. But to place him on a level with his betters is to confound every sound principle of criticism.

It follows that a kind of collateral test of poetical excellence may be found by extracting the philosophy from the poetry. The test is, of course, inadequate. A good philosopher may be an execrable poet. Even stupidity is happily not inconsistent with sound doctrine, though inconsistent with a firm grasp of ultimate principles. But the vigour with which a man grasps and assimilates a deep moral doctrine is a test of the degree in which he possesses one essential condition of the higher poetical excellence. A continuous illustration of this principle is given in the poetry of Wordsworth, who, indeed, has expounded his ethical and philosophical views so explicitly, one would rather not say so ostentatiously, that great part of the work is done to our hands. Nowhere is it easier to observe the mode in which poetry and philosophy spring from the same root and owe their excellence to the same intellectual powers. So much has been said by the ablest critics of the purely poetical side of Wordsworth's genius, that I may willingly renounce the difficult task of adding or repeating. I gladly take for granted—what is generally acknowledged—that Wordsworth in his best moods reaches a greater height than any other modern Englishman. The word "inspiration" is less forced when applied to his loftiest poetry than when used of any of his contemporaries. With defects too obvious to be mentioned, he can yet pierce furthest behind the veil; and embody most efficiently the thoughts and emotions which come to us in our most solemn and reflective moods. Other poetry becomes trifling when we are making our inevitable passages through the Valley of the Shadow of Death. Wordsworth's alone retains its power. We love him the more as we grow older and become more deeply impressed with the sadness and seriousness of life; we are apt to grow weary of his rivals when we have finally quitted the regions of youthful enchantment. And I take the explanation to be that he is not merely a melodious writer, or a powerful utterer of deep emotion, but a true philosopher. His poetry wears well because it has solid substance. He is a prophet and a moralist as well as a mere singer. His ethical system, in particular, is as distinctive and capable of systematic exposition as that of Butler. By endeavouring to state it in plain prose we shall see how the poetical power implies a sensitiveness to ideas which, when extracted from the symbolical embodiment, fall spontaneously into a scientific system of thought.

There are two opposite types to which all moral systems tend. They correspond to the two great intellectual families to which every man belongs by right of birth. One class of minds is distinguished by its firm grasp of facts, by its reluctance to drop solid substance for the loveliest shadows, and by its preference of concrete truths to the most symmetrical of theories. In ethical questions the tendency of such minds is to consider man as a being impelled by strong but unreasonable passions towards tangible objects. He is a loving, hating, thirsting, hungering—anything but a reasoning—being. As Swift—a typical example of this intellectual temperament—declared, man is not an *animal rationale*, but at most *capax rationis*. At bottom, he is a machine worked by blind instincts. Their tendency cannot be deduced by *à priori* reasoning, though reason may calculate the consequences of indulging them. The passions are equally good, so far as equally pleasurable. Virtue means that course of conduct which secures the maximum of pleasure. Fine theories about abstract rights and correspondence to eternal truths are so many words. They provide decent masks for our passions; they do not really govern them, or alter their nature, but they cover the ugly brutal selfishness of mankind, and soften the shock of conflicting interests. Such a view has something in it congenial to the English love of reality and contempt for shams. It may be represented by Swift or Mandeville in the last century; in poetry it corresponds to the theory attributed by some critics to Shakespeare; in a tranquil and reasoning mind it leads to the utilitarianism of Bentham; in a proud, passionate, and imaginative mind it manifests itself in such a poem as "Don Juan." Its strength is in its grasp of fact; its weakness, in its tendency to cynicism. Opposed to this is the school which starts from abstract reason. It prefers to dwell in the ideal world, where principles may be contemplated apart from the accidents which render them obscure to vulgar minds. It seeks to deduce the moral code from eternal truths without seeking for a groundwork in the facts of experience. If facts refuse to conform to theories, it proposes that facts should be summarily abolished. Though the actual human being is, unfortunately, not always reasonable, it holds that pure reason must be in the long run the dominant force, and that it reveals the laws to which mankind will ultimately conform. The revolutionary doctrine of the "rights of man," expressed one form of this doctrine, and showed in the most striking way a strength and weakness, which are the converse of those exhibited by its antagonist. It was strong as appealing to the loftier motives of justice and sympathy; and weak as defying the appeal to experience. The most striking example in English literature is in Godwin's "Political Justice." The existing social order is to be calmly abolished because founded upon blind prejudice; the constituent atoms called men are to be rearranged in an ideal order as in a mathematical diagram. Shelley gives the translation of this theory into poetry. The "Revolt of Islam" or the "Prometheus Unbound," with all its unearthly beauty, wearies the imagination which tries to soar into the thin air of Shelley's dreamworld; just as the intellect, trying to apply the abstract formulae of political metaphysics to any concrete problem, feels as though it were under an exhausted receiver. In both cases we seem to have got entirely out of the region of real human passions and senses into a world, beautiful perhaps, but certainly impalpable.

The great aim of moral philosophy is to unite the disjoined element, to end the divorce between reason and experience, and to escape from the alternative of dealing with empty but symmetrical formulae or concrete and chaotic facts. No hint can be given here as to the direction in which a final solution must be sought. Whatever the true method, Wordsworth's mode of conceiving the problem shows how powerfully he grasped the questions at issue. If his doctrines are not systematically expounded, they all have a direct bearing upon the real difficulties involved. They are stated so forcibly in his noblest poems that we might almost express a complete theory in his own language. But, without seeking to make a collection of aphorisms from his poetry, we may indicate the cardinal points of his teaching.[2]

The most characteristic of all his doctrines is that which is embodied in the great ode upon the "Intimations of Immortality." The doctrine itself—the theory that the instincts of childhood testify to the pre-existence of the soul—sounds fanciful enough; and Wordsworth took rather unnecessary pains to say that he did not hold it as a serious dogma. We certainly need not ask whether it is reasonable or orthodox to believe that "our birth is but a sleep and a forgetting." The fact symbolised by the poetic fancy—the glory and freshness of our childish instincts—is equally noteworthy, whatever its cause. Some modern reasoners would explain its significance by reference to a very different kind of pre-existence. The instincts, they would say, are valuable, because they register the accumulated and inherited experience of past generations. Wordsworth's delight in wild scenery is regarded by them as due to the "combination of states that were organised in the race during barbarous times, when its pleasurable activities were amongst the mountains, woods, and waters." In childhood we are most completely under the dominion of these inherited impulses. The correlation between the organism and its medium is then most perfect, and hence the peculiar theme of childish communion with nature.

Wordsworth would have repudiated the doctrine with disgust. He would have been "on the side of the angels." No memories of the savage and the monkey, but the reminiscences of the once-glorious soul could explain his emotions. Yet there is this much in common between him and the men of science whom he denounced with too little discrimination. The fact of the value of these primitive instincts is admitted, and admitted for the same purpose. Man, it is agreed, is furnished with sentiments which cannot be explained as the result of his individual experience. They may be intelligible, according to the evolutionist, when regarded as embodying the past experience of the race; or, according to Wordsworth, as implying a certain mysterious faculty imprinted upon the soul. The scientific doctrine, whether sound or not, has modified the whole mode of approaching ethical problems; and Wordsworth, though with a very different purpose, gives a new emphasis to the facts, upon a recognition of which, according to some theorists, must be based the reconciliation of the great rival schools—the intuitionists and the utilitarians. The parallel may at first sight seem fanciful; and it would be too daring to claim for Wordsworth the discovery of the most remarkable phenomenon which modern psychology must take into account. There is, however, a real connection between the two doctrines, though in one sense they are almost antithetical. Meanwhile we observe that the same sensibility which gives poetical power is necessary to the scientific observer. The magic of the ode, and of many other passages in Wordsworth's poetry, is due to his recognition of this mysterious efficacy of our childish instincts. He gives emphasis to one of the most striking facts of our spiritual experience, which had passed with little notice from professed psychologists. He feels what they afterwards tried to explain.

The full meaning of the doctrine comes out as we study Wordsworth more thoroughly. Other poets—almost all poets —have dwelt fondly upon recollections of childhood. But not feeling so strongly, and therefore not expressing so forcibly, the peculiar character of the emotion, they have not derived the same lessons from their observation. The Epicurean poets are content with Herrick's simple moral—

> Gather ye rosebuds while ye may—

and with his simple explanation—

> That age is best which is the first,
> When youth and blood are warmer.

Others more thoughtful look back upon the early days with the passionate regret of Byron's verses:

> There's not a joy the world can give like that it takes away,
> When the glow of early thought declines in feeling's dull
> decay;
> 'Tis not on youth's smooth cheek the blush alone which fades
> so fast,
> But the tender bloom of heart is gone, ere youth itself be
> past.

Such painful longings for the "tender grace of a day that is dead" are spontaneous and natural. Every healthy mind feels the pang in proportion to the strength of its affections. But it is also true that the regret resembles too often the maudlin meditation of a fast young man over his morning's soda-water. It implies, that is, a non-recognition of the higher uses to which the fading memories may still be put. A different tone breathes in Shelley's pathetic but rather hectic moralisings, and his lamentations over the departure of the "spirit of delight." Nowhere has it found more exquisite expression than in the marvellous "Ode to the West Wind." These magical verses—his best, as it seems to me—describe the reflection of the poet's own mind in the strange stir and commotion of a dying winter's day. They represent, we may say, the fitful melancholy which oppresses a noble spirit when it has recognised the difficulty of forcing facts into conformity with the ideal. He still clings to the hope that his "dead thoughts" may be driven over the universe,

Like withered leaves to quicken a new birth.

But he bows before the inexorable fate which has cramped his energies:

A heavy weight of years has chained and bowed
One too like thee; tameless and swift and proud.

Neither Byron nor Shelley can see any satisfactory solution, and therefore neither can reach a perfect harmony of feeling. The world seems to them to be out of joint, because they have not known how to accept the inevitable, nor to conform to the discipline of facts. And, therefore, however intense the emotion, and however exquisite its expression, we are left in a state of intellectual and emotional discontent. Such utterances may suit us in youth, when we can afford to play with sorrow. As we grow older we feel a certain emptiness in them. A true man ought not to sit down and weep with an exhausted debauchee. He cannot afford to confess himself beaten with the idealist who has discovered that Rome was not built in a day, nor revolutions made with rose-water. He has to work as long as he has strength; to work in spite of, even by strength of, sorrow, disappointment, wounded vanity, and blunted sensibilities; and therefore he must search for some profounder solution for the dark riddle of life.

This solution it is Wordsworth's chief aim to supply. In the familiar verses which stand as a motto to his poems—

The child is father to the man,
And I could wish my days to be
Bound each to each by natural piety—

the great problem of life, that is, as he conceives it, is to secure a continuity between the period at which we are guided by half-conscious instincts, and that in which a man is able to supply the place of these primitive impulses by reasoned convictions. This is the thought which comes over and over again in his deepest poems, and round which all his teaching centred. It supplies the great moral, for example, of the "Leech-gatherer:"

> My whole life I have lived in pleasant thought,
>   As if life's business were a summer mood:
> As if all needful things would come unsought
>   To genial faith still rich in genial good.

When his faith is tried by harsh experience, the leech-gatherer comes,

> Like a man from some far region sent
> To give me human strength by apt admonishment;

for he shows how the "genial faith" may be converted into permanent strength by resolution and independence. The verses most commonly quoted, such as—

> We poets in our youth begin in gladness,
> But thereof come in the end despondency and sadness,

give the ordinary view of the sickly school. Wordsworth's aim is to supply an answer worthy not only of a poet, but a man. The same sentiment again is expressed in the grand "Ode to Duty," where the

> Stern daughter of the voice of God

is invoked to supply that "genial sense of youth" which has hitherto been a sufficient guidance; or in the majestic morality of the "Happy Warrior;" or in the noble verses on "Tintern Abbey;" or, finally, in the great ode which gives most completely the whole theory of that process by which our early intuitions are to be transformed into settled principles of feeling and action.

Wordsworth's philosophical theory, in short, depends upon the asserted identity between our childish instincts and our enlightened reason. The doctrine of a state of pre-existence as it appears in other writers—as, for example, in the Cambridge Platonists[3]—was connected with an obsolete metaphysical system, and the doctrine—exploded in its old form—of innate ideas. Wordsworth does not attribute any such preternatural character to the "blank misgivings" and "shadowy recollections" of which he speaks. They are invaluable data of our spiritual experience; but they do not entitle us to lay down dogmatic propositions independently of experience. They are spontaneous products of a nature in harmony with the universe in which it is placed, and inestimable as a clear indication that such a harmony exists. To interpret and regulate them belongs to the reasoning faculty and the higher imagination of later years. If he does not quite distinguish between the province of reason and emotion—the most difficult of philosophical problems—he keeps clear of the cruder mysticism, because he does not seek to elicit any definite formulae from those admittedly vague forebodings which lie on the borderland between the two sides of our nature. With his invariable sanity of mind, he more than once notices the difficulty of distinguishing between that which nature teaches us and the interpretations which we impose upon nature.[4] He carefully refrains from pressing the inference too far.

The teaching, indeed, assumes that view of the universe which is implied in his pantheistic language. The Divinity really reveals Himself in the lonely mountains and the starry heavens. By contemplating them we are able to rise into that "blessed mood" in which for a time the burden of the mystery is rolled off our souls, and we can "see into the life of things." And here we must admit that Wordsworth is not entirely free from the weakness which generally besets thinkers of this tendency. Like Shaftesbury in the previous century, who speaks of the universal harmony as emphatically though not as poetically as Wordsworth, he is tempted to adopt a too facile optimism. He seems at times to have overlooked that dark side of nature which is recognised in theological doctrines of corruption, or in the scientific theories about the fierce struggle for existence. Can we in fact say that these early instincts prove more than the happy constitution of the individual who feels them? Is there not a teaching of nature very apt to suggest horror and despair rather than a complacent brooding over soothing thoughts? Do not the mountains which Wordsworth loved so well, speak of decay and catastrophe in every line of their slopes? Do they not suggest the helplessness and narrow limitations of man, as forcibly as his possible exaltation? The awe which they strike into our souls has its terrible as well as its amiable side; and in moods of depression the darker aspect becomes more conspicuous than the brighter. Nay, if we admit that we have instincts which are the very substance of all that afterwards becomes ennobling, have we not also instincts which suggest a close alliance with the brutes? If the child amidst his newborn blisses suggests a heavenly origin, does he not also show sensual and cruel instincts which imply at least an admixture of baser elements? If man is responsive to all natural influences, how is he to distinguish between the good and the bad, and, in short, to frame a conscience out of the vague instincts which contain the germs of all the possible developments of the future?

To say that Wordsworth has not given a complete answer to such difficulties, is to say that he has not explained the origin of evil. It may be admitted, however, that he does to a certain extent show a narrowness of conception. The voice of nature, as he says, resembles an echo; but we "unthinking creatures" listen to "voices of two different natures." We do not always distinguish between the echo of our lower passions and the "echoes from beyond the grave." Wordsworth sometimes fails to recognise the ambiguity of the oracle to which he appeals. The "blessed mood" in which we get rid of the burden of the world, is too easily confused with the mood in which we simply refuse to attend to it. He finds lonely meditation so inspiring that he is too indifferent to the troubles of less self-sufficing or clear-sighted human beings. The ambiguity makes itself felt in the sphere of morality. The ethical doctrine that virtue consists in conformity to nature becomes ambiguous with him, as with all its advocates, when we ask for a precise definition of nature. How are we to know which natural forces make for us and which fight against us?

The doctrine of the love of nature, generally regarded as Wordsworth's great lesson to mankind, means, as interpreted by himself and others, a love of the wilder and grander

objects of natural scenery; a passion for the "sounding cata-
ract," the rock, the mountain, and the forest; a preference,
therefore, of the country to the town, and of the simpler to
the more complex forms of social life. But what is the true
value of this sentiment? The unfortunate Solitary in the
"Excursion" is beset by three Wordsworths; for the Wan-
derer and the Pastor are little more (as Wordsworth indeed
intimates) than reflections of himself, seen in different mirrors. The Solitary represents the anti-social lessons to be
derived from communion with nature. He has become a
misanthrope, and has learnt from "Candide" the lesson that
we clearly do not live in the best of all possible worlds.
Instead of learning the true lesson from nature by penetrating
its deeper meanings, he manages to feed

> Pity and scorn and melancholy pride

by accidental and fanciful analogies, and sees in rock pyra-
mids or obelisks a rude mockery of human toils. To confute
this sentiment, to upset "Candide,"

> This dull product of a scoffer's pen,

is the purpose of the lofty poetry and versified prose of the
long dialogues which ensue. That Wordsworth should call
Voltaire dull is a curious example of the proverbial blindness
of controversialists; but the moral may be equally good. It is
given most pithily in the lines—

> We live by admiration, hope, and love;
> And even as these are well and wisely fused,
> The dignity of being we ascend.

"But what is Error?" continues the preacher; and the
Solitary replies by saying, "somewhat haughtily," that love,
admiration, and hope are "mad fancy's favourite vassals."
The distinction between fancy and imagination is, in brief,
that fancy deals with the superficial resemblances, and imagination with the deeper truths which underlie them. The
purpose, then, of the "Excursion," and of Wordsworth's
poetry in general, is to show how the higher faculty reveals a
harmony which we overlook when, with the Solitary, we

> Skim along the surfaces of things.

211

The rightly prepared mind can recognise the divine harmony which underlies all apparent disorder. The universe is to its perceptions like the shell whose murmur in a child's ear seems to express a mysterious union with the sea. But the mind must be rightly prepared. Everything depends upon the point of view. One man, as he says in an elaborate figure, looking upon a series of ridges in spring from their northern side, sees a waste of snow, and from the south a continuous expanse of green. That view, we must take it, is the right one which is illuminated by the "ray divine." But we must train our eyes to recognise its splendour; and the final answer to the Solitary is therefore embodied in a series of narratives, showing by example how our spiritual vision may be purified or obscured. Our philosophy must be finally based, not upon abstract speculation and metaphysical arguments, but on the diffused consciousness of the healthy mind. As Butler sees the universe by the light of conscience, Wordsworth sees it through the wider emotions of awe, reverence, and love, produced in a sound nature.

The pantheistic conception, in short, leads to an unsatisfactory optimism in the general view of nature, and to an equal tolerance of all passions as equally "natural." To escape from this difficulty we must establish some more discriminative mode of interpreting nature. Man is the instrument played upon by all impulses, good or bad. The music which results may be harmonious or discordant. When the instrument is in tune, the music will be perfect; but when is it in tune, and how are we to know that it is in tune? That problem once solved we can tell which are the authentic utterances and which are the accidental discords. And by solving it, or by saying what is the right constitution of human beings, we shall discover which is the true philosophy of the universe, and what are the dictates of a sound moral sense. Wordsworth implicitly answers the question by explaining, in his favourite phrase, how we are to build up our moral being.

The voice of nature speaks at first in vague emotions, scarcely distinguishable from mere animal buoyancy. The boy,

212

hooting in mimicry of the owls, receives in his heart the voice of mountain torrents and the solemn imagery of rocks, and woods, and stars. The sportive girl is unconsciously moulded into stateliness and grace by the floating clouds, the bending willow, and even by silent sympathy with the motions of the storm. Nobody has ever shown, with such exquisite power as Wordsworth, how much of the charm of natural objects in later life is due to early associations, thus formed in a mind not yet capable of contemplating its own processes. As old Matthew says in the lines which, however familiar, can never be read without emotion—

> My eyes are dim with childish tears,
>   My heart is idly stirred;
> For the same sound is in my ears
>   Which in those days I heard.

And the strangely beautiful address to the cuckoo might be made into a text for a prolonged commentary by an æsthetic philosopher upon the power of early association. It curiously illustrates, for example, the reason of Wordsworth's delight in recalling sounds. The croak of the distant raven, the bleat of the mountain lamb, the splash of the leaping fish in the lonely tarn, are specially delightful to him, because the hearing is the most spiritual of our senses; and these sounds, like the cuckoo's cry, seem to convert the earth into an "unsubstantial fairy place." The phrase "association" indeed implies a certain arbitrariness in the images suggested, which is not quite in accordance with Wordsworth's feeling. Though the echo depends partly upon the hearer, the mountain voices are specially adapted for certain moods. They have, we may say, a spontaneous affinity for the nobler affections. If some early passage in our childhood is associated with a particular spot, a house or a street will bring back the petty and accidental details: a mountain or a lake will revive the deeper and more permanent elements of feeling. If you have made love in a palace, according to Mr. Disraeli's prescription, the sight of it will recall the splendour of the object's dress or jewelry; if, as Wordsworth would prefer, with a

213

background of mountains, it will appear in later days as if they had absorbed, and were always ready again to radiate forth, the tender and hallowing influences which then for the first time entered your life. The elementary and deepest passions are most easily associated with the sublime and beautiful in nature.

> The primal duties shine aloft like stars;
> The charities that soothe, and heal, and bless,
> Are scattered at the feet of man like flowers.

And therefore if you have been happy enough to take delight in these natural and universal objects in the early days, when the most permanent associations are formed, the sight of them in later days will bring back by preordained and divine symbolism whatever was most ennobling in your early feelings. The vulgarising associations will drop off of themselves, and what was pure and lofty will remain.

From this natural law follows another of Wordsworth's favourite precepts. The mountains are not with him a symbol of anti-social feelings. On the contrary, they are in their proper place as the background of the simple domestic affections. He loves his native hills, not in the Byronic fashion, as a savage wilderness, but as the appropriate framework in which a healthy social order can permanently maintain itself. That, for example, is, as he tells us, the thought which inspired the "Brothers," a poem which excels all modern idylls in weight of meaning and depth of feeling, by virtue of the idea thus embodied. The retired valley of Ennerdale, with its grand background of hills, precipitous enough to be fairly called mountains, forces the two lads into closer affection. Shut in by these "enormous barriers," and undistracted by the ebb and flow of the outside world, the mutual love becomes concentrated. A tie like that of family blood is involuntarily imposed upon the little community of dalesmen. The image of sheep-tracks and shepherds clad in country grey is stamped upon the elder brother's mind, and comes back to him in tropical calms; he hears the tones of his waterfalls in the piping shrouds; and when he returns, recognises every fresh scar made by winter storms on the mountain sides, and knows by sight every unmarked grave in the little churchyard. The fraternal affection sanctifies the scenery, and the sight of the scenery brings back the affection with over-powering force upon his return. This is everywhere the sentiment inspired in Wordsworth by his beloved hills. It is not so much the love of nature pure and simple, as of nature seen through the deepest human feelings. The light glimmering in a lonely cottage, the one rude house in the deep valley, with its "small lot of life-supporting fields and guardian rocks," are necessary to point the moral and to draw to a definite focus the various forces of sentiment. The two veins of feeling are inseparably blended. The peasant noble, in the "Song at the Feast of Brougham Castle," learns equally from men and nature:—

> Love had he found in huts where poor men lie;
>   His daily teachers had been woods and hills,
> The silence that is in the starry skies,
>   The sleep that is among the lonely hills.

Without the love, the silence and the sleep would have had no spiritual meaning. They are valuable as giving intensity and solemnity to the positive emotion.

The same remark is to be made upon Wordsworth's favourite teaching of the advantages of the contemplative life. He is fond of enforcing the doctrine of the familiar lines, that we can feed our minds "in a wise passiveness," and that

> One impulse from the vernal wood
>   Can teach you more of man,
> Of moral evil and of good,
>   Than all the sages can.

And, according to some commentators, this would seem to express the doctrine that the ultimate end of life is the cultivation of tender emotions without reference to action. The doctrine, thus absolutely stated, would be immoral and illogical. To recommend contemplation in preference to action is like preferring sleeping to waking; or saying, as a full expression of the truth, that silence is golden and speech silvern. Like that familiar phrase, Wordsworth's teaching is not to be interpreted literally. The essence of such maxims is to be one-sided. They are paradoxical in order to be emphatic. To have seasons of contemplation, of withdrawal from the world and from books, of calm surrendering of ourselves to the influences of nature, is a practice commended in one form or other by all moral teachers. It is a sanitary rule, resting upon obvious principles. The mind which is always occupied in a multiplicity of small observations, or the regulation of practical details, loses the power of seeing general principles and of associating all objects with the central emotions of "admiration, hope, and love." The philosophic mind is that which habitually sees the general in the particular, and finds food for the deepest thought in the simplest objects. It requires, therefore, periods of repose, in which the fragmentary and complex atoms of distracted feeling which make up the incessant whirl of daily life may have time to crystallise round the central thoughts. But it must feed in order to assimilate; and each process implies the other as its correlative. A constant interest, therefore, in the joys and sorrows of our neighbours is as essential as quiet, self-centred rumination. It is when the eye "has kept watch o'er man's mortality," and by virtue of the tender sympathies of "the human heart by which we live," that to us

> The meanest flower which blows can give
> Thoughts that do often lie too deep for tears.

The solitude which implies severance from natural sympathies and affections is poisonous. The happiness of the heart which lives alone,

> Housed in a dream, an outcast from the kind,
> .   .   .   .
> Is to be pitied, for 'tis surely blind.

Wordsworth's meditations upon flowers or animal life are impressive because they have been touched by this constant sympathy. The sermon is always in his mind, and therefore every stone may serve for a text. His contemplation enables him to see the pathetic side of the small pains and pleasures which we are generally in too great a hurry to notice. There are times, of course, when this moralising tendency leads him

216

to the regions of the namby-pamby or sheer prosaic plati-
tude. On the other hand, no one approaches him in the
power of touching some rich chord of feeling by help of the
pettiest incident. The old man going to the fox-hunt with a
tear on his cheek, and saying to himself,

> The key I must take, for my Helen is dead;

or the mother carrying home her dead sailor's bird; the
village schoolmaster, in whom a rift in the clouds revives the
memory of his little daughter; the old huntsman unable to
cut through the stump of rotten wood—touch our hearts at
once and for ever. The secret is given in the rather prosaic
apology for not relating a tale about poor Simon Lee:

> O reader! had you in your mind
>   Such stores as silent thought can bring,
> O gentle reader! you would find
>   A tale in everything.

The value of silent thought is so to cultivate the primitive
emotions that they may flow spontaneously upon every common incident, and that every familiar object becomes symbolic of them. It is a familiar remark that a philosopher or
man of science who has devoted himself to meditation upon
some principle or law of nature, is always finding new illustrations in the most unexpected quarters. He cannot take up
a novel or walk across the street without hitting upon appropriate instances. Wordsworth would apply the principle to
the building up of our "moral being." Admiration, hope,
and love should be so constantly in our thoughts, that innumerable sights and sounds which are meaningless to the
world should become to us a language incessantly suggestive
of the deepest topics of thought.

This explains his dislike to science, as he understood the
word, and his denunciations of the "world." The man of
science is one who cuts up nature into fragments, and not
only neglects their possible significance for our higher feelings, but refrains on principle from taking it into account.
The primrose suggests to him some new device in classification, and he would be worried by the suggestion of any

spiritual significance as an annoying distraction. Viewing all objects "in disconnection, dead and spiritless," we are thus really waging

> An impious warfare with the very life
> Of our own souls.

We are putting the letter in place of the spirit, and dealing with nature as a mere grammarian deals with a poem. When we have learnt to associate every object with some lesson

> Of human suffering or of human joy;

when we have thus obtained the "glorious habit,"

> By which sense is made
> Subservient still to moral purposes,
> Auxiliar to divine;

the "dull eye" of science will light up; for, in observing natural processes, it will carry with it an incessant reference to the spiritual processes to which they are allied. Science, in short, requires to be brought into intimate connection with morality and religion. If we are forced for our immediate purpose to pursue truth for itself, regardless of consequences, we must remember all the more carefully that truth is a whole, and that fragmentary bits of knowledge become valuable as they are incorporated into a general system. The tendency of modern times to specialism brings with it a characteristic danger. It requires to be supplemented by a correlative process of integration. We must study details to increase our knowledge; we must accustom ourselves to look at the detail in the light of the general principles in order to make it fruitful.

The influence of that world which "is too much with us late and soon" is of the same kind. The man of science loves barren facts for their own sake. The man of the world becomes devoted to some petty pursuit without reference to ultimate ends. He becomes a slave to money, or power, or praise, without caring for their effect upon his moral character. As social organisation becomes more complete, the social unit becomes a mere fragment instead of being a complete whole in himself. Man becomes

The senseless member of a vast machine,
Serving as doth a spindle or a wheel.

The division of labour, celebrated with such enthusiasm by Adam Smith,[5] tends to crush all real life out of its victims. The soul of the political economist may rejoice when he sees a human being devoting his whole faculties to the performance of one subsidiary operation in the manufacture of a pin. The poet and the moralist must notice with anxiety the contrast between the old-fashioned peasant who, if he discharged each particular function clumsily, discharged at least many functions, and found exercise for all the intellectual and moral faculties of his nature, and the modern artisan doomed to the incessant repetition of one petty set of muscular expansions and contractions, and whose soul, if he has one, is therefore rather an incumbrance than otherwise. This is the evil which is constantly before Wordsworth's eyes, as it has certainly not become less prominent since his time. The danger of crushing the individual is a serious one according to his view; not because it implies the neglect of some abstract political rights, but from the impoverishment of character which is implied in the process. Give every man a vote, and abolish all interference with each man's private tastes, and the danger may still be as great as ever. The tendency to "differentiation"—as we call it in modern phraseology—the social pulverisation, the lowering and narrowing of the individual's sphere of action and feeling to the pettiest details, depends upon processes underlying all political changes. It cannot, therefore, be cured by any nostrum of constitution-mongers, or by the negative remedy of removing old barriers. It requires to be met by profounder moral and religious teaching. Men must be taught what is the really valuable part of their natures, and what is the purest happiness to be extracted from life, as well as allowed to gratify fully their own tastes; for who can say that men encouraged by all their surroundings and appeals to the most obvious motives to turn themselves into machines, will not deliberately choose to be machines? Many powerful thinkers have illustrated Wordsworth's doctrine more elaborately, but nobody has gone more decisively to the root of the matter.

219

One other side of Wordsworth's teaching is still more significant and original. Our vague instincts are consolidated into reason by meditation, sympathy with our fellows, communion with nature, and a constant devotion to "high endeavours." If life run smoothly, the transformation may be easy, and our primitive optimism turn imperceptibly into general complacency. The trial comes when we make personal acquaintance with sorrow, and our early buoyancy begins to fail. We are tempted to become querulous or to lap ourselves in indifference. Most poets are content to bewail our lot melodiously, and admit that there is no remedy unless a remedy be found in "the luxury of grief." Prosaic people become selfish though not sentimental. They laugh at their old illusions, and turn to the solid consolations of comfort. Nothing is more melancholy than to study many biographies, and note—not the failure of early promise which may mean merely an aiming above the mark—but the progressive deterioration of character which so often follows grief and disappointment. If it be not true that most men grow worse as they grow old, it is surely true that few men pass through the world without being corrupted as much as purified.

Now Wordsworth's favourite lesson is the possibility of turning grief and disappointment into account. He teaches in many forms the necessity of "transmuting" sorrow into strength. One of the great evils is a lack of power,

> An agonising sorrow to transmute.

The Happy Warrior is, above all, the man who in face of all human miseries can

> Exercise a power
> Which is our human nature's highest dower;
> Controls them, and subdues, transmutes, bereaves
> Of their bad influence, and their good receives;

who is made more compassionate by familiarity with sorrow, more placable by contest, purer by temptation, and more enduring by distress.[6] It is owing to the constant presence of this thought, to his sensibility to the refining influence of sorrow, that Wordsworth is the only poet who will bear reading in times of distress. Other poets mock us by an impossible optimism, or merely reflect the feelings which, however we may play with them in times of cheerfulness, have now become an intolerable burden. Wordsworth suggests the single topic which, so far at least as this world is concerned, can really be called consolatory. None of the ordinary commonplaces will serve, or serve at most as indications of human sympathy. But there is some consolation in the thought that even death may bind the survivors closer, and leave as a legacy enduring motives to noble action. It is easy to say this; but Wordsworth has the merit of feeling the truth in all its force, and expressing it by the most forcible images. In one shape or another the sentiment is embodied in most of his really powerful poetry. It is intended, for example, to be the moral of the ''White Doe of Rylstone.'' There, as Wordsworth says, everything fails so far as its object is external and unsubstantial; everything succeeds so far as it is moral and spiritual. Success grows out of failure; and the mode in which it grows is indicated by the lines which give the keynote of the poem. Emily, the heroine, is to become a soul

> By force of sorrows high
> Uplifted to the purest sky
> Of undisturbed serenity.

The ''White Doe'' is one of those poems which make many readers inclined to feel a certain tenderness for Jeffrey's dogged insensibility; and I confess that I am not one of its warm admirers. The sentiment seems to be unduly relaxed throughout; there is a want of sympathy with heroism of the rough and active type, which is, after all, at least as worthy of admiration as the more passive variety of the virtue; and the defect is made more palpable by the position of the chief actors. These rough borderers, who recall William of Deloraine and Dandie Dinmont, are somehow out of their element when preaching the doctrines of quietism and submission to circumstances. But, whatever our judgment of this particular embodiment of Wordsworth's moral philosophy, the inculcation of the same lesson gives force to many of his finest poems. It is enough to mention the "Leechgatherer," the "Stanzas on Peele Castle," "Michael," and, as express-ing the inverse view of the futility of idle grief, "Laodamia," where he has succeeded in combining his morality with more than his ordinary beauty of poetical form. The teaching of all these poems falls in with the doctrine already set forth. All moral teaching, I have sometimes fancied, might be summed up in the one formula, "Waste not." Every element of which our nature is composed may be said to be good in its proper place; and therefore every vicious habit springs out of the misapplication of forces which might be turned to account by judicious training. The waste of sorrow is one of the most lamentable forms of waste. Sorrow too often tends to produce bitterness or effeminacy of charac-ter. But it may, if rightly used, serve only to detach us from the lower motives and give sanctity to the higher. That is what Wordsworth sees with unequalled clearness, and he therefore sees also the condition of profiting. The mind in which the most valuable elements have been systematically strengthened by meditation, by association of deep thought with the most universal presences, by constant sympathy with the joys and sorrows of its fellows, will be prepared to convert sorrow into a medicine instead of a poison. Sorrow is deteri-orating so far as it is selfish. The man who is occupied with his own interests makes grief an excuse for effeminate indulgence in self-pity. He becomes weaker and more fretful. The man who has learnt habitually to think of himself as part of a greater whole, whose conduct has been habitually directed to noble ends, is purified and strengthened by the spiritual convulsion. His disappointment, or his loss of some beloved object, makes him more anxious to fix the bases of his happiness widely and deeply, and to be content with the consciousness of honest work, instead of looking for what is called success.

But I must not take to preaching in the place of Words-worth. The whole theory is most nobly summed up in the grand lines already noticed on the character of the Happy Warrior. There Wordsworth has explained in the most forc-ible and direct language the mode in which a grand charac-

ter can be formed; how youthful impulses may change into
manly purpose; how pain and sorrow may be transmuted into
new forces; how the mind may be fixed upon lofty purposes;
how the domestic affections—which give the truest happiness
—may also be the greatest source of strength to the man who
is

> More brave for this, that he has much to lose;

and how, finally, he becomes indifferent to all petty ambition—

> Finds comfort in himself and in his cause;
> And, while the mortal mist is gathering, draws
> His breath in confidence of Heaven's applause.
> This is the Happy Warrior, this is he
> Whom every man in arms should wish to be.

We may now see what ethical theory underlies Wordsworth's teaching of the transformation of instinct into reason.
We must start from the postulate that there is in fact a Divine
order in the universe; and that conformity to this order
produces beauty as embodied in the external world, and is
the condition of virtue as regulating our character. It is by
obedience to the "stern lawgiver," Duty, that flowers gain
their fragrance, and that "the most ancient heavens" preserve their freshness and strength. But this postulate does not
seek for justification in abstract metaphysical reasoning. The
"Intimations of Immortality" are precisely intimations, not
intellectual intuitions. They are vague and emotional, not
distinct and logical. They are a feeling of harmony, not a
perception of innate ideas. And, on the other hand, our
instincts are not a mere chaotic mass of passions, to be
gratified without considering their place and function in a
certain definite scheme. They have been implanted by the
Divine hand, and the harmony which we feel corresponds to
a real order. To justify them we must appeal to experience,
but to experience interrogated by a certain definite procedure. Acting upon the assumption that the Divine order
exists, we shall come to recognise it, though we could not
deduce it by an *à priori* method.

The instrument, in fact, finds itself originally tuned by its Maker, and may preserve its original condition by careful obedience to the stern teaching of life. The buoyancy common to all youthful and healthy natures then changes into a deeper and more solemn mood. The great primary emotions retain the original impulse, but increase their volume. Grief and disappointment are transmuted into tenderness, sympathy, and endurance. The reason, as it develops, regulates, without weakening, the primitive instincts. All the greatest, and therefore most common, sights of nature are indelibly associated with "admiration, hope, and love;" and all increase of knowledge and power is regarded as a means for furthering the gratification of our nobler emotions. Under the opposite treatment, the character loses its freshness, and we regard the early happiness as an illusion. The old emotions dry up at their source. Grief produces fretfulness, misanthropy, or effeminacy. Power is wasted on petty ends and frivolous excitement, and knowledge becomes barren and pedantic. In this way the postulate justifies itself by producing the noblest type of character. When the "moral being" is thus built up, its instincts become its convictions, we recognise the true voice of nature, and distinguish it from the echo of our passions. Thus we come to know how the Divine order and the laws by which the character is harmonised are the laws of morality.

To possible objections it might be answered by Wordsworth that this mode of assuming in order to prove is the normal method of philosophy. "You must love him," as he says of the poet,

> Ere to you
> He will seem worthy of your love.

The doctrine corresponds to the *crede ut intelligas* of the divine; or to the philosophic theory that we must start from the knowledge already constructed within us by instincts which have not yet learnt to reason. And, finally, if a persistent reasoner should ask why—even admitting the facts—the higher type should be preferred to the lower, Wordsworth may ask, Why is bodily health preferable to disease? If a man

224

likes weak lungs and a bad digestion, reason cannot convince him of his error. The physician has done enough when he has pointed out the sanitary laws obedience to which generates strength, long life, and power of enjoyment. The moralist is in the same position when he has shown how certain habits conduce to the development of a type superior to its rivals in all the faculties which imply permanent peace of mind and power of resisting the shocks of the world without disentegration. Much undoubtedly remains to be said. Wordsworth's teaching, profound and admirable as it may be, has not the potency to silence the scepticism which has gathered strength since his day, and assailed fundamental—or what to him seemed fundamental—tenets of his system. No one can yet say what transformation may pass upon the thoughts and emotions for which he found utterance in speaking of the Divinity and sanctity of nature. Some people vehemently maintain that the words will be emptied of all meaning if the old theological conceptions to which he was so firmly attached should disappear with the development of new modes of thought. Nature, as regarded by the light of modern science, will be the name of a cruel and wasteful, or at least of a purely neutral and indifferent power, or perhaps as merely an equivalent for the Unknowable, to which the conditions of our intellect prevent us from ever attaching any intelligible predicate. Others would say that in whatever terms we choose to speak of the mysterious darkness which surrounds our little island of comparative light, the emotion generated in a thoughtful mind by the contemplation of the universe will remain unaltered or strengthen with clearer knowledge; and that we shall express ourselves in a new dialect without altering the essence of our thought. The emotions to which Wordsworth has given utterance will remain, though the system in which he believed should sink into oblivion; as, indeed, all human systems have found different modes of symbolising the same fundamental feelings. But it is enough vaguely to indicate considerations not here to be developed.

It only remains to be added once more that Wordsworth's poetry derives its power from the same source as his philosophy. It speaks to our strongest feelings because his speculation rests upon our deepest thoughts. His singular capacity for investing all objects with a glow derived from early associations; his keen sympathy with natural and simple emotions; his sense of the sanctifying influences which can be extracted from sorrow, are of equal value to his power over our intellects and our imaginations. His psychology, stated systematically, is rational; and, when expressed passionately, turns into poetry. To be sensitive to the most important phenomena is the first step equally towards a poetical or a scientific exposition. To see these truly is the condition of making the poetry harmonious and the philosophy logical. And it is often difficult to say which power is most remarkable in Wordsworth. It would be easy to illustrate the truth by other than moral topics. His sonnet, noticed by De Quincey, in which he speaks of the abstracting power of darkness, and observes that as the hills pass into twilight we see the same sight as the ancient Britons, is impressive as it stands, but would be equally good as an illustration in a metaphysical treatise. Again, the sonnet beginning

> With ships the sea was sprinkled far and wide,

is at once, as he has shown in a commentary of his own, an illustration of a curious psychological law—of our tendency, that is, to introduce an arbitrary principle of order into a random collection of objects—and, for the same reason, a striking embodiment of the corresponding mood of feeling. The little poem called "Stepping Westward" is in the same way at once a delicate expression of a specific sentiment and an acute critical analysis of the subtle associations suggested by a single phrase. But such illustrations might be multiplied indefinitely. As he has himself said, there is scarcely one of his poems which does not call attention to some moral sentiment, or to a general principle or law of thought, of our intellectual constitution.

Finally, we might look at the reverse side of the picture, and endeavour to show how the narrow limits of Wordsworth's power are connected with certain moral defects; with the want of quick sympathy which shows itself in his dramatic feebleness, and the austerity of character which caused him to

lose his special gifts too early and become a rather commonplace defender of conservatism; and that curious diffidence
(he assures us that it was "diffidence") which induced him to
write many thousand lines of blank verse entirely about
himself. But the task would be superfluous as well as ungrateful. It was his aim, he tells us, "to console the afflicted; to add
sunshine to daylight by making the happy happier; to teach
the young and the gracious of every age to see, to think,
and therefore to become more actively and securely virtuous;" and, high as was the aim, he did much towards its
accomplishment.

5

An Agnostic's Apology

Poisonous Opinions

Mr. Froude, in his 'Life of Carlyle,' incidentally sets forth a theory of toleration. Cromwell, he tells us, held Romanism to be 'morally poisonous'; therefore Cromwell did not tolerate. We have decided that it is no longer poisonous; therefore we do tolerate. Cromwell's intolerance implied an intense 'hatred of evil in its concrete form'; our tolerance need not imply any deficiency in that respect, but merely a difference of opinion as to facts. Upon this showing, then, we are justified in extirpating, by fire and sword, any doctrine, if only we are sincerely convinced that it is 'morally poisonous.' I do not take this as a full account either of Carlyle's theory or of Mr. Froude's. I quote it merely as a pointed statement of a doctrine which in some ways would appear to follow more directly from the utilitarianism which Carlyle detested. The argument is simple. A 'poisonous opinion' is one which causes a balance of evil. The existence of such opinions is admitted. Nor, again, is it denied that under certain conditions an opinion may be suppressed by persecution. The persecution, then, of a poisonous opinion must do some good, and must produce a balance of good if the evil effects of the opinion suppressed exceed the various evils due to the

Reprinted from *An Agnostic's Apology* (1876).

persecution. But that which causes a balance of good is right according to utilitarians; and therefore persecution may sometimes be right. If you have to suppress a trifling error at the cost of much suffering, you are acting wrongly, as it would be wrong to cure a scratch by cutting off a finger. But it may be right to suppress a poisonous opinion when the evil of the opinion is measured by the corruption of a whole social order, and the evil of the persecution by the death, say, of twelve apostles. In such a case it is expedient, and therefore right, that one man or a dozen should perish for the good of the people.

Mill attacked the applicability, though not the first principle, of this reasoning in the most forcible part of his 'Liberty.' He argues in substance that the collateral evils due to persecution are always, or almost always, excessive. He could not, as a utilitarian, deduce toleration from some absolute à priori principle. But by pointing out evil consequences generally overlooked, he could strengthen the general presumption against its utility in any particular case. His utilitarian opponents may still dispute the sufficiency of his reasoning. They urge, in substance, that the presumption is not strong enough to justify an absolute rule. Granting that there is a presumption against persecution generally, and that all the evils pointed out by Mill should be taken into account, yet, they say, it is still a question of expediency. We must be guided in each particular case by a careful balance of the good and evil, and must admit this general presumption only for what it is worth; that is, as a guiding rule in doubtful cases, or where we do not know enough to balance consequences satisfactorily, but not as possessing sufficient authority to override a clear conclusion in the opposite sense. Practically, we may assume, the difference comes to very little. Mill's opponents might often be as tolerant as himself. He says, indeed, that toleration is the universal rule; yet even he might admit that, as in other moral problems, a casuist might devise circumstances under which it would cease to be an absolute rule. On the other hand, his opponents, though holding in theory that each case has to be judged on its merits, would, in fact, agree that no case ever occurs at the present time in which the balance is not in favour of toleration. The discussion, therefore, has less practical application than one might at first sight suppose. One man says, 'Toleration is always right, but at times this, like other moral rules, may be suspended.' The other, 'It is not a question of right or wrong, but of expediency; but, on the other hand, in almost every conceivable case, toleration is clearly expedient.' It is only, therefore, as illustrating an interesting ethical problem—interesting, that is, to people capable of feeling an interest in such gratuitous logic-chopping—that I would consider the problem.

I remark, therefore, in the first place, that one argument of considerable importance scarcely receives sufficient emphasis from Mill. The objection taken by the ordinary common-sense of mankind to persecution is, very often, that the doctrines enforced are false. Toleration, beyond all doubt, has been advanced by scepticism. It is clearly both inexpedient and wrong to burn people for not holding erroneous beliefs. Mill extends the argument to cases where power and truth are on the same side; but he scarcely brings out what may be called the specifically moral objection. I may hold that Romanism is false and even 'poisonous.' I may still admit that a sincere Romanist is not only justified in believing—for, so far as his belief appears to him to be reasonable, he cannot help believing—but also that he is morally bound to avow his belief. He is in the position of a man who is sincerely convinced that a food which I hold to be poisonous is wholesome, or, rather, an indispensable medicine. If he thinks so, it is clearly his duty to let his opinion be known. A man holds that prussic acid will cure, when it really kills. He is mistaken, but surely he is bound to impart so important a truth to his fellows. So long, indeed, as men held that it was not only foolish, but wicked, to hold other religious opinions than their own, this argument did not apply. But I need not argue that sincere errors are in themselves innocent. The most virtuous of men will be a Calvinist in Scotland, a Catholic in Spain, and a Mohammedan in Turkey. And so far as this possibility is admitted, and as the contrary conviction spreads—namely, that the leaders of heresies are generally virtuous, because it requires virtue to uphold an unpopular opinion—the dilemma becomes pressing. The persecutor, as a rule, is punishing the virtuous for virtuous conduct, and, moreover, for conduct which he admits to be virtuous. For this is not one of those cases with which casuists sometimes puzzle themselves. The fact that a man thinks himself acting rightly, or is wicked on principle, is not a sufficient defence against legal punishment. If a man is a Thug, the Government is not the less bound to hang him because he thinks murder right. A thief must be punished, though he objects to property in general; and a man who deserts his wife, though he disapproves of marriage. A man is in such cases punished for an action which the ruler holds to be immoral. But the persecutor has to punish a man precisely for discharging a duty admitted even by the persecutor to be a duty, and a duty of the highest obligation. If the duty of truthfulness be admitted, I am bound not to express belief in a creed which I hold to be false. If benevolence be a duty, I am bound to tell my neighbour how he can avoid hellfire. The dilemma thus brought about—the necessity of crushing conscience by law—will be admitted to be an evil, though it may be an inevitable evil. The social tie carries with it the necessity of sometimes forcing particular people to do that which both they and we admit to be wrong. But the scandal so caused is one main cause of the abhorrence felt for the persecutor, and the sympathy for his victims. The ordinary statement of the impolicy of making men martyrs testifies to the general force of the impression. And it must, in fact, be taken into account upon any method of calculation, in so far, at least, as the revulsion of feeling excited by persecution tells against the efficacy of the method adopted. The persecutor, that is, must clearly remember that by burning a man for his honesty he is inevitably exciting the disgust of all who care for honesty, even though they do not prize it more than orthodoxy. It must be in all cases a great, even if a necessary, evil, that the law should outrage the conscience of its subjects. And whatever conclusion may be reached, it is desirable to consider how far and on what principles the acceptance of this dilemma can be regarded as unavoidable.

231

The utilitarian can, of course, give a consistent reply. The ultimate criterion, he says, of virtue is utility. Sincerity is a virtue because it is obviously useful to mankind. That men should be able to trust each other is a first condition of the mutual assistance upon which happiness depends. But here is a case in which we—that is, the rulers—are convinced that sincerity does harm. We shall be illogical if we allow the general rule derived from particular cases to govern us in the case where it plainly does not apply. We admit all the evils alleged: the suffering of a sincere man because of his sincerity, the encouragement to hypocrisy, the demoralisation of those whose lips are closed; but, after admitting all this, we still see so clearly the mischief which will follow from the spread of the opinions in question, that we pronounce it to exceed all the other admitted mischief, and are therefore still bound to persecute. Turn it and twist it as you will, the question still comes to this: Which way does the balance of happiness incline? Is it better that virtuous Romanists should go to the stake and Romanism be so stamped out, or that so poisonous an opinion be allowed to spread? We fully admit all the evils which you have noted, and willingly put them in the balance; but we must weigh them against the evils which will follow from the toleration, and our action must be determined by a final comparison.

Undoubtedly the argument has great apparent strength. It fixes the issues which are generally taken; and when helped by the assumption that belief in a creed may determine a man's happiness for all eternity, and that men or some body of men may possess infallibility, it makes a very imposing show. Nor do I wish to dispute the fundamental principle; that is, the principle that utility is in some sense to be the final criterion of morality. I think, however, that here, as in other cases, a thoroughgoing application of that criterion will lead us to a different conclusion from that which results from a first inspection. And, in order to show this, I must try to point out certain tacit assumptions made in the application of this principle to the facts. Granting that we must test persecution by its effects upon human happiness, I must add that we cannot fairly measure these effects without looking a little more closely into the conditions under which they are necessarily applied. The argument starts from the generalisation of something like a truism. The alleged fact is simply this: that pain, threatened or inflicted, will stop a man's mouth. It can hardly convert him, but it will prevent him from converting others. I do not dispute the statement; I will not undertake to say that there is any creed which I would not avow or renounce rather than be burnt alive. I think that I might possibly prefer distant damnation to immediate martyrdom. Many men, happily for the race, have been more heroic; but burning stopped even their mouths, and so far suppressed their influence. We have, however, to modify this statement before we can apply it to any serious purpose. We have to show, that is, that we not only suppress the individual, but eradicate the opinion from society; and this raises two questions. There is a difficulty in catching the opinion which is to be suppressed, and there is a difficulty about arranging the machinery through which the necessary force is to be supplied. When we examine the conditions of success in the enterprise, it may turn out that it is impossible in many cases, and possible in any case only at the cost of evils which would more than counterbalance any possible benefit. Only by such an investigation can we really measure the total effect of persecution, and it will, I think, appear to be still more far-reaching and disastrous than is implied even by Mill's cogent reasoning.

Mill, in fact, conducts the argument as though he made an assumption (for I will not say that he actually made it) which appears to me, at least, to be curiously unreal. His reasoning would be sometimes more to the purpose if we could suppose an opinion to be a sort of definite object, a tangible thing like the cholera bacillus, existing in a particular mind, as the germ in a particular body, and therefore capable of being laid hold of and suppressed by burning the person to whom it belongs, as the germ is suppressed by being dipped in boiling water. This corresponds to what one may call the 'happy thought' doctrine of scientific discovery. Popular writers used sometimes to tell the story of Newton's great discovery as though Newton one day saw an apple fall, and exclaimed, 'Ah! an apple is a kind of moon!' This remark had occurred to no one else, and might never have struck anybody again. If, therefore, you had caught Newton on the spot and stamped him out, the discovery of gravitation might have been permanently suppressed. Mill would, of course, have perceived the absurdity of such a statement as clearly as anyone; yet he seems to make a very similar assumption in his 'Liberty.' It is, he is arguing, a 'piece of idle sentimentality' that truth has any intrinsic power of prevailing against persecution. 'The real advantage which truth has consists in this—that when an opinion is true it may be extinguished once, twice, or many times, but in the course of ages there will generally be found persons to rediscover it'; and when, he adds, it is rediscovered in a propitious age, it may 'make such head' as to resist later attempts at suppression. Surely this is a most inadequate account of the strength of truth. The advantage dependent upon a chance of rediscovery is equally possessed by error; old superstitions are just as much given to reappearance as old truths. Everyone who has examined stupid lads knows very well that the blunders which they make are just as uniform as the truths which they perceive. Given minds at a certain stage, and exposed to certain external conditions, we can predict the illusions which will be generated. So, to take the familiar instances, the mass of mankind still believes that the sun goes round the earth, and is convinced that a moving body will stop of itself, independently of external resistance. The advantage of truth is surely dependent upon the other fact that it can, as Mill says, 'make head.' It gathers strength by existing; it gathers strength, that is, because it can be verified and tested, and every fresh test confirms the belief; and it gathers strength, again, in so far as it becomes part of a general system of truths, each of which confirms, elucidates, and corroborates the others, and which together form the organised mass of accepted knowledge which we call science. So far as we are possessed of anything that can be called scientific knowledge, we have not to deal with a list of separate assertions, each of which has to be judged upon its own merits, and each of which may stand or fall independently of all the others; but with a system of interdependent truths, some of which are supported by irresistible weight of evidence, whilst the remainder are so inextricably intertwined with the central core of truth that they cannot be separately rejected. To talk, therefore, of suppressing an opinion as if it were not part of a single growth, but a separable item in a chaotic aggregate of distinguishable theories, is to overlook the most essential condition of bringing any influence to bear upon opinion generally.

Consider, first, the case of any scientific theory. Newton's great achievement was supposed to lead to questionable theological inferences; as, indeed, whatever may be the logical inferences, there can be no doubt that it was fatal to the mythological imagery in which the earth appeared as the centre of the universe. Suppose, then, that it had been decided that the opinion was poisonous, and that anybody who maintained that the earth went round the sun should be burnt. Had such a system been carried out, what must have happened? If we suppose it to be comparable with the continued progress of astronomical and physical inquiries, this particular conclusion might still be ostensibly conceded. Kepler's discoveries, and all the astronomical observations assumed by Newton, might have been allowed to be promulgated, as affording convenient means of calculation, and Newton's physical theories might have been let pass as interesting surmises in speculation, or admitted as applicable to other cases. It might still be asserted that, so far as the solar system was concerned, the doctrines possessed no 'objective truth.' Something of the kind was, I believe, actually attempted. It needs, however, no argument to show that such a persecution would be childish, and would be virtually giving over the key of the position to the antagonist, with some feeble, ostensible stipulation that he should not openly occupy one dependent outwork. The truth would not have been suppressed, but the open avowal of the truth. The only other alternative would have been to suppress physical theories and astronomical observation altogether, in order to avoid the deduction of the offensive corollary. In such a case, then, the only choice, by the very nature of the case, is not between permitting or suppressing 'an opinion,' but between permitting or suppressing scientific inquiry in general. There are, no doubt, bigots and stupid people enough to be ready to suppress speculation at large, but they would find it hard to induce people to suppress things of obvious utility; they cannot suppress the study of astronomy for purposes of navigation, and yet, when the truth has been acquired for this end, its application to others follows by a spontaneous and irresistible process. The victory is won, and the only question is, whether the conqueror shall march in openly or in a mask.

This familiar example may illustrate the extreme difficulty of catching, isolating, and suppressing so subtle an essence as an opinion. Stop all thought, and of course you can annihilate the particular doctrine which it generates. But the price to pay is a heavy one, and clearly not to be measured by the particular sets of consequences which result from the specified dogma. The same principle is everywhere operative. The greatest shock lately received by the conservative theologians has been due to the spread of Darwinian theories. How, granting that rulers and priests had at their disposal any amount of persecuting power, would they have proposed to suppress those theories? They object to the belief that men have grown out of monkeys. Would they, then, allow men to hold that the horse and ass have a common ancestor; or to question the permanency of genera and species of plants? Would they prohibit Darwin's investigations into the various breeds of pigeons, or object to his exposition of the way in which a multiplication of cats might be unfavourable to the fertilisation of clover? The principle shows itself in the most trifling cases; once established there, it spreads by inevitable contagion to others; the conclusion is obvious to all men, whether tacitly insinuated or openly drawn. To suppress it you must get rid of the primitive germ. When once it has begun to spread, no political nets or traps can catch so subtle an element. It would be as idle to attempt to guard against it as to say that small-pox may rage as it pleases everywhere else, but you will keep it out of Pall Mall by a cordon of policemen to stop people with an actual eruption. The philosophy of a people is the central core of thought, which is affected by every change taking place on the remotest confines of the organism. It is sensitive to every change in every department of inquiry. Every new principle discovered anywhere has to find its place in the central truths; and unless you are prepared to superintend, and therefore to stifle, thought in general, you may as well let it alone altogether. Superintendence means stifling. That is not the less true, even if the doctrine suppressed be erroneous. Assuming that Darwinianism is wrong, or as far as you please from being absolutely true, yet its spread proves conclusively that it represents a necessary stage of progress. We may have to pass beyond it; but in any case we have to pass through it. It represents that attitude of mind and method of combining observations which is required under existing conditions. It may enable us to rise to a point from which we shall see its inadequacy. But even its antagonists admit the necessity of working provisionally, at least, from this assumption, and seeing what can be made of it; and would admit, therefore, that a forcible suppression, if so wild an hypothesis can be entertained, would be equivalent to the suppression, not of this or that theory, but of thought.

The conclusion is, briefly, that, so far as scientific opinion is concerned, you have to choose between tolerating error and suppressing all intellectual activity. If this be admitted in the case of what we call 'scientific' knowledge, the dilemma presents itself everywhere. We are becoming daily more fully aware of the unity of knowledge; of the impossibility of preserving, isolating, and impounding particular bits of truth, or protecting orthodoxy by the most elaborate quarantine. It is idle to speak of a separation between the spheres of science and theology, as though the contents of the two were entirely separate. There is, doubtless, much misconception as to the nature of the relation; false inferences are frequently made by hasty thinkers; but the difference, whatever it may be, is not such as divides two independent series of observations, but such that every important change in one region has a necessary and immediate reaction on the other. If we accept the principle of evolution—whether we take the Darwinian version or any other as our guide—as applied to the history of human belief, we more and more realise the undeniable facts that the history must be considered as a whole; that the evolution, however it takes place, has to follow certain lines defined by the successive stages of intellectual development; that it consists of a series of gradual approximations, each involving positive errors, or at least provisional assumptions accepted for the moment as definitive truths; and that every widely-spread belief, whether accurate or erroneous, has its place in the process, as representing at least the illusions which necessarily present themselves to minds at a given point of the ascending scale. The whole process may be, and, of course, frequently has been, arrested. But, if it is to take place at all, it is impossible to proscribe particular conclusions beforehand. The conclusions forbidden may, of course, be such as would never have been reached, even if not forbidden. In that case the persecution would be useless. But if they are such as would commend themselves to masses of men but for the prohibition, it follows that they are necessary 'moments' in the evolution of thought, and therefore can only be suppressed by suppressing that evolution.

The vagueness of the argument stated in these general terms is no bar to its value in considering more special cases. It suggests, in the first place, an extension of one of Mill's arguments, which has been most frequently criticised. He tries to prove this advantage of persecution by a rather exaggerated estimate of the value of contradiction. 'Even admitted truths,' he says, 'are apt to lose their interest for us unless stimulated by collision with the contradictory error.' It is, of course, obvious to reply that we believe in Euclid or in the ordinary principles of conduct, though nobody ever denies that two sides of a triangle are greater than the third, or doubts that water quenches thirst. An opinion, I should say, gains vividness rather from constant application to conduct than from habitual opposition. But, so far as Mill's argument has to do with toleration, it seems to be cogent, and to derive its strength from the principle I am defending. Many opinions, if left alone, would doubtless die out by inherent weakness. It would be idle to punish men for maintaining that two and two make five, because the opinion would never survive a practical application. The prohibition of a palpably absurd theory would be a waste of force, and might possibly suggest to a few eccentric people that there must, after all, be something to say for the absurdity, and therefore, if for no other reason, it is undesirable. But it was, of course, not of such opinions that Mill was thinking. The only opinions which anyone would seriously desire to suppress are plausible opinions—opinions, that is, which would flourish but for persecution; and every persecutor justifies himself by showing, to his own satisfaction, that his intervention is needed. He rejects the argument by which Gamaliel defended the first plea for toleration. He holds that opinions, though coming from God, require human defence. He thinks that even the devil's creed would flourish but for a stake, and this assumption is the sole justification of the stake. That is to say, persecution is always defended, and can only be defended, on the ground that the persecuted opinion is highly plausible, and the same plausibility of an opinion is a strong presumption that it is an essential part of the whole evolution. Even if it be wrong, it must represent the way in which a large number of people will think, if they think at all. It corresponds to one aspect, though an incomplete or illusory aspect, of the facts. If there be no reason, there must be some general cause of the error; a cause which, in the supposed case, must be the prevalence of some erroneous or imperfect belief in the minds of many people. The predisposing cause will presumably remain, even if this expression of opinion be silenced. And, in all such cases, the effect of suppression will be prejudicial to the vigour even of the true belief. The causes, whatever they be, which obstruct its acceptance will operate in a covert form. Real examination becomes impossible when the side which is not convicted is not allowed to have its reasons for doubt tested; and we reach the dilemma just stated. That is to say, if thought is not suppressed, the error will find its way to the surface through some subterranean channels; whilst, if thought is suppressed, the truth and all speculative truth will of course be enfeebled with the general enfeeblement of the intellect. To remedy a morbid growth you have applied a ligature which can only succeed by arresting circulation and bringing on the mortification of the limb. To treat intellectual error in this fashion must always be to fall into the practice of quackery, and suppress a symptom instead of attacking the source of the evil.

The assertion is, apparently, at least, opposed to another doctrine in which Mill agrees with some of his antagonists. He says, as we have seen, that a belief in the natural prevalence of truth is a piece of idle sentimentality; it is a 'pleasant falsehood' to say that truth always triumphs; 'history teems with instances of successful persecution'; and he confirms this by such cases as the failure of the Reformers in Spain, Italy, and Flanders, and of the various attempts which preceded Luther's successful revolt. Arguments beginning 'all history shows' are always sophistical. The most superficial knowledge is sufficient to show that, in this case at least, the conclusion is not demonstrated. To prove that persecution 'succeeded' in suppressing truth, you must prove that without persecution truth would have prevailed. The argument from the Reformation must surely in Mill be an *argumentum ad hominem*. He did not hold that Luther, or Knox, or the Lollards preached the whole truth; hardly, even, that they were nearer the truth than Ignatius Loyola or St. Bernard. And the point is important. For when it is said that the Reformation was suppressed in Italy and Spain by persecution, we ask at once whether there is the slightest reason to suppose that, if those countries had been as free as England at the present day, they would have become Protestant? Protestantism had its day of vitality, and in some places it is still vigorous; but with all the liberty of conscience of modern Italy, the most enthusiastic Protestant scarcely expects its conversion before the millennium. If, when there is a fair field and no favour, Protestantism stands still, why should we suppose that it would once have been advanced? Many writers have insisted upon the singular arrest of the Protestant impulse. The boundaries between Protestantism and Catholicism are still drawn upon the lines fixed by the first great convulsion. It is at least as plausible to attribute this to the internal decay of Protestantism as to the external barriers raised by persecution. In the seventeenth century philosophical intellects had already passed beyond the temporary compromise which satisfied Luther and his contemporaries. Protestantism, so far as it meant a speculative movement, was not the name of a single principle or a coherent system of opinion, but of a mass of inconsistent theories approximating more or less consciously to pure deism or 'naturalism.' Victories over Romanism were not really won by the creed of Calvin and Knox, but by the doctrines of Hobbes and Spinoza. Otherwise we may well believe the Protestant creed would have spread more rapidly, instead of ceasing to spread at all precisely when persecution became less vigorous. When we look more closely at the facts, the assumption really made shows its true nature. Persecution might strike down any nascent Protestantism in Spain; but it can hardly be said that it created the very zeal which it manifested. If no persecution had been possible, the enthusiasm of Loyola and his successors might (even if I may not say would) have burnt all the more brightly. And if the orthodox had been forbidden to strike a foul blow, they might have been equally successful when confined to legitimate methods. The reasoning, in fact, is simple. Protestantism died out when persecution flourished. But persecution flourished when zeal was intense. It is impossible, then, to argue that the extinction of heresy was due to the special fact of the persecution in order to account for the fact that it did not spread in the regions where faith was strongest. In any case, if we assume, as we must assume, that the old faith was congenial to a vast number of minds, we might be sure that it would triumph where it had the most numerous and zealous followers. Under the conditions of the times, that triumph of course implied persecution; but it is an inversion of all logic to put this collateral effect as the cause of the very state of mind which alone could make it possible. So, again, Protestantism died out in France (which Mill does not mention) and survived in England; and in England, says Mill, the death of Elizabeth or the life of Mary would 'most likely' have caused its extirpation. Possibly, for it is difficult to argue 'might have beens.' But it is equally possible that the English indifference which made the country pliable in the hands of its rulers would have

AN AGNOSTIC'S APOLOGY

prevented any effective persecution, and the ineffectual persecution have led only to a more thoroughgoing revolution when the Puritan party had accumulated a greater stock of grievances. If, again, Protestantism had been really congenial to the French people, is it not at least probable that it would have gathered sufficient strength in the seventeenth century —whatever the disadvantages under which it actually laboured—to make a subsequent revival of vigorous persecution impossible? One ultimate condition of success lay, partly, at any rate, in the complex conditions, other than the direct action of rulers, which predisposed one society to the Catholic and others to the Protestant doctrine; and if we are not entitled to assume that this was the sole ultimate and determining condition of the final division, we are certainly not entitled to seek for it in the persecution which is in any land a product of a spiritual force capable of acting in countless other ways.

Once more we come across that 'happy thought' doctrine which was natural to the old method of writing history. Catholics were once content to trace the English Reformation to the wickedness of Henry VIII. or Elizabeth; Protestants, to the sudden inspiration of this or that Reformer. Without attempting to argue the general question of the importance of great religious leaders, this at least is evident: that the appropriate medium is as necessary as the immediate stimulus. There were bad men before Henry VIII., and daring thinkers and Reformers before Luther. The Church could resist plunder or reform whilst it possessed sufficient vital force; and the ultimate condition of that force was that its creeds and its worship satisfied the strongest religious aspirations of mankind. Luther himself at an earlier period would have been a St. Bernard. Its weakness and the success of assailants, good or bad, was due, as no one will now deny, to the morbid condition into which it had fallen, from causes which could only be fully set forth by the profoundest and most painstaking investigation. If this be granted, it follows that Protestantism, whether a wholesome or a pernicious movement, meant the operation of certain widely-spread and deeply-seated causes rendering some catastrophe inevitable.

242

To apply an effective remedy it would have been necessary to remove the causes, to restore the old institutions in working order, and to renew the vitality of the faiths upon which its vigour essentially depended. So far as the opponents of reform relied upon persecution, they were driving the disease inwards instead of applying an effectual remedy. Such observations—too commonplace to be worth more than a brief indication—must be indicated in order to justify the obvious limitations to Mill's estimate of the efficacy of persecution. In the first place, it is not proved that it was properly 'efficacious' at all; that is, that the limits of the creeds would not have been approximately the same had no persecution been allowed. Secondly, if efficacious, it was efficacious at a cost at which the immediate suffering of the martyrs is an absurdly inadequate measure. In Spain, Protestantism was stamped out, when it might have died a natural death, at the price of general intellectual atrophy. Had the persecutors known that the system from which persecution resulted was also a system under which their country would decline from the highest to the most insignificant position, their zeal might have been cooled. In France, again, if Protestantism was suppressed by the State, Catholics of to-day may reckon the cost. Thought, being (upon that hypothesis) forced into a different mode of expressing dissent, has not only brought about the triumph of unbelief, but the production of a type of infidelity not only speculatively hostile to Catholicism, but animated by a bitter hatred which even the most anti-Catholic of reasoners may regret. I am unable to decide the problem whether it is worth while to save a few souls at the moment with the result of ultimately driving a whole nation to perdition; but it is one which even those who rely upon the hell-fire argument may consider worth notice. And if in England we have escaped some of these mischiefs, we may ask how much good we have done by an ineffectual persecution of Catholics in Ireland—a point upon which it is needless to insist, because everyone admits the folly of ineffectual persecution.

The facts, so considered, seem to fit best with the doctrine which I am advocating. Persecution may be effective at the cost of strangling all intellectual advance; it may be successful for a time in enforcing hypocrisy, or, in other words, taking the surest means of producing a dry-rot of the system defended; or, finally, it may be ineffectual in securing its avowed object, but singularly efficacious in producing bitter antipathy and accumulating undying ill-will between hostile sections of society. When, therefore, the argument is stated as though all the evils to be put in the balance against persecution were the pain of the immediate sufferers and the terror of sympathisers, I should say that the merest outside of the case has really been touched. One other consideration is enough for this part of the question. Persecution may discourage unbelief, but it cannot be maintained that it has the least direct tendency to increase belief. Positively it must fail, whatever it may do negatively. The decay of a religion means a decline of 'vital faith'—of a vivid realisation of the formulae verbally accepted. That is the true danger in the eyes of believers; and, if it be widely spread, no burning of heretics can tend to diminish it. People do not believe more vigorously because believers in a different creed are burnt. They only become more cowardly in all their opinions; and some other remedy of a totally different nature can alone be efficacious. You can prevent people from worshipping another God, but you cannot make them more zealous about their own. And perhaps a lukewarm believer is more likely to be damned, certainly he is not less likely to be mischievous, than a vigorous heretic.

To complete the argument, however, or rather the outline of the argument, it would be necessary to follow out another set of considerations. Granting that you can suppress your heresy by persecution enough, we have to ask how you can get persecution enough. Persecution which does not suppress is a folly as well as a crime. To irritate without injuring is mischievous upon all hypotheses. In that case, if not in others, even cynics allow that the blood of the martyrs is the seed of the Church. The danger of advertising your opponent is pretty well understood by this time, and popular riots suppressed by the police are the very thing desirable for the Salvation Army. It is agreed, then, that the weapon is one to be used solely on condition that it is applied with sufficient stringency. Now, if we ask further how this is to be obtained, and especially if we ask that question in the light of the preceding inquiry, we shall arrive at a conclusion difficult to state in adequate terms. It may be possible to stamp out what we call a particular opinion. The experiment, at least, has often been tried, though I do not know that it has often succeeded. When it was criminal to speak of a king's vices, the opinion entertained about particular kings was hardly more flattering—though flatterers alone could speak openly —than it is now. But to suppress so vague and penetrating a thing as a new religious opinion is a very different and a very serious matter. The change may not be the less efficacious because it is not overt. Nothing, for example, could be easier than to advocate the most infidel opinions in the language of perfect orthodoxy. The belief in God is generally taken to be a cardinal article of faith. But the words may be made to cover any state of mind. Spinoza and Hobbes both professed to believe in a God who, to their opponents, is no God at all. The quaint identification of 'deist' with 'atheist,' by ortho-dox writers, is an illustration of the possible divergence of meaning under unity of phrase. One set of theologians hold to the conception of a Being who will help a pious leader to win a battle if a proper request be made. Another set, equally sincere and devout, regard any such doctrine as presumptu-ous and profane. Briefly, what is common to all who use the word, is a substance known only by attributes which are susceptible of indefinite variation. And what is true of this is true of all articles of faith. I will be a believer in any theologi-cal dogma to-morrow, if you will agree that I shall define the words precisely as I please; nor do I think that I should often have to strain them beyond very respectable precedents in order to cover downright positivism. How is this difficulty to be met? How is a nominal belief in Christianity to be guarded from melting away without any change of phraseology into some vague pantheism or agnosticism, or, in the other direc-tion, to a degrading anthropomorphism? A mere chain of words is too easily borne to be cared for by anybody. You may crash a downright Tom Paine; but how are you to restrain your wily latitudinarian, who will swallow any formula as if he liked it? Obviously, the only reply can be that you must give discretionary powers to your Inquisition. It must be empowered to judge of tendencies as well as of definite opinions; to cross-examine the freethinker, and bring his heresy to open light; to fashion new tests when the old ones break down, and to resist the very first approaches of the insidious enemy who would rationalise and extenuate. And, further, as I have said, the same authority must lay his grasp, not only on theologians and philosophers, but upon every department of thought by which they are influenced; that is to say, upon speculation in general. Without this, the substance may all slip away, and leave you with nothing but an empty shell of merely formal assertion. The task is, of course, practicable in proportion to the rarity of intellectual activity. In ages when speculation was only possible for a rare philosopher here and there, it might be easy to make the place too hot to hold him, even if he escaped open collision with authority. But in any social state approaching at all to the present, the magnitude of the task is obvious beyond all need of explanation.

This suggests a final conclusion. No serious politician assumes offhand that a law will execute itself. It may be true that drunkenness and heresy would expire together if every drunkard and heretic could be hanged. But before proposing a law founded upon that opinion, the legislator has to ask, not only whether it would be effective if applied, but whether it could be applied. What are the conditions of efficiency of law itself? Opponents of toleration seem to pass over this as irrelevant. If heretics were burnable, heresy would die out. Suppose that granted, how does it apply? The question as to the possibility of carrying out a law is as important as any other question about it. The Legislature is omnipotent in the sense that whatever it declares to be a law is a law, for that is the meaning of a law; but it is as far as possible from omnipotence in the sense of being able to impose any rule in practice. For anything to be effective persecution you require your Inquisition—a body endowed with such authority as to be able not merely to proscribe a given dogma, but all the various disguises which it may assume; and to suppress the very germs of the doctrines by which the whole of a creed may be sapped without ostensible assaults upon its specific statements; to silence, not only the conscious heretic, but the more dangerous reasoner who is unintentionally furthering heretical opinions; to extend its dominion over the whole field of intellectual activity, and so stamp out, not this or that objectionable statement, but to arrest those changes in the very constituent principles of reasoning, which, if they occur, bring with them the necessity of correlative changes in particular opinions, and which can only be hindered from occurring by arresting the development of thought itself. When faith in the supernatural is decaying, it is idle to enforce internal homage to this or that idol. The special symptom is the result of a constitutional change which such measures have no tendency to remedy. How, then, is an administrative machinery equal to such purposes to be contrived, or the necessary force supplied for its effective working? Obviously it implies such an all-embracing and penetrating despotism as can hardly be paralleled in history; a blind spirit of loyalty which will accept and carry out the decisions of the political rulers, and that in the face of the various influences which, by the hypothesis, are bringing about an intellectual change, and presumably affecting the rulers as well as their subjects. And even so much can only be reached by limiting or asphyxiating the intellectual progress, with all which it implies. The argument, it must be added, applies to the case of erroneous, as well as of sound, opinions. That is to say, it is in all cases idle to attack the error unless you can remove the predisposing cause. I may hold, as in fact I do hold, that what is called the religious reaction of recent times involves the growth of many fallacies, and that it is far more superficial than is generally asserted. But, whatever its origin, it has its causes. So far as they are not to be found in the purely intellectual sphere, they must be sought in social conditions, or in the existence of certain emotional needs not yet provided for by the newer philosophy. To try to suppress such movements forcibly—if any such enterprise could be seriously proposed—would be idiotic. However strong our conviction of intellectual error, we must be content to have error as long as we have fools. For folly, education in the widest sense is the sole, though singularly imperfect, remedy; and education in that sense means the stimulation of all kinds of intellectual energy. The other causes can only be removed by thorough social reforms, and the fuller elaboration of a satisfactory philosophy. Persecution, were such a thing really conceivable, could at most drive the mischief to take other forms, and would remove one of the most potent stimulants to the more satisfactory variety of regenerating activity.

My reply, then, to the question, Why do you not extirpate poisonous opinions by force? is, briefly, the old one—Because I object to quack remedies: to remedies, in this case, which can at most secure a negative result at the cost of arresting the patient's growth. When I come to the strictly ethical problem, Is persecution wicked? and, if so, why? I must answer rather more fully. All that I have said is a simple expansion of familiar and obvious arguments. Not only must Mill, whom I have criticised in particular points, have recognised all the alleged evils in a general way, but I am certain that others less favourable to toleration would admit them in any given case. If, that is, a systematic attack upon any opinion, or upon general freedom of thought, were proposed, everyone would admit the futility of a partial persecution, and the impossibility of an effectual one. It is only the form into which the general argument is cast that perplexes the general theory. It is so plain that a special utterance may be stopped by a sufficient penalty; and, again, it seems so easy to assume that a dogma is a kind of entity with a particular and definable set of consequences adhering to it, that reasoners overlook the unreality which intrudes in the course of their generalisations. They neglect what, according to me, is an essential part of the case—all the secondary implications, that is, of an effectual persecution; the necessity of arresting a mental phase as well as a particular error, and of altering the whole political and social organisation in order to provide an effectual censorship. If these necessities are more or less recognised, they are thrust out of the argument by a simple device. The impossibility of organising an effectual persecution now is admitted; but then it is said that this is a proof of modern effeminacy—sentimentalism, or anarchy, or some other objectionable peculiarity. This is virtually to say that, though toleration must be admitted as a transitional phase, it implies a weakness, not strength, and, in brief, that the advocate of persecution would prefer a totally different social state—namely, such a one as combines all the requisites for an adequate regulation of opinion. Persecution is wrong, here and now, for you and me, because our teeth are drawn, and we can only mumble without biting; but we will hope that our teeth may grow again. The admission, in whatever terms it may be made, is perhaps enough for us. Virtually it is an admission that persecution cannot be justified unless certain conditions are realised which are not now realisable; and this admission is not less important because made in terms calculated to extenuate the importance and the permanence of these conditions. From my point of view, on the other hand, the circumstances thus treated as removable and trifling accidents are really of the very essence of the case, and it is only by taking them into account that we can give a satisfactory theory of toleration. Toleration presupposes a certain stage of development, moral and intellectual. In the ruder social order, toleration is out of the question for familiar reasons. The rudimentary Church and State are so identified that the kingly power has the spiritual sanctity, and the priest can wield the secular arm. Heresy is a kind of rebellion, and the gods cannot be renounced without an attack upon political authority. Intellectual activity is confined to a small class, and opinions change by an imperceptible and unconscious process. Wherever such a condition is actually in existence, controversy can only be carried on by the sword. A change of faith is not caused by argument, but is part of the process by which a more powerful race conquers or extirpates its neighbours. The higher belief has a better chance, perhaps, so far as it is characteristic of a superior race, but owes little to its logical or philosophical merits. And, in such a state of things, toleration is hardly to be called a virtue, because it is an impossibility. If the equilibrium between sects, as between races, depends upon the sword, the propagator or the defender of the faith must use the sword as the essential condition of his success. If individuals perceive that toleration is desirable, they perceive also that it can only be achieved through an elevation of the whole race to a higher social condition. It remains as an unattainable ideal, dimly fore-shadowed in some higher minds.

In the more advanced stage, with which we have to do, the state of things is altered. Church and State are no longer identified; a society has a political apparatus discharging one set of functions, and an ecclesiastical apparatus (or more than one) which discharges another set. Some such distinction exists as a plain matter of fact. There remains, indeed, the perplexed controversy as to its ultimate nature, and the degree in which it can be maintained. The priest is a different person from the ruler, and each individual is governed in part of his conduct by a reference to the political order, and in other parts by a reference to the spiritual order. On the other hand, it is urged, and, indeed, it is undeniable, that the distinction is not a complete separation. Every spiritual rule has its secular aspect, and every secular rule its spiritual. Each power has an influence over the whole sphere of conduct, and it is idle to draw a line between theory and practice, inasmuch as all theory affects practice, and all practice is based upon theory. How are the conflicting claims of two powers to be reconciled, when each affects the whole sphere of thought and conduct, without making one absolutely dependent upon the other?

This opens a wide field of controversy, upon which I must touch only so far as the doctrine of toleration is concerned. How are we to reconcile any such doctrine with the admission that the State must enforce certain kinds of conduct, that it must decide (unless it is to be absolutely dependent upon the Church, or, in other words, unless the Church is itself a State) what kinds of conduct it will enforce; and, therefore, that it may have to forbid practices commended by the Church, or to punish men, indirectly at least, for religious opinions—that is, to persecute? We may argue about the expediency in particular cases; but how can we lay down a general principle?

Before answering, I must begin by one or two preliminary considerations. The existence of any society whatever clearly presupposes an agreement to obey certain elementary rules, and therefore the existence of a certain desire for order and respect for constituted authority. Every society also contains anti-social elements, and must impose penalties upon anti-social conduct. It can, of course, deal with a small part only of such conduct. It can punish murder, but not ill-will. And, further, though it cannot punish all immorality, it may punish no conduct which is not immoral. The criminal law covers only a part of the field of the moral law, and may nowhere extend beyond it. The efficacy, again, of all State action depends upon the existence of the organic instincts which have been evolved in its growth. Churches, like all other forms of association, depend upon the existence of similar instincts or sentiments, some of which are identical with those upon which the State is also founded, whilst others are not directly related to any particular form of political organisation. Many different Churches may arise, corresponding to differences of belief upon questions of the highest importance, of which the members may yet be capable of uniting for political purposes, and of membership of the same State. Agnostics, Protestants, and Catholics may agree to hang murderers and enforce contracts, though they go to different Churches, and some of them to no Church at all; or hold the most contradictory opinions about the universe at large. The possibility, within some undefined limits, is proved by experience; but can we define the limits or deny the contrary possibility? May not a Church be so constituted that membership is inconsistent with membership of the State? If a creed says 'Steal,' must not believers go to prison? If so, and if the State be the sole judge on such points, do we not come back to persecution?

I reply, first, that the difficulty is in one way exaggerated, and in a way which greatly affects the argument. Respect, for example, for human life or for property represents different manifestations of that essential instinct which is essential to all social development. Unless murderers and thieves were condemned and punished, there could be no society, but only a barbarous chaos. These are fundamental points which are and must be settled before the problem of toleration can even be raised. The ethical sentiment which condemns such crimes must exist in order that priests and policemen may exist. It is not a product, but a precedent condition, of their activity. The remark is needed because it is opposed to a common set of theories and phrases. Theologians of one class are given to assert that morality is the creation of a certain set of dogmas which have somehow dropped out of the skies. The prejudice against theft, for example, is due to the belief, itself due to revelation—that is, to a communication from without—that thieves will have their portion in the lake of fire. So long as this theory, or one derived from it, holds its ground, we are liable to the assumption that all morality is dependent upon specific beliefs about facts of which we may or may not be ignorant, and has, therefore, something essentially arbitrary about it. It is a natural consequence that religion may change in such a way as to involve a reversal of the moral law, and therefore a total incompatibility between the demands of the religion and the most essential conditions of social life. I hold, as I have argued elsewhere, that this represents a complete inversion of cause and effect; that morality springs simply from the felt need of human beings living in society; that religious beliefs spring from and reflect the prevalent moral sentiment instead of producing it as an independent cause; that a belief that murderers will be damned is the effect, and not the cause, of our objection to murder. There is, doubtless, an intimate connection between the two beliefs. In the intellectual stage at which hell seems a reasonable hypothesis, we cannot express our objection to murder without speaking in terms of hell-fire. But the hell is created by that objection when present to minds at a certain stage; and not a doctrine communicated from without and generating the objection. From this it follows that the religious belief which springs from the moral sentiments (amongst other conditions) cannot, as a rule, be in conflict with them, or with the corollaries deduced from them by the legislator. In other words, agreement between the State and the Church as to a very wide sphere of conduct must be the rule, because the sentiment upon which their vitality depends springs from a common root, and depends upon general conditions, independent of special beliefs and forms of government. In spite of these considerations, the difficulty may undoubtedly occur. A religion may command criminal practices, and even practices inconsistent with the very existence of the society. Nihilists and Communists may order men to steal or slay. Are they to be permitted to attack the State because they attack it in the name of religion? The answer, of course, is plain. Criminals must be punished, whatever their principle. The fact that a god commands an action does not make it moral. There are very immoral gods going about, whose followers must be punished for obeying their orders. Belief in his gods is no excuse for the criminal. It only shows that his moral ideas are confused. If the god has no better principles than a receiver of stolen goods, his authority gives no better justification for the act. The punishment does not violate the principle that none but immoral acts should be punished, unless we regard morality as a mere name for actions commanded by invisible beings. Nor, leaving this for the moment, is this properly a case of persecution. Toleration implies that a man is to be allowed to profess and maintain any principles that he pleases; not that he should be allowed in all cases to act upon his principles, especially to act upon them to the injury of others. No limitation whatever need be put upon this principle in the case supposed. I, for one, am fully prepared to listen to any arguments for the propriety of theft or murder, or, if it be possible, of immorality in the abstract. No doctrine, however well established, should be protected from discussion. The reasons have been already assigned. If, as a matter of fact, any appreciable number of persons is inclined to advocate murder on principle, I should wish them to state their opinions openly and fearlessly, because I should think that the shortest way of exploding the principle and of ascertaining the true causes of such a perversion of moral sentiment. Such a state of things implies the existence of evils which cannot be really cured till their cause is known, and the shortest way to discover the cause is to give a hearing to the alleged reasons. Of course, this may lead to very difficult points of casuistry. We cannot always draw the line between theory and practice. An attack upon the evils of landed property delivered in a certain place and time may mean—shoot this particular landlord. In all such cases, it can only be said that the issue is one of fact. It is most desirable that the principles upon which property in land can be defended should be thoroughly discussed. It is most undesirable that any landlord should be assassinated. Whether a particular speech is really a part of the general discussion, or an act in furtherance of a murderous conspiracy, is a question to be decided by the evidence in the case. Sometimes it may be almost impossible to draw the line; I only urge that it should be drawn in conformity with the general rule. The propriety of every law should be arguable; but whilst it is the law, it must be enforced.

This brings us to a further difficulty. Who, it is asked, is to decide these cases? The State is to punish acts which are inconsistent with its existence or immoral. But if the State is to decide, its decision is ultimate; and it may decide, for example, as Cromwell decided, that the Mass was an immoral ceremony, and therefore as much to be suppressed as an act of theft. Simply to traverse the statement of fact would be insufficient. If we merely deny the immorality of the Mass, we say that Cromwell was mistaken in his facts, not that his conduct was immoral in itself. He was mistaken, as he would have been mistaken had he supposed that the congregation was collected to begin a political rising, when it simply came together for a religious ceremonial. The objection (if we may fairly judge Cromwell by a modern standard, which need not be here considered) is obviously different. It assumes that the suppression of the Mass was an act done in restraint of opinion. Nobody alleged that the Mass had any other ill-consequences than its tendency to encourage the spread of a religion. A simple act of idolatry is not of itself injurious to my neighbour. I am not injured because you, being a fool, do an act of folly which is nothing but an open avowal of your folly. The intention of the persecutor was to restrain the spread of an opinion by terror; and just so far as that was the intention it was an act of intolerance. It is easy to put different cases. If, for example, a creed commanded human sacrifices, it might be (I should say that it would be) right to suppress an anti-social practice. The murder would not be justified because of the invisible accomplice, though he were called a god. The action should therefore be punished, though we ought not to punish the promulgation of an argument in favour of the practice, nor to punish other harmless practices dictated by the same creed. But in the case of the Mass the conduct would be admittedly harmless in every other respect than in its supposed effect upon opinion. The bare act of eating a wafer with certain ceremonies only became punishable because the actor attached to it, and encouraged others to attach to it, a particular religious significance. Restraint of opinion, or of its free utterance, by terror is the essence of persecution, and all conduct intended to achieve that purpose is immoral. The principle is entirely consistent with the admission that a legislator must decide for himself whether or not that is the real tendency of his legislation. There is no appeal from the Legislature, and therefore it must decide in the last resort. But it does not follow that a court from which there is no appeal follows no rules in fact, nor that all its decisions are morally right. In laying down such a principle, or any other first principle, we are not proposing a rule which can be enforced by any external authority. It belongs to a sphere which is antecedent to all legislation. We say simply that a legislator will accept it so far as he legislates upon sound principles. Nor is it asserted that the principle is always free from ambiguity in its applications. Granting that persecution is wrong, it may still be a fair question whether this or that law implies persecution. There may be irreconcilable differences of opinion. The legislator may declare that a particular kind of conduct is immoral, or, in other words, that the practice is irreconcilable with the essential conditions of social welfare. The priest may assert that it is commanded by his deity, and, moreover, that it is really moral in the same sense in which the legislator declares it to be immoral. Who is to decide? The principle of toleration does not of itself answer that question. It only lays down certain conditions for conducting the argument. It decides that the immorality must consist in something else than the evil tendency of any general doctrine. A man must not be punished for openly avowing any principles whatever. Any defence of the proposed rule is irrelevant unless it contains an allegation that the punishment is inflicted for something else than a defence of opinion. And, further, if agreement be still impossible, the principle does not say who is to give the decision; it only lays down a condition as to the mode of obtaining the decision. In the last resort, we may say, the question must be fought out, but it must be fought out with fair weapons. The statesman, so long as he is seriously convinced, must uphold the law, but he must allow its policy and justice to be freely discussed. No statement can be made as to the result. The statesman appeals directly to one class of motives; the priest to others, not identical, though not disparate. The ultimate success of one or the other will depend upon the constitution of the society, and the strength of all the various forces by which authority is supported and balanced. Toleration only ensures fair play, and implies the existence of conditions necessary for securing a possibility of ultimate agreement. The relevant issues are defined, though the question of fact remains for discussion. Even where brute force has the most unrestricted play, and rule is most decidedly based upon sheer terror, all power ultimately rests upon the beliefs and sentiments of the society. The advantage of toleration is to exclude that kind of coercion which tries to restrain opinion by sheer terror, and therefore by considerations plainly irrelevant to the truth of the opinions.

This leads to what are really the most difficult problems at the present day. No moral principle, I should say, and certainly not the principle of toleration, can lay down a distinct external criterion of right and wrong applicable at once to all concrete cases. No test, by the nature of the case, can be given which will decide at once whether a particular rule does or does not transgress the principle of toleration. This is especially true in the controversies where the question of toleration is mixed up with the other question as to the proper limits of State interference. A great deal has been said, and very little has been decided, as to the latter problem. We may argue the propriety of the State undertaking the management of railways, or interfering between labourers and capitalists, without considering the principle of toleration in the sense in which I have taken it. But when we come to such controversies as that about the Established Church or the national systems of education, the problem becomes more intricate. The briefest glance must suffice to show the bearing of my principles upon such problems. An Established Church was clearly open to objection on the ground of intolerance so long as it was virtually and avowedly an organisation for propagating a faith. When it was supported on the ground that its doctrines were true, and dissent was regarded as criminal because heretical, persecution was accepted in principle and carried into practice. At the present day its advocates have abandoned this ground. All that can be said is, that the State confers certain privileges upon, and assigns certain revenues to, persons who will discharge certain functions and accept certain tests. Dissenters, therefore, are excluded from the privileges on account of their faith. But it may be urged that the functions discharged by the Church are useful to the people in general, even to unbelievers, and that in the opinion of unbelievers themselves. And, again, it is argued that the formularies of the Church are maintained, not as true, but simply as expressing the opinions of the majority. There is no direct persecution, for anyone may dissent as much as he pleases, and (with hardly an exception) attack any doctrines whatever. The existence of such an institution must, of course, act to some extent as a bribe, if not as a threat; but implies so little of direct intolerance that it is frequently defended expressly and sincerely on the ground that it is favourable to freedom of thought. To argue all the issues here suggested would require a treatise. I should certainly hold that, so long as an Establishment exists, the free play of opinion is trammelled, in spite of some plausible arguments to the contrary. But I certainly hold also, that it is impossible to condemn an Establishment purely and simply on the ground of toleration without doing violence to fair argument. All that can be said is, that questions of toleration are here involved, along with many other questions possibly of more importance in this particular case, and I am not prepared to cut the knot by any unqualified assertion. And this is equally true of national education. It does not necessarily imply any intolerance whatever. Not only may it be possible or easy in many cases to solve the problem by giving an education which all sects approve, and to leave the religious education to each sect, but there is another consideration. Toleration implies that each man must have a right to say what he pleases. It does not imply a right both to impress his own doctrines upon other people and to exclude the influence of other teachers. If I take the child of a Protestant and bring him up as a Catholic, or *vice versâ*, I am guilty, undoubtedly, of a gross act of tyranny. But I am not necessarily more intolerant than if I decided that a slave was to be educated by the State instead of by his master. The moral question falls under a different head. The Legislature in such a case is altering the relation between parents and children. It is handing over to others the authority over the children hitherto possessed by their parents. This is a very grave and, beyond narrow limits, a most objectionable proceeding, but it is not so objectionable as intolerant. It simply implies the exchanging one kind of influence for another. The parent's right to his own opinions and their utterance is not the same as his right to instil them into other minds; the tyranny implied is the tyranny of limiting his power over his children; and that limitation, upon other grounds, may be most oppressive. But if the child was sent to a school where he was allowed to hear all opinions, and his parents had access to him, amongst others, he would clearly be freer to form his own creed, and, so far, there would be more room for the free play of opinion. To give the rule over him exclusively to his parents is, so far, to sanction private intolerance, though for other reasons this may be fully justifiable. The question of intolerance is raised at a different point. If, for example, one creed should be favoured at the expense of others, if all the schools of a country should be Protestant whilst some of the people were Catholic, we should clearly have a case of limiting opinion by force; and so, if any uniform creed were prescribed by the State, all Dissenters might complain of persecution. It may, further, be urged that some such result is a natural result of a State system. I do not argue the question, which I only notice to show how the simple doctrine of toleration may be mixed up with other problems—here, for example, with the enormously important question of the proper limits of parental authority—which render impossible any offhand decision. The principle of toleration may be simple; the importance of so organising society that it may be carried out without exceptions is enormous; but it is not the sole principle of conduct, and in a complex condition of society, full of fragments of institutions which have more or less deviated from their original functions, we must sometimes be content with an imperfect application, and permit it to be overridden by other principles which spring from the same root of social utility, and cannot be brought into harmony with it without changes which, for the moment, are impracticable.

How far, then, does the principle, thus understood, differ from the simple doctrine of expediency, and therefore exclude the admission that we have in every case to decide by the calculation of consequences? The final reply to this question will sum up what I have to say, by indicating what I take to be the weakness or inadequacy of the simple utilitarian doctrine. I entirely agree with Mill that conduct is proved to be immoral by proving it to be mischievous, or, in other words, productive of a balance of misery. But I hold that his neglect of the conditions of social development deprives his argument of the necessary coherency. For the reasons already set forth, I say that toleration becomes possible and desirable at a certain stage of progress. If this condition be overlooked or insufficiently recognised, we fall into errors at the beginning and the end of our argument. The advocate of toleration tries to prove that persecution is bad irrespectively of this condition, and therefore that it was bad at the earliest as well as the latest stages. Since this is not true, and therefore cannot be proved, his argument seems to break down; and so we find that the arguments from history are indiscriminately joined, and that the advocates of persecution argue as if precedents drawn from primitive social stages were applicable without modification to the latest. They frequently try to defend this explicitly by assuming that human nature is always the same, and inferring that, if people once argued with the fist, we must always use that controversial weapon. That human nature always retains certain fundamental properties may be fully granted; but if this inference be sound, civilisation, which consists in great measure in learning to limit the sphere of brute force, must be an illusory phenomenon. From my point of view, on the other hand, the recognition that society does in fact grow is an essential point of the case. When we have to deal with the later stages, Mill's argument fails of cogency just so far as he treats its essential characteristics as though they were mere accidents. So, as we have seen, he says, virtually, that persecution may be effective in suppressing an opinion; and passes lightly over the consideration of the real meaning of this 'may be.' It 'may be' efficient if it is so vigorous as to choke thought as well as to excise particular results of thought, and if, therefore, a political organisation exists which becomes altogether impossible as society advances beyond a certain stage. But when we restore the condition thus imperfectly indicated to its proper place in the argument, Mill's arguments, cogently stated already, acquire fresh cogency. At that stage toleration becomes an essential condition of development, and therefore it becomes at the same time an essential condition of promoting happiness. Given such a social organisation as exists at present, the only kind of persecution which is possible is that which is condemned by everyone as ineffectual. To persecute without suppressing, to stimulate hypocrisy without encouraging faith, is clearly to produce suffering without compensating advantage. Persecution is an anachronism, and becomes a blunder, and upon this showing it is so palpably impolitic, and therefore immoral, that even a theoretical advocate of persecution admits that it is wicked under the conditions. The chief point of difference is that he does not recognise the necessity of the conditions, or fancies that he implicitly gets rid of them by saying that he dislikes them.

This suggests one further explanation. You assume, it is said, that progress is a blessing. We prefer the mediaeval, or the pagan, or the savage state of society, and deny that progress deserves the admiration lavished upon it by professors of claptrap. I make no such assumption, whatever my private opinion; I simply allege the fact of progress as showing historically what is the genesis of toleration, and therefore the conditions under which it has become essential. But whether progress be a good or a bad thing, whether men are happier or less happy than monkeys, the argument is unaffected. Perhaps a child is happier than a man; but a man does not therefore become happier by adopting childish modes of life. When society is at a given stage, you cannot restore the previous stage, nor can you adopt the old methods. The modes by which society progresses determine a certain organisation, and when that exists it becomes an essential part of the problem. It is still possible to be intolerant; but it is not possible to restore the conditions under which intolerance could be carried out as a principle, and therefore you can only tease and hamper and irritate, without gaining any proportional advantage, if any advantage whatever. Even if there be a period at which it is still possible to arrest progress, you do not ensure a maintenance of the existing stage, but rather ensure actual decay. The choice is not between advancing and standing still, but between growing and rotting; and the bitterest denouncers of progress may think it less objectionable than actual decline. We have, fortunately, advanced beyond the early stage, and may therefore say that, given the existing order, toleration is not merely conducive on the average, but is unconditionally and necessarily conducive, to happiness. I do not, of course, deny that in this, as in all moral principles, there may not be found, here and there, exceptional cases which may amuse a casuist; but they can be only such rare cases as might cause doubt to one thoroughly convinced of the essential importance of a complete permeation of society by tolerant principles. Something, indeed, remains to be done, perhaps much, before the principle can be thoroughly carried out. There is a region of difficulties or anomalies not yet cleared up. Toleration, in fact, as I have understood it, is a necessary correlative to a respect for truthfulness. So far as we can lay it down as an absolute principle that every man should be thoroughly trustworthy, and therefore truthful, we are bound to respect every manifestation of truthfulness. In many cases a man's opinions are really determined by his character, and possibly by bad characteristics. He holds a certain creed because it flatters him as a cowardly, or sensual, or selfish animal. In that case it is hard,

261

but it is right, to distinguish between our disapproval of the passions, and our disapproval of the open avowal of the doctrines which spring from them. The virtue of truthfulness was naturally recognised in particular cases before the virtue of toleration. It was obviously necessary to social welfare that men should be able to trust each other, and, therefore, that in all private relations a man's word should be as good as his bond. The theory was virtually limited by the understanding that there were certain opinions which could not be uttered without endangering the social order. If an avowal of disbelief in the gods necessarily meant disloyalty, the heretic was punishable upon that ground, whatever might be thought of his virtue. The conflict began as soon as a respect for such sincerity was outraged by a punishment still held to be necessary. It is solved when society is organised in such a way that this necessity is removed; when, therefore, the outrage is not compensated even apparently, and the suppression of free utterance is seen to be in itself an inappropriate mode of meeting the difficulty. It is clenched by the spread of a general conviction that the only safe basis for any theory is the encouragement of its full discussion from every point of view. By a strange inconsistency, toleration is still sometimes denounced, even by acute reasoners, as a product of absolute scepticism. It may spring from scepticism as to the particular doctrines enforced; but it is certainly inseparable from the conviction, the reverse of sceptical, that truth is attainable, and only attainable, by the free play of intelligence. Toleration, it is said, is opposed to the 'principle of authority'; as if there could be a principle of authority in the abstract! To say that we are to accept authority in the abstract, is to say that we are to believe anything that anybody tells us; that is, to believe direct contradictions. Toleration is, in fact, opposed to any authority which does not rest upon the only possible ground of rational authority—the gradual agreement of inquirers free from all irrelevant bias, and therefore from the bias of sheer terror of the evils inflicted by persons of different opinion.

The principle, I have said, is not yet fully developed. Intolerance of the crudest kind is discredited, and has come to be regarded as wicked. It is admittedly wrong to burn any man because he does not think as I think. But there are the cases already noticed in which, though heretical opinion is not punishable as such, it carries with it certain disqualifications, or is marked by a certain stigma in consequence of the survival of old institutions and hereditary prejudices. Such anomalies may be gradually removed, but they cannot be adequately discussed under the simple heading of tolerance. We are, in regard to them, in the same position as our ancestors in regard to the primary questions of toleration. The concrete facts are still so ravelled that we have (if I may say so) to make a practical abstraction before we can apply the abstract theory. And, besides this, further corollaries may be suggested. It is a recognised duty not to punish people for expressing opinion; but it is not a recognised duty to let our opinions be known. The utterance of our creed is taken to be a right, not a duty. And yet there is a great deal to be said for objecting to passive as well as active reticence. If every man thought it a duty to profess his creed openly, he would be doing a service not only by helping to remove the stigma which clings to unpopular creeds, but very frequently by making the discovery that his opinions, when articulately uttered, were absurd, and the grounds upon which they are formed ludicrously inadequate. A man often excuses himself for bigotry because he locks it up in his own breast instead of openly avowing it. Brought into daylight, he might see its folly, and recognise the absurdity of the principle which makes it a duty to be dogmatic about propositions which we are palpably unable to understand or appreciate. If, however, the right of holding one's tongue be still considered as sacred, though it seems to be justified only by the remnant of the bigotry directed against free speech, there is an application of the principle in the sphere of politics which requires explicit notice. The doctrine of toleration requires a positive as well as a negative statement. It is not only wrong to burn a man on account of his creed, but it is right to encourage the open avowal and defence of every opinion sincerely maintained. Every man who says frankly and fully what he thinks is, so far, doing a public service. We should be grateful to him for attacking most unsparingly our most cherished opinions. I do not say that we should be grateful to

263

him for attacking them by unfair means. Proselytism of all varieties is, to my mind, a detestable phenomenon; for proselytism means, as I understand it, the attempt to influence opinion in an underhand way, by appeals to the passions which obscure reason, or by mere personal authority. The only way in which one human being can properly attempt to influence another is the encouraging him to think for himself, instead of endeavouring to instil ready-made doctrines into his mind. Every sane person, of course, should respect the authority of more competent inquirers than himself, and not less in philosophical or religious than in scientific questions. But he should learn to respect because the authority is competent, not because it is that of someone whom he respects for reasons which have nothing to do with such competence.

I have thus argued that all legal restraint of opinion is wrong; and wrong because it tends to enervate the vital principle of intellectual development. In doing so, I have partly indicated the method in which I should attempt to approach a more general problem: How, in point of fact, are opinions constructed? When we try to form a clear conception of social dynamics, we are naturally led to ask what is the true theory of the intellectual factor. We possess philosophies of history and religion in abundance; and I think that it is generally impossible to read them without a strange sense of unreality. They may show infinite ingenuity and great plausibility, but they become unsatisfactory when we try to translate them into facts, and bring them face to face with history. When we try to give a theory of history, we are naturally tempted to convert history into a theory; and, therefore, to represent it as a purely logical process. The successive stages correspond to deductions from first principles; and the whole process becomes an 'evolution' in the purely logical, as distinguished from the empirical, sense; the explication of a dogma, not the elaboration of an institution. The race, we suppose, lays down a major premiss in one century, supplies the minor in a second, and in a third draws the inference. This conception is the natural heir to the theological doctrine of a revelation. The history of a religion traces back all later developments to certain first principles which were introduced into the world from without. A Divine Being presented us with a set of axioms and definitions, and we, still, perhaps, under Divine guidance, have drawn from them a series of propositions and corollaries which constitute the orthodox system of dogma, as the deductions of Euclid constitute a system of geometry. On this showing, the revelation of the axioms, whether they announce themselves as 'innate ideas' or are injected by some miraculous process, is the starting-point of the religion. We must, of course, recur to empirical observation in order to describe the actual process of their acceptance, diffusion, and development. But we never get further back than the promulgation of the primary truths. By faith, that is, by assimilating these truths, men accept the religion, and the religion shapes all their lives, thoughts, and actions. On this showing, then, the purely intellectual factor is, if not the sole, the sole original and independent force. A history of religion is a history of the development of the primitive belief, or of the errors by which they have been obscured; but those beliefs themselves are an ultimate cause, and, as such, incapable of further explanation. We have traced the river to its source, or to its first emergence in the world of fact. Even disbelievers in a particular religion often continue to make this assumption. The founder of the new creed is regarded as its ultimate creator. We trace Mahomedanism back to Mahomet, and no further. Had Mahomet died before he had written the Koran, the whole history of the world, in the accepted phrase, would have been different. To the true believer, he was the channel through which came a revelation from the outside; to outsiders, he is still the ultimate source of the new doctrine, and of all the effects attributed to it. Without discussing these assumptions in the abstract, I will say something of the facts which, to me, seem to necessitate a reconstruction of the theory.

We have lately been led to look back to the primitive ages for the explanation of all institutions. A savage has a certain system of 'beliefs' and customs. He does not distinguish between his philosophical, his religious, his political, and his ethical beliefs; they exist in him, so far as they exist, only in germ, and they take the form of an acceptance of certain concrete facts. He believes in the god of his tribe as he believes in the chief whom he follows, or in the enemy whom he fights. He adheres to certain customs by instinct, and it would be as idle to ask him why he observes them, as to ask him why he eats or drinks, or to ask a bird why it builds nests. An instinct—even the instinct of an animal—is of course 'reasonable' in the sense that we can ascertain the rules according to which it acts, and explain by conditions of its existence. It only becomes reason, in the full sense, when reflection makes the agent himself conscious of the rule already implicitly given, and of the place which it holds in his constitution and in his system of life. But until reflection is possible, and is, to some extent, systematised, the instinct is an ultimate fact for the agent; no explanation or justification is demanded, or even conceived as possible. Such development, then, as takes place must take place, not by any conscious reasoning, but, as I have said, by natural selection. A superior creed must generally accompany higher intelligence and a better organisation of society. The religion is an indistinguishable part of the instincts which hold a tribe together and determine its efficiency. The savage does not argue with his enemy, but knocks him on the head. But the tribe which has the best brains and the most appropriate instincts will generally exterminate its antagonists. Even while I write, the Catholics and Protestants of Uganda are propagating their faiths after this method, and their arguments receive additional point from the Maxim guns of their apostolic allies. Whatever the precise relation between the primitive creed and the instincts in which it is embedded, the creed which conduces to, or which is generated by, supreme qualities will tend to prevail. The men of the flint weapons were not converted by the worshippers of Odin, but their creed, whatever it may have been, was effectually suppressed. Again, if one savage creed contains more truth than another, we may suppose that it is so far the better. There must to every period be a certain conformity between the beliefs of a race and the facts asserted, or the race would disappear. Science, even in its germ, must approximately state facts. The lowest savage must believe that fire burns and water drowns. But this test of truthfulness is not so easily applied to the beliefs in which we find the germ of later ethics, or which animate the collective action of the tribe. The power of united action, the primitive public spirit of a tribe, must be of primary importance. But this is recognised in the savage dialect by help of grotesque hypotheses. A group of savages believes that it is descended from a mythical animal, or that the ghost of its great-grandfather looks after its common interests. The theory, taken as a statement of fact, is absurd; but, in its name, the tribe may destroy the less intelligent savages who are not drilled, even by a ghost. Such a belief indicates qualities of the highest utility; but is, one must suppose, a symptom, not a cause, of the useful qualities. It corresponds to the only way in which a truth could be dimly apprehended by the savage. It is the projection upon the imaginary world of a sentiment, not of a perception of fact. 'Union among kinsmen is useful' would be the ultimate formula, which could only present itself by the fancy; 'you and I must not kill each other, because we are connected by an imaginary Totem.' In other words, social relations of the highest utility give rise to mythological fancies, which, as reflection awakens, are put forward as the reasons or 'sanctions' of the practices. The practice prevailed because it was useful, not because it was seen to be useful; that is, because the race which had that instinct was successful in the struggle for existence; although the perception of its utility was not even dimly present to the savage mind; and, when a justification was required, the embodiment in symbols of the belief was given as the cause of the belief itself.

How far is the case altered when we advance to comparatively civilised races? Do we ever reach a stage in which reason is substituted for instinct? In what sense is reason specifically distinct from instinct? A germ of reason is already present in instinct, and to become rational is never to suppress, but to rationalise, instinct. We still start from beliefs which are also instincts, but they are instincts which have been verified by observation. The reasoned belief is still propagated by identical methods. If the doctrine of the 'survival of the fittest' be true nowhere else, it seems certainly to be true of intellectual development. The world of thought grows by the development of countless hypotheses, among which those

267

which are useless die out, and those which are useful, because they correspond to fruitful combinations of thought, become fixed, and serve as the nucleus of more complex constructions. We call men reasonable so far as their beliefs are formed by some conscious logical process; by a deliberate attempt to frame and to verify general rules as to phenomena of all kinds, and which can, therefore, be propagated by argument or persuasion as well as by the more roundabout method which depends upon the survival of the most intelligent races. When people have sat at the feet of philosophers and filled libraries with argumentative treatises, pure reasoning has some influence. And yet it is still only a part, and a subordinate part, of the process by which creeds are elaborated. For, in the first place, the intellect of the millions is altogether indifferent to the logic of the dogmatists, and ignorant of the data to which the logic is applied. It must take its beliefs for granted, and is so far from asking how they are proved that it does not see that proof is required. There are two or three hundred millions of human beings in our Indian Empire, and perhaps not as many hundreds who could, in the old phrase, give a reason for their belief, except the fact that their fathers believed. There are six hundred and seventy members of Parliament, of whom we may certainly doubt whether the odd seventy have ever reasoned, or could really reason, about the fundamental doctrines of Christianity. If, again, we take the few who have some sort of reasoned persuasion, we know as a fact that a man generally accepts Catholicism or Protestantism much as he accepts the shape of his hat, from the conditions under which he has been brought up; that even if he reasons, he generally seeks for reasons to support his creed, instead of finding a creed to suit his reason; and that, in any case, he necessarily starts with an established set of opinions, which he may gradually modify, but which, even in the keenest and most candid minds, are still traceable as transformed, rather than replaced, in his latest convictions. And then, finally, it is clear that in any case his reason is but one factor in his total system of beliefs. His opinions are necessarily influenced by his whole character, his emotional and active, as well as by his intellectual, nature, and, moreover, by his social position. As holding a religion, he belongs to a Church. A Church is a social organisation which supposes a certain corporate spirit, no more to be fully expressed by its dogmas than the patriotism of an Englishman by the beliefs which he holds about the characteristics of his nation or the peculiarities of its political constitution. The Church is invested with historical associations; it has provided channels for our thoughts, activities, and emotions; it supplies the intellect with ready-made beliefs, tacitly instilled in infancy; it has established forms of worship which fascinate the imagination and provide utterance for the emotions; it presents an ideal of life; it has in its system of discipline a powerful machinery for regulating the passions; and it is more or less elaborately organised with a view to discharging a variety of important social functions. The vast majority of its members take its beliefs on trust, and, of those who examine, a large proportion only examine in order to be convinced. We may, therefore, safely assume that, although a religion supposes certain beliefs in its adherents, we have gone but a little way to explain the whole complex phenomenon when we have formulated the beliefs and stated the reasons upon which they are founded. They are, for the enormous majority, mere expressions of belief still in the stage of instinct; and so far as they imply genuine reasoning, they correspond to a modification of a previously-existing creed, slowly developed, and worked into conformity with philosophical doctrines by a gradual and often imperceptible process. A genuine historian of religion would, therefore, still have to regard the whole record as an enlarged process of natural selection. The Church and the creed thrive by reason of their adaptation to the whole of human nature and the needs of the society in which they are planted; and the purely intellectual process is merely one factor, which we may, indeed, consider apart, but which is in reality a subordinate factor in the concrete history. It must, of course, be a source of weakness if a religion includes incredible statements, or its theories represent deficient moral and social ideals. That is, the intellectual state has an influence upon the vitality of the religion, but it is through that influence, and not

269

by an explicit reasoning process, that it really acts. We still have to deal with a survival of the fittest, and the 'fitness' includes much besides logic.

Indeed, it is only necessary to lay stress upon this because the obvious facts seem to have been so often ignored by theories not yet quite obsolete. The Protestant writers upon the 'evidences,' for example, very properly held that they were bound to prove the propositions which they asked others to believe. But their method of reasoning showed that they not only supposed themselves capable of giving a proof, but thought that everybody else had followed the same method. They held that the Evangelists were not merely recording the beliefs of their day, but giving evidence like witnesses in a court of justice. They imagined that St. Paul had convinced himself of the truth of the Resurrection by a method of inquiry which would have passed muster in an English criminal trial. They held, therefore, that a statement of a miracle proved the fact, instead of proving the credulity of the witness. They could see the fallacy of such an argument when applied, say, to the deification of the Virgin Mary; but when the traditional view had been put in writing a little earlier, it became a 'proof' of the divinity of Christ. Therefore the whole proof of their religion and, as they often held, the proof of facts upon which even morality was dependent, came to be the truth of certain statements which really prove only the mental condition of the writers. Such a conception of a rational religion is a curious proof of the unreality of the whole way of regarding the question. The pyramid is balanced upon its apex. The truth of Christianity, with all that it is supposed to involve, including all genuine morality, was made to rest upon the possibility of proving that certain events took place two thousand years ago. The position was indefensible, but scarcely more grotesque than the implied conception that a religion is, in fact, propagated after this fashion: that apostles go about proving things by 'evidence'; that miracles are the cause, and not the consequence, of a vast moral and social crisis; and, in brief, that any religion which wants facts to support it will have the slightest difficulty in making any evidence that is desirable for the purpose. Yet it is hardly more impossible to suppose that a

270

religion is a product of 'evidence' in the technical, juristic sense than to suppose that it is a product of conscious philosophy. The grave humourists, indeed, who call themselves historians of philosophy seem to be at times under the impression that the development of the world has been affected by the last new feat of some great man in the art of logical hair-splitting. They imagine that the true impulse to the greatest changes of thought and character is to be sought in the metaphysical lectures which supply new puzzles for half a dozen eccentric recluses. To me, though I cannot argue the point, it seems clear that what a philosopher does—and it is quite enough—is not to govern speculation, but to codify and bring into clearer light the principles already involved in the speculations of the more concrete sciences. But, in any case, the problem occurs how the promulgation of a philosophical doctrine, especially if it is of an intuitive or self-evident truth, comes to produce the gigantic influence attributed to a new religion. We must surely consider, not simply the doctrine, true or false, but the moral state of the recipients. Even in such a case as pure mathematics, where the progress is a simple question of reasoning, we can only account for the historical phenomenon, for the development of mathematical knowledge at certain periods, and for its absolutely stationary condition at others, by assigning the conditions which lead to a study of mathematics. But in the case of a philosophical theory this necessity is more obvious. If the truth of monotheism be self-evident, and if upon any theory it is a doctrine dependent on the simplest grounds, and resting upon arguments familiar to the earliest speculator, why should its enunciation at a particular period suddenly transform the world? A syllogism, or a 'self-evident truth,' is not a thing walking about on two legs, which suddenly catches hold of people and converts them. The more evident the truth, the more difficult to understand its efficacy at a particular conjecture. The truth was always there, and the secret must lie in the variable, not in the constant, factor. It is a favourite view of many people that the essence of the Christian revelation consisted in the promulgation of its ethical teaching. I, of course, have no doubt that the moral ideal implied in the Christian teaching played a great part in the growth of the new religion. But I do not think, nor would it, I suppose, be even the orthodox view, that the secret lay in the propounding of a new (so far as it was a new) thesis in ethical philosophy. On this showing, the sudden revelation of the truth that a man should love his neighbour as himself brought about the revolution. Why should people who did not love their neighbours already be so much attracted? or, if they loved them already, why should they be startled as by a novelty? The morality of the Sermon on the Mount has been universally admired, but it is so far from having been generally accepted, that to take it seriously even now would be to adopt a position of eccentric originality; and it may be doubted whether the whole progress of the race has not depended upon the limitation of this by other moral principles, and whether its full acceptance would not have meant a destruction of social order and welfare. But, in any case, it was not as a simple proposition in ethics, but as part of a system of teaching, that it really impressed the imagination of the new Church. The morality was one aspect of an ideal of life which, for some reason, became widely spread at that period, and has had a wide influence ever since.

What, then, was the reason? The answer which, I suppose, everyone would now admit in some form or other, would be, in the first place, that it was not the proof of miracles, nor the enunciation of new dogmas, but the development of that spirit which has been called the 'enthusiasm of humanity,' the widely-spread and powerful desire for a reconstruction of society and a regeneration of the individual. To the believer in supernatural interferences, this presents itself as the sudden infusion of a new spiritual force; and so far as he argues against the inadequacy of the doctrines invented by evidence writers and abstract philosophers, I should think that he has a strong case. But the conditions of such a development must, even by him, be sought in the 'environment' as well as in the new creed. We can only explain the spread of the organism by showing how and why the soil was congenial. The Christian doctrine obviously spread, as every doctrine spreads, just so far as it was adapted to men at a given stage. If, therefore, it spread through a certain section of the human race, and never spread further, the circumstances of that section must be relevant to the explanation. Nor can there be any doubt of the direction in which explanation must be sought, though there is ample room for the most elaborate researches before we can put any explanation into a definitive shape. The explanation, in fact, must include nothing less than an analysis of the vast religious, social, and political changes which were fermenting throughout the Roman Empire. The destruction of the old national systems of government, and of the creeds with which they were bound up, the mixture and transfusion of various races and institutions, the growth of a vast population which could not find satisfaction within the old social framework, form, of course, essential data for any comprehension of the greatest revolution which ever transformed the world. Amidst the struggle for existence of various modes of thought, the Christian doctrine formed in some sense the centre round which the classic elements ultimately crystallised into a certain unity. No one, I presume, would undertake to say confidently how much was due in the final result to the personal character of the founders of the creed, and how much to the countless multitudes who found in it what they wanted. We cannot try experiments on such points, nor say what would have been the prevalent form of religion, had St. Paul, for example, been killed before he was converted. The tendency of more scientific thinkers, I take it, will be to attribute less to the single voice which uttered the appropriate solution, and more to the millions who were ready for a solution, and were certain ultimately to find one to suit them. When the passions are roused, the man will come who sets them to a tune. Given the ferment, a crystallisation upon some point is a practical certainty. We may infer what was required for success from what ultimately succeeded. The demand was for a Kingdom of Heaven—that is, for a new society, apart from all the rotting fabrics which had served their time; cosmopolitan instead of national, with hopes fixed upon another world, since this world appeared to be hopeless, with the assertion of a brotherhood of suffering poor throughout the nations, and with a prophecy of a good time for the saints when their tyrants would be cast into the lake of fire. How that society was formed and grew, and was in time fused with the order against which it protested, is the greatest of themes for a philosophical historian. The scarcity of facts will give him an ample field for imaginative construction. But we, at least, are in a position, at the present time, to appreciate the general nature of the position. Looking on, daily, hopefully or doubtfully, at the growth of a new social creed, which is rejecting the outworn and assimilating the living elements of the old, we can surely not be amazed at the parallel phenomenon of the development of a new society, though at a time when possibilities of aspirations were very unlike those now existing, and the dialect which men had to use involved a very different terminology. Certainly we can be at no loss to understand why the new creed is to include an element representative of ignorance and superstition. What, then, was the influence of the purely intellectual factor in this complex revolution? We see a vast struggle of philosophies and religions, and a confused hubbub of controversy, dead long ago, and buried in the stately mausoleums of official dogma. How did it come to pass, we ask with wonder, that men grew so heated over the famous diphthong? Even Gibbon is moved by the personal greatness of Athanasius; but the greater the man, the greater is the wonder of the historian that he should have laboured so zealously in such a cause. The orthodox may be tolerably sure that, whatever false opinions may arise, there will be no heresies in future about the relations of the Persons of the Trinity. No one will grudge them the possession of dogmas which refer to the mere exuviae of long-extinct speculation. Yet no rational historian can now doubt that there once was really fire under all the smoke. Even the early Fathers must have meant something; and we must do them the bare justice to suppose that the subtleties in which they spent their brains were symbols of a profound and important underlying principle. Whatever the full explanation of this principle, one point seems to be sufficiently clear for our purpose.

The great theological controversies are the conflict of rival solutions of one great problem: how to reconcile philosophy to superstition. A vigorous creed has to appeal to the populace, and yet to be acceptable to the higher intellects. Stoicism might satisfy a Marcus Aurelius, but the mass required a concrete duty; not a philosophical theory of the universe, but a historical, if invisible being, capable of being definitely presented to the average imagination. There must be an official monotheism, and yet some substitute must be found for the old polytheistic fancies. Christianity had to embody philosophical doctrines of a first cause, and yet to frame a pantheon with a hierarchy of angels, saints, and devils, which was, in fact, a simple survival of the old pagan mode of thought. It had in its own phrase to provide a God-man; to bring together into some sort of unity two conceptions so heterogeneous as that of the ground of all existence and that of a particular peasant in Galilee. One use of language is to conceal, not thought, but flat contradictions of thought. Since the conception of God corresponds to a historical development from the tribal deity to the inconceivable and infinite Being whose attributes can only be expressed by negatives, the use of the same phrase could bridge the apparently infinite distance, and bring together, verbally at least, the most contradictory opinions. If the traditional element of the creed raised difficulties, they could be evaded by the help of 'spiritualisation' and allegory; and if the philosophical element led to contradictions, they had only to be called mysteries. If, in fact, the creed covered absolutely heterogeneous philosophies, that was, for the time, its strength, and not its weakness. The religious society could thrive precisely because its formulæ represented a *modus vivendi* acceptable both to the people and their teachers. The religion was to be cosmopolitan, but not universal. It required one God for Jew and Gentile, but he was still to be the God of a historical creed. He had to be identified historically with the national ruler of a tribe, and on the other hand with the First Principle of the universe. Monotheism may mean either belief in one particular deity, or belief in the essential unity which is independent of all particular events. The unity may be accidental or essential. That the two conceptions are logically irreconcilable matters little. People did not look so close as to care for contradictions. They must have both elements, the superstitious and the philosophical, however superficial the logical connection. A rationalism which could really trust to abstract reasoning alone, and which could really set aside all tradition, was in danger of being sublimated into a shifting phantasmagoria of mystical metaphysics. The unqualified deification of the historical Christ was therefore necessary in order to suppress the drift of philosophers into hopeless cosmological speculations. The Church must have for its head a conceivable Deity. The essential practical object was to set up a concrete theology which would satisfy the needs of the popular imagination. As much philosophy might be introduced as was consistent with the traditional creed; but in any case there must be a creed which would work, and any dangerous incursions into speculation must be rigidly suppressed. It is for the learned critic to tell us precisely how this was accomplished. We need not doubt for a moment that the great men who worked out the problem, starting from the ethical side, and regarding the practical requirements of the time, were perfectly sincere in subordinating the philosophical requirements. They believed that it was not only morally right, but theoretically reasonable, to start from the traditional belief, and work in the philosophy as far as it would go. When people have learnt to distinguish between an esoteric and exoteric creed, when they hold that philosophy teaches scepticism, while morality requires dogmatism, they come face to face with an unpleasant problem, and sometimes escape from it by something disagreeably like lying. That issue was probably not so distinctly presented to the framers of the early creed. But it is not the less true that, in point of fact, reason was put in chains: forced to grind in the theological mill, and bring out the orthodox dogma, and therefore that the claims of truth were subordinated to the immediate practical necessities. Difficulties were seen—some difficulties are too palpable not to have been seen by every serious thinker; but they were judiciously skimmed over by convenient formulae. The real deity had to be the anthropomorphic deity; and was only identified with the philosophical deity when it was convenient to confute heretics. God was the head of the celestial hierarchy; and the Devil was his adversary. Practically, the Devil ruled this lower world, and human beings had fallen under his power. Such a scheme would suit a polytheistic creed. But as God was also the God of philosophers, it was equally declared that the evil was a mere negation or nonentity, and that the Devil, unpleasantly active as he was for the present, would be suppressed in time, and that his existence was therefore compatible with universal benevolence. It was hard to bring together the finite and the infinite, or to combine a tradition with an abstract theory. But anything can be done by words. All good impulses, it was said, come from God; press the doctrine, and we have predestination and arbitrary grace as the sole basis of morality. But man must be allowed the mysterious attribute of free-will. Since God is reason, and will help all men impartially, it would seem on this showing that one determining factor of the result depends absolutely upon ourselves. We are in presence of two really contradictory theories, but they can be forced into one by the help of judicious verbal distinctions. The whole history of theological controversies is a history of such devices, by which awkward questions could be suppressed or relegated to the time when reason would insist upon its rights. 'For God's sake, hold your tongue!' is the plain answer to impertinent inquirers.

Whether from conscious reflection or unconscious instinct, the true problem was to hit off that mixture of philosophy and superstition which was best adapted to secure the efficiency and authority of the Church. While the ecclesiastical system acquired unity and vigour, the philosophical doctrine only covered profound incoherencies by a judicious manipulation of official dogma. The reasoning faculty was strictly subordinated to the needs of the evolution of the organism. The result is especially obvious in that part of the system which applies to the theory of toleration. The relations of God to the world at large, or to the soul of the individual, the theories of creation and of grace, present difficulties enough when we have to combine tradition with philosophy, the anthropomophic with the philosophical conception of the deity. But there is also the problem of the relations of God to

277

the Church—the great organisation whose needs determined the whole process of evolution. Does the Church mean the saints, or does it mean the visible hierarchy, which includes a good many people who are not saints? The question received different answers, and underlay some critical controversies. In the early period the two could be identified; to become a member of the Kingdom of Heaven was the same thing as to be saved, and the rite of baptism was the mark of adhesion. But when the Church became a vast institution, including men of all sorts; when a man joined it as an infant by hereditary right; when it came into relations, hostile or friendly, with the political institutions, the question became more complex. The Church retained the old claim appropriate to the early conception. To be a Christian was still to have a certain spiritual status; all outsiders were still without the privilege which admitted to heaven, and as membership of the Church implied acceptance of certain doctrines, there grew up the theory of salvation by dogma. To be a Christian gave a certain right, without which none could be saved, but which, of course, required to be supplemented by compliance with other conditions. The subjects of the new kingdom must be obedient to its regulations. But though the Church includes both sinners and fallible men, the divine character still adhered to the Church in its corporate capacity. It could be infallible in matters of doctrine and the sole dispenser of the means of grace, that is, of the means of keeping out of hell. From the philosophical point of view, the only difference between the relations of men to a Supreme Being must depend upon their intrinsic quality. But if you believe in an anthropomorphic being, he may have special relations to a favoured race or a favoured society; he may confer a monopoly upon a particular corporation; and prescribe compliance with a special set of external regulations as a condition of his favour. From the preservation, therefore, of this anthropomorphic element there follows logically the whole system of priestly magic, and of the transcendent value of external rites and observances. The God in whom you believe is far above the god of savages; but he has to be conceived as the legislator of a particular historical system, and his authority must be represented by its regulations. It was consistent still to believe that the whole heathen world—that is, the vast majority of the race—would be damned for not obeying rules of which they had never heard; that their virtues, since they did not come from the grace of God, which flows only in its prescribed channels, were 'splendid vices'; and that a baby born when a certain charm has been said will be saved eternally, and its brother, who has accidentally been overlooked, be eternally damned. No doubt, as Butler suggested, babies are lost or rescued in cases of physical illness by the action of their parents, and the God of Revelation may be expected to act in the same way as the God of Nature. The vital question is, what we mean by God. The word covered two opposite senses, and the difficulties which arise when the same word is applied to contradictory meanings were latent in the results. The elaborate theory of sacraments, of their nature, effects, conditions of efficacy, mode of administering, and so forth, is all perfectly intelligible and coherent if the sacraments are regarded as the regulations of a human society, intended to secure order and discipline within the corporation, and to stimulate an interest by appropriate observances. It is, on this understanding, simply a case of legislation worked out by minds imbued with theories of jurisprudence, as was natural to members of a vast organisation with an elaborate constitution. But when they are regarded as regulations emanating from a divinity, we must necessarily suppose a thoroughly anthropomorphic being, capable, like human legislators, of applying only external tests, though he chooses to communicate supernatural influences by means of them; and when their being is identified with the First Cause, or even with the ruler of all men, as well as of the members of his special society, the doctrine is in danger of becoming blasphemous. The system of legislation was no doubt intended, like the English or any other system of law, in the interests of morality. Some such system was inevitable when men were at a certain stage of development, and in the hands of well-meaning people it may still be worked, especially with the help of judicious explanations and reticences, so as to promote good habits and avoid gross shocks to a healthy conscience. Still, a God who is represented by a particular human corporation, however august, will suffer in his character. He will have, like a human legislator, to look at the outside action instead of the inmost consciousness, to be responsible for all the slips and irregularities inevitable in a human system of regulation, and to extend his favour to a class or a race on the most arbitrary and immoral principles.

To look at the problem historically is, therefore, to recognise the weakness, though not to diminish the importance, of the purely reasoning faculty. The love of abstract truth is the feeblest of all human passions. There is no passion, according to Bacon, which will not overpower the fear of death. Certainly there is none which will not suppress the love of logical consistency. A Spinoza—a man in whom the passion for logical harmony is really dominant—is the rarest of all human types. Even the most vigorous of thinkers have found their stimulus in some practical need, and reasoning has been only the instrument for securing some end prescribed by the emotions. They have seen that the achievement of a social reform involved the refutation of some error: but if the reasoning process did not lead them to the desired end, it has generally been the logic, and not the desired conclusion, which was finally sacrificed. To the great mass of mankind a sacrifice of consistency or of rigid proof is, of course, no sacrifice at all. There is nothing, as every schoolmaster knows, which the average mind resents so much as the demand for reasons. It will gladly accept any rule, provided that it has not to answer the troublesome question, Why? Tell me how to answer: but, for heaven's sake! don't explain the reasons of the answer. We are sometimes told that men of science have to encounter the natural desire of mankind to extend the limits of knowledge. That seems to me to be an inversion of the truth. What a man naturally desires is to put a fixed stop to inquiry. To-day, says the man of science, must be explained by yesterday; and the same process must be repeated for every period to which we can push our researches. The popular instinct stops this indefinite regress by a summary hypothesis. This planet is the universe; never mind the stars. The world was created 6,000 years ago, and there is an end of it. Ask no more. The 'explanation' turns out to be that an inconceivable being performed an inconceivable process; but, if accepted verbally, it supplies an excuse for dropping a troublesome operation, which fatigues the imagination, though it is still demanded by the reason. We want a world limited in every direction; we desire to lay down definite bounds to the labour of investigation; and we make our limits by an arbitrary hypothesis. The inertness of the average mind, not its desire for knowledge, is the real obstacle; and if it nominally asks for an infinite and the absolute, that means that it wants to put a final stop to the restless activity of the genuine inquirer.

This, of course, is pre-eminently true of that part of religious beliefs which corresponds, not to a statement of fact, but to the promulgation of laws. You must do so and so; you must obey this or that rule of the society to which you belong. To ask why is to be not only impertinent but profane. Society depends upon the observation of certain primary rules; and the question why they should be obeyed is, in fact, the question why they are essential to the welfare of the society, or what is the value of society itself to its members. Obviously, these are questions inconvenient in the highest degree to the society which embodies the working of the laws. The dumb sense of their necessity has embodied itself in a set of imaginary sanctions; and the imagination has attributed them to the supernatural agents whose existence is assumed as the ultimate groundwork of all authority; that is, as belonging to the region about which it is wicked to ask questions. The authority must be taken for granted in practice, and therefore in theory. A government cannot be carried on if the subjects are entitled to go behind the Constitution. That is a practical necessity. It is now thought almost as wicked to ask why a majority should be obeyed, as it would have been to ask why a king should be obeyed, and to ask that was once to ask why a god should be obeyed. If obedience to the moral law is interpreted as obedience to the will of a god, his authority must not be questioned in practice; for to 'question' there means to dispute; and it must not be questioned in theory, so long as no answer can possibly be given. It is taken to be part

of the primary data, assumed in all social action, and therefore to be enforced by society. Nothing can be more simple,
though it involves the assumption that to inquire is the same
thing as to deny. It is only when we have reached the conclusion that free inquiry can be constitutive as well as destructive
that we can give full play to the activity of reason, even in
those sacred regions where assumptions are necessary in the
sphere of conduct, and where, therefore, assumptions are
made into ultimate or unquestionable truths in the sphere of
speculation.

The normal attitude of the religious mind is therefore
conservative. Even the founders of a new religion profess to
be restoring an ancient creed, or in some way base their
authority upon the creed which already exists. They are at
most getting rid of accretions, not introducing novelties.
They advance from the old base. A religion, on its practical
side, is a system of rules of conduct, and therefore involves an
appeal to some authority which must not be disputed, even
in argument. In the earlier period, it is an indistinguishable
part of the political creed. It does not persecute because it
only extirpates. The rival tribe has as good a claim to its god
as to its chief, and its conversion can be only an incident of its
conquests, or of the subjection of its deities to the hostile
deities. When the creed has both philosophical and 'empirical,' or historical, elements, persecution becomes logical. The
faith of a foreigner is not merely different, but wrong; his
god is not another god, but a devil; for my creed, as philosophical, should be universal. But, in so far as it includes
historical elements, a recognition of the sanctity of beings
only known to me, and of facts of which you have never
heard, I can enforce your allegiance only by the universally
intelligible argument of the sword. You are a Turk, whom,
perhaps, I should like to conquer for other reasons, and it
must be right to prevent forcibly your allegiance to a devil.
The same argument applies within the ecclesiastical society,
so long as the creed includes elements which are not demonstrable by reason. If the central core depends upon mysteries,
which rest upon authority in this sense, that the individual
must take them without asking questions, a recalcitrant in-

dividual can only be suppressed by force. The Church is the embodiment of the Divine element in human affairs; its decisions must belong to the region in which all question is profane: and every attempt to go 'behind the record' must be suppressed by every applicable means. The inquirer has shown by the very act of inquiring that, in his case, reason is not an efficient weapon, and we must therefore try what can be done by the stake.

The reason, then, is a faculty which, by the nature of the case, has to intrude itself tacitly and gradually, and under disguises. It may slowly disintegrate old opinions under cover of ambiguities and the gradual infiltration of new meanings into old words. The determining factors are evident when we consider a Church as a great society, intended to meet certain practical requirements, and not as a system of philosophy developed by abstract thinkers. It has to rule by obeying; to adapt itself to the state of mind of the believers, to incorporate old superstitions, to make use of the imaginative construction embodied in the previous half-instinctive conceptions of the universe, to sanction whatever appeals to the crude masses of mankind, and only to consider the requirements of the more thoughtful so far as is necessary to secure their co-operation. If they will accept the official formulae, they may be allowed, within limits, to introduce elements really inconsistent, so long as the inconsistency is carefully hidden away. A vigorous religion is a superstition which has enslaved a philosophy. Slowly, and by soft degrees, indeed, the new leaven of thought may produce a vast revolution. If the philosopher is tolerated on condition of proving the orthodox conclusions, the admission that a proof is desirable leads to a recognition that it will not always work in the desired direction. But the reason is still bound by inexorable necessity to present itself as a development instead of a contradiction. Its successes are won only when it can point to some conclusion comprehensible by the majority. The abstract arguments against the authority of the Church will be regarded with indifference until abuses have grown up which supply a palpable *reductio ad absurdum*. The theory of indulgences might be illogical, but no one cared till they were obviously used for commercial purposes. Persecution may be wrong, but the abstract arguments were of little efficacy till the persecuted were able to fight. When, as a matter of fact, men of different creeds had to live in the same country, and to deal with each other in ordinary affairs, they came to see that the differences were not so vast as to imply that one creed came from God and the other from the Devil. The way to teach toleration is to force Protestants and Catholics to live together on terms of equality. The ordinary mind still needs some kind of picture-writing, a concrete instance, not a general principle. A theory confutes itself by some logical application which revolts even the instinct out of which it originally sprang. Then, and not before, it becomes evident that there must be something wrong—somewhere. When we have learnt by experience that freethinkers may be decent people, we cannot make up our minds to burn them. By degrees the moral instincts have broken through the dogmatic bondage, and forced the most dogged theologians to find means of importing liberal theories even into the heart of their formulae. Persecution has been discredited, till even the most dogmatic disavow indignantly the principles of which they once boasted. All that remains is a survival of certain claims carefully divorced from their practical application. Although the dogmatic system renounces the aid of the secular arm, it is forced to claim the same spiritual position. It still represents the one body of truth upon which the salvation of men hereafter, and their morality and welfare in this world, are essentially dependent. Its antagonists are still instruments, though not the conscious instruments, of the Devil. So long as it claims to be a supernatural revelation, it must invert the true order of thought, and represent itself, not as one stage in a slow development, one step in an approximation, but as whole, pure, and perfect, and differing from all other doctrine, not in degree, but in kind.

Persecution clearly implies authority. Does authority necessarily imply persecution? That question can only be answered when the vague phrase is made specific. All men have to take most of their opinions upon authority—that is, to believe because others believe; and the reason is often a very good one. In the doctrines, again, which form the substance of a religious creed, the great bulk of mankind inevitably depends upon authority—that is, they must accept the beliefs of the few who can reason. In that sense I take my astronomy and nearly all my mathematics upon authority, as well as my belief in Rome or in Julius Caesar. I have not personally investigated the arguments in one case, or the evidence for facts in the other. Again, men's religious beliefs are, as a fact, chiefly determined by the society into which they are born, and the true history of a religion must be sought, not in an examination of the logical relations of its official creed, but in the development of the organised society which we call a Church. And, therefore again, it is sufficiently obvious that the religious belief is a development of traditions, and is impressed upon the individual by the more or less organised action of the society. The other side of the same fact is that the Church can only thrive by embodying the beliefs and satisfying the instincts of its members. It is not an arbitrary form imposed from without, but simply a development and co-ordination of the various elements of the popular creed by means of the social organ. The fact, therefore, that most people believe on authority is the explanation of the fact that most people believe so much nonsense: that every creed hitherto established includes survival of superstitions, and inadequate solutions of difficulties, and unstable combinations of heterogeneous elements of thought. A belief in the fact of authority is, therefore, really incompatible with a belief in the fact of infallible authority. When we see how creeds are formed, we see why they must be full of error and inconsistency.

But, again, the Church is developed by its practical utility: its power of satisfying certain human aspirations and imaginations. The utility of a doctrine is only indirectly related to its truth; or rather, before we can say what is the element of truth or falsehood, we have to consider the doctrine from outside: to ask, as we have done in the case of the savage tribe, whether the value of a belief in a certain deity lies in the fact that such a deity exists, or in the fact that a certain youthful instinct is connected in the savage mind with the existence of the deity. Is the real pith and meaning of the belief in the direct meaning of the words, or in the utility which it indirectly ascribes to certain modes of conduct? The meaning of dogmas in a semi-civilised race is that a certain organisation is invested with sanctity, and can, therefore, secure obedience and co-operation. The Church may have been a highly useful organisation, as a counterpoise to the more brutal system of a military aristocracy. But it does not follow that the utility depended upon the superstitious attributes, a belief in which may, in a historical sense, have been necessary to its efficiency. They may have been the mere trappings, the ceremonial outside, which could be advantageously abolished when men became more reasonable. We can be loyal to a king now without believing that kingship involves any mysterious or supernatural attributes, and we may believe that a Church was useful though the magical powers attributed to it were a mere appendage to its utility.

The authority of the Church, when the Church is regarded as a social organisation, is simply a translation into eccelesiastical of the loyal doctrine of sovereignty. The lawyer shows that every political Constitution implies the existence of a sovereign somewhere. That is to say, simply, that the condition of unity of action is the existence of some ultimate body for deciding upon the action of the whole. There must be some ultimate court of appeal, or disputes cannot be decided, as the corporate body cannot act as a unit. The unity of the Church implies an ecclesiastical, as the unity of the State implies a political, sovereign, whether the sovereign be the Pope or any other body, constituted according to certain rules. Authority, in this sense, is the antithesis of authority in the philosophical sense. The authority of a number of people, considered politically, varies with their mutual dependence. They can act more energetically as each individual is subordinated to the rest. The authority, in a philosophical sense, varies as the independence. If two qualified people come to the same conclusion, its value is doubled, or more than doubled. If one accepts the opinion of the other, the authority is only the authority of the first. If every member of the Royal Society told me that he had reached a scientific truth independently, I should probably believe it to be established. If each told me he accepted it because the President of the Society had declared it to be true, I should have only the authority of one man. Therefore, the closer the political union, the less the real philosophical authority. While, however, we believe in the supernatural character of a Church, and are prepared to accept miracles, we can, of course, believe in its uniting authorities of both kinds. The fact of the unity, of the antecedent resolution to agree, which is really fatal to the philosophical authority, because it proves that the unity is the result of other than philosophical considerations, may induce me to accept the creed, so long as I consider faith to be a matter of obedience instead of conviction. As politicians used to consider a Constitution to be the cause of all the supposed political virtues of a country, instead of seeing in it a product of the political qualities, so the organisation of a miraculous Church which could reveal the truth and bestow the means of salvation because it could suppress dissent and enforce conformity, was supposed to be the source of all the instincts to which it really owed its origin.

Where such a confusion exists between the two kinds of 'authority,' the power to suppress and the capacity to know, persecution cannot be inconsistent. If I know that a certain body is the manifestation of God upon earth, and that its regulations are parts of the divine law, they may be enforced by either branch of 'authority.' And so long as the creed includes 'empirical,' or purely historical elements, persecution must be necessary. If the divine power is identified with an institution existing only within certain limits of time and place, the theory must include an arbitrary element: and such a theory cannot be propagated by pure reason. A scientific doctrine gives general, not particular, laws; a science of mechanics is true wherever there is existing and moving matter; and a science of psychology, wherever there are human beings. Doctrines of such a nature can be, therefore, taught independently of particular conditions. The scientific doctrine, as such, has not to deal with this or that bit of matter— with St. Paul's Church in London, or the Observatory at Greenwich—but with all matter; not with Paul or Caesar, but with human beings. Therefore the arguments are as applicable at the Antipodes as in England. So the arguments for theology, so long as they are philosophical, are equally good in London or China, now or 10,000 years ago. But if your theology asserts that a particular person who appeared at a given time and place was also God Almighty, it includes an element of which the vast majority of the race have been necessarily ignorant, and which is irrelevant to pure philosophy. In such a case, authority is at least highly convenient. You have got to believe simply because I tell you to believe; and, as belief is essential to your eternal happiness, I shall make you believe. My 'telling' shall have the force of an order, not simply of a bit of useful information. So long as such an empirical element remains, the door is open for some fragment of persecution. So long as the religion supposes a belief in facts which are not capable of establishment by reason, it has a natural affinity to support by 'authority' in the sense of coercion. The duty is allied to a particular set of institutions and events. Though persecution, in the grosser sense, has gone out of fashion, and, we may hope, for ever, the spirit is still left wherever this element remains. For if the creed is divine, its opponents are diabolical. The heretical view is taken to be—not part of the imperfect process of clumsy dialectics by which the human mind gradually works out a trustworthy creed—but an absolute denial of the truth. We are learning, in political questions, that a revolution in some sense justifies itself. It proves that the old order was defective, though it does not prove that the innovation gives the final solution. So the growth of materialism, and atheism, and agnosticism, and other wicked doctrines, should be recognised as proving, at least, that the system of thought, which has broken down in practice, was defective in theory. But so long as opinions are regarded, not as moments in a great intellectual development, but as things injected from without, suggested by the Devil or revealed by a deity; so long, therefore, as there is something essentially arbitrary in the whole process; so long as a particular creed or Church can be regarded as monopolising the whole divine element, and only the anti-divine can be left to its opponents, there is a natural leaning to coercion of some kind, whether the bigotry can use appropriate instruments or must relieve itself by simply anathematising its opponents. The final and adequate solution can only be reached when 'authority' in matters of opinion means simply that kind of authority which is in principle also demonstration; the authority of the coincidence of independent thinkers, not of the agreement of a body to put down all dissent. In that case the superstitious, arbitrary, and temporary element might disappear, and philosophy be the ally instead of the slave of religion. But it is difficult to say how much of the old creed will have to be sacrificed before such a consummation comes within a distance measurable by the imagination.

Notes

Editor's Introduction

1. To Basil Willey, for instance; see his *More Nineteenth Century Studies* (London, 1956), p. 260.
2. John W. Bicknell, "Leslie Stephen's 'English Thought in the Eighteenth Century': A Tract for the Times," *Victorian Studies* vol. 6, no. 2 (December 1962). Indispensable reading for anyone studying Stephen as an historian of ideas.
3. *English Thought in the Eighteenth Century*, 3d ed., 1:13.
4. Ibid., 2:331.
5. Bicknell, "Leslie Stephen's 'English Thought in the Eighteenth Century,'" pp. 114–15.
6. See Q. D. Leavis, *Scrutiny*, March 1939, p. 407; and F. R. Leavis, *The Common Pursuit* (1952), pp. 255–60. But see also Sheldon Rothblatt, *The Revolution of the Dons* (1968), and John Gross, *The Rise and Fall of the English Man of Letters* (1969).
7. Leslie Stephen, *The English Utilitarians* (London, 1900), 1:10.
8. Ian Watt, *The Rise of the Novel* (London, 1967).
9. F. W. Maitland, *The Life and Letters of Leslie Stephen* (London, 1906), p. 283.

1. English Thought in the Eighteenth Century

1. Boswell, July 21, 1763.
2. 'Tour to the Hebrides.' October 1, 1773.
3. I have seen another pamphlet by Philanthropos, upon Butler's sixth chapter. London, 1737.

4. Butler's Works, i. 7.

5. Ib. i. 130.

6. See it fully stated, Clarke's Works, iii. 795-799.

7. Ib. iii. 881.

8. Clarke's Works, iii. 833.

9. The same illustration, it may be noticed, appears in a similar controversy between Mr. Martineau and Mr. Herbert Spencer. See 'Contemporary Review,' April and May 1872. Professor Tyndall refers to the same illustration, 'Fortnightly Review,' November 1875.

10. See Clarke's Works, pp. 788, 789, 810.

11. Butler, i. 21.

12. Ib. p. 22.

13. Ib. p. 23.

14. Ib. p. 28.

15. Ib. p. 31.

16. Butler, i. 38.

17. See *e.g.* Warburton, Works, iii. 15; Conybeare against Tindal, p. 389; Leland against Tindal, p. 234.

18. Butler's Works, i. 37.

19. Ib. i. 49.

20. Butler's Works, i. 186.

21. Ib. i. 235.

22. Ib. i. 187.

23. Ib. i. 190.

24. Ib. i. 343.

25. Ib. i. 136, and note.

26. Butler's Works, i. 80.

27. Ib. i. 81.

28. Ib. i. 83.

29. Analogy, part i. ch. vii.

30. Butler's Works, i. 162.

31. Butler's Works, i. 42.

32. Ib. i. 79.

33. See especially the dissertation on the nature of virtue, where the utilitarian view is emphatically rejected. The language of some writers might, he thinks, lead to the impression that virtue consists in aiming at the promotion of human happiness in this life, and vice in the contrary; 'than which mistakes none can be conceived more terrible' (Butler's Works, i. 382).

34. Butler hesitates as to calling prudence a virtue. In part i. ch. iii., and in the 'Dissertation on the Nature of Virtue,' he inclines to call it a part of virtue. In part i. ch. iii. the stress laid on the analogy between prudence and virtue seems to imply that one cannot be part of the other. But the argument does not seem to be really affected.

35. P. 90.

36. Butler's Works, i. 122.

37. Butler's Works, i. 98.

38. Ib. i. 120, 121.
39. Butler's Works, i. 109.
40. Butler's Works, i. 128.
41. Ib. i. 132.
42. Butler's Works, i. 129.
43. Ib. i. 136.
44. Butler's Works, i. 145-6.
45. Butler's Works, i. 245.
46. Ib. i. 254.
47. Butler's Works, i. 332.
48. Ib. i. 258, 335.
49. Ib. i. 272.
50. Ib. i. 331.
51. See this doctrine burlesqued in the concluding chapter of Price's 'Morality.'
52. Butler's Works, i. 343.
53. Butler's Works, i. 346.
54. Hume's Works, iv. 89.
55. The first reference to Hume's Essay which I have noticed is in Skelton's 'Ophiomachia, or Deism Revealed,' vol. ii. 20, &c., London, 1749. It is said that the bookseller was determined to publish this treatise by the advice of Hume, who accidentally saw it in MS. at the bookseller's shop. See Chalmers's 'Biog. Dictionary.' Hume passed most of the year 1748 in London, and his Essays were published by the same bookseller, Millar. The first answer, according to Mr. Burton, was Adams's Essay, in 1751. See Burton's 'Life of Hume,' i. 285.
56. That on 'A Particular Providence and a Future State.'
57. Locke's Works, iii. 495.
58. 'Treatise,' i. 524.
59. Ib. part iv. sec. v.
60. 'Treatise,' i. 523.
61. Ib. pp. 526, 527.
62. Ib. p. 530.
63. 'Dialogues,' ii. 390.
64. Ib. ii. 405.
65. Ib. ii. 407.
66. Ib. ii. 432.
67. 'Dialogues,' ii. 432.
68. Reid, p. 430.
69. 'Dialogues,' ii. 433.
70. Ib. ii. 403.
71. Ib. ii. 434.
72. 'Dialogues,' ii. 443.
73. Ib. ii. 467.
74. 'Dialogues,' ii. 392.
75. Ib. ii. 393.
76. Ib. ii. 396.

77. 'Dialogues,' ii. 424.
78. Ib. pp. 408-11.
79. 'Dialogues,' ii. 412.
80. Ib. ii. 413.
81. Ib. ii. 414.
82. 'Dialogues,' ii. 419-20.
83. Ib. ii. 428.
84. 'Dialogues,' ii. 413-14. See the illustration of the ship worked out very ingeniously by Mandeville, though for a different purpose ('Fable of the Bees,' pt. ii. dial. 3).
85. Ib. ii. 426.
86. Ib. ii. 430.
87. Ib. ii. 398.
88. Essays, iv. 121 ('Essay on a Particular Providence').
89. 'Dialogues,' ii. 443.
90. Ib. ii. 444.
91. 'Dialogues,' ii. 446.
92. This is certainly a curious argument from the opponent of miracles. If such miracles could happen without our knowledge, how do we know they have not happened? Perhaps this may suggest a new mode of assailing Hume to his orthodox antagonists; but the argument would require delicate handling.
93. Ib. ii. 446-452.
94. 'Dialogues,' ii. 452.
95. Ib. ii. 459.
96. It was originally called 'Of the Practical Consequences of Natural Religion'—a title which seems to correspond more accurately to the contents.
97. Essays, iv. 112.
98. Ib. iv. 113.
99. Ib. iv. 112.
100. Ib. iv. 115.
101. Essays, iv. 118.
102. Ib. iv. 119.
103. Essays, iv. 116.
104. Essays, iv. 116-7.
105. The excellent Beattie recommends a perusal of Butler as an antidote to the cavils of this 'flimsy essay.' He is right in noticing their opposition (Beattie's 'Essay on Truth,' part i. ch. ii. sec. 5).
106. 'Natural History' &c. iv. 317.
107. 'Natural History' &c. iv. 320-325.
108. Ib. iv. 325-328.
109. Ib. iv. 329.
110. Ib. iv. 330.
111. Ib. iv. 332.
112. 'Natural History' &c. iv. 333-6.
113. Ib. iv. 355.

114. Ib. iv. 359.
115. Ib. iv. 362.
116. Ib. iv. 363.
117. Hume, 'Natural History' &c. iv. 320. 'These pretended religionists' (i.e. the polytheists) 'are really a kind of superstitious atheists.'
118. Hume, 'Dialogues,' ii. 388.
119. The reluctance of Adam Smith to publish the papers committed to him by his friend, though not unnatural, is scarcely creditable.
120. Lowth's 'Letter to Warburton' (2nd edition), p. 64.
121. Letters to Hurd, p. 346.
122. Warburton's Works, iv. 79.
123. Ib. iv. 74.
124. See table of contents to fourth and fifth books, vol. iv.
125. Warburton, v. 124.
126. Letters to Hurd, p. 239.
127. See Kilvert's 'Life of Hurd.'
128. See Cradock's 'Memoirs,' i. 180. It is fair to say that Cradock, who saw a good deal of him, considered him to be 'intrinsically good.'
129. Letters, p. 161.
130. Ib. p. 473.
131. Letters, p. 458.
132. Ib. p. 377.
133. Ib. p. 378.
134. Ib. p. 387.
135. Ib. p. 367.
136. Ib. p. 439.
137. Ib. p. 285.
138. Ib. p. 278. This means that 10,000 copies of Smollett's History were said to have been sold.
139. Ib. p. 442.
140. Ib. p. 466.
141. See Watson's 'Life of Warburton,' pp. 440, 441. Hurd's pamphlet is republished in Parr's 'Tracts by a Warburtonian,' and fully justifies the above description.
142. Letters, p. 207.
143. Ib. p. 210.
144. Letters, pp. 270, 271.
145. The same might be said of Churchill's abuse of Warburton in the third book of the 'Duellist,' which is about worthy of its victim. Churchill is to Dryden what Warburton was to Bentley.
146. Warburton's Works, viii. 343.
147. Preface to Shakespeare.
148. Warburton's Works, xii. 59. The last reference is to a pamphlet attributed to Morgan, the Moral Philosopher, but really by Annet. See above, ch. iv. sec. 60.
149. Ib. iv. 12.
150. Warburton's Works, xii. 352. One specimen of Warburton's

remarks upon Hume may be noticed, as it seems to imply that he could not have read the essay which he is attacking with ordinary attention. Hume 'confesses,' says Warburton, 'that there are popular religions in which it is expressly declared that nothing but morality can gain the divine favour' (xii. 373). Hume's words are: 'Nay, if I should suppose, *what never happens,* that a popular religion were found, in which it was expressly declared, &c. (Works, iv. 357). Hume wisely maintained silence.

151. Ib. v. 9.

152. Ib. ii. 263. This passage, in an appendix to the 'Divine Legation,' is a polished version of a coarser form in the Letters on Bolingbroke (xii. 185).

153. Ib. xi. 404.

154. Ib. iv. 347.

155. Warburton's Works, vi. 256. See also Letters, p. 31, as to Collins, and a similar remark about Tindal, p. 267.

156. Ib. viii. 281.

157. Warburton's Works, viii. 289.

158. Ib. iii. 315.

159. I must confess that I do not even know to what particular writings Warburton alludes in this main assumption. Certainly the point is not commonly urged by the deists whom he chiefly assails.

160. Warburton's Works, vi. 228.

161. Ib. i. 199.

162. Warburton's Works, i. 200.

163. Warburton's Works, ii. 254.

164. 'Literary Remains,' p. 179.

165. Warburton's Works, iii. 243.

166. Ib. v. 164.

167. Warburton's Works, v. 167.

168. Warburton's Works, iv. 323.

169. Ib. ii. 292.

170. Ib. iii. 323.

171. Ib. vi. 251.

172. A learned Dutch theologian (1636–1708), who, amongst other writings, maintained against Spenser that the Egyptians had borrowed from the Jews.

173. Warburton's Works, iv. 324.

174. Ib. iv. 312.

175. See 'Ethics,' part ii. prop. iii.

176. Warburton's Works, viii. 390.

177. Ib. viii. 138.

178. Warburton's Works, viii. 319.

179. Warburton's Works, viii. 309.

180. Ib. viii. 315.

181. Ib. i. 230.

182. Dr. Whitaker, in the 'Quarterly Review,' vol. vii.

183. See Disraeli's 'Quarrels of Authors,' in the 'Miscellanies' (edition 1840), p. 158.

4. Hours in a Library

1. See, for example, the great debate on February 13, 1741.

2. J. S. Mill and Whewell were, for their generation, the ablest exponents of two opposite systems of thought upon such matters. Mill has expressed his obligations to Wordsworth in his "Autobiography," and Whewell dedicated to Wordsworth his "Elements of Morality" in acknowledgment of his influence as a moralist.

3. The poem of Henry Vaughan, to which reference is often made in this connection, scarcely contains more than a pregnant hint.

4. As, for example, in the *Lines on Tintern Abbey:* "If this be but a vain belief."

5. See Wordsworth's reference to the *Wealth of Nations,* in the *Prelude,* book xiii.

6. So, too, in the *Prelude:*—

Then was the truth received into my heart,
That, under heaviest sorrow earth can bring,
If from the affliction somewhere do not grow
Honour which could not else have been, a faith,
An elevation, and a sanctity;
If new strength be not given, nor old restored,
The fault is ours, not Nature's.